Teaching Writing Using Blogs, Wikis, and Other Digital Tools

Teaching Writing Using Blogs, Wikis, and Other Digital Tools

Richard Beach

Chris Anson

Lee-Ann Kastman Breuch

Thom Swiss

Christopher-Gordon Publishers, Inc.
Norwood, Massachusetts

Copyright Acknowledgments

Christopher~Gordon Publishers, Inc.
Bridging Theory and Practice

1420 Providence Highway, Suite 120 • Norwood, MA 02062
800-934-8322 • 781-762-5577 • www.Christopher-Gordon.com

Printed in Canada
10 9 8 7 6 5 4 3 2 1   14 13 12 11 10 09

ISBN: 978-1-933760-28-5
Library of Congress Catalogue Number: 2008938521

Contents

Preface

This book is about the use of digital tools such as such as blogs, wikis, online chat, digital storytelling, podcasts, and e-portfolios to teach writing. These tools have been described as Web 2.0 tools because they go beyond simply accessing material from the Web to having students create their own material, what Will Richardson (2006, p. 3) describes as uses of the "Read/Write Web."

It is certainly the case that students are already using some of these tools outside school, participating in online social networking sites, IMing, and writing blogs (Lenhart, Arafeh, Smith, & MacGill, 2008). They create multimodal, often narrative material readily accessible by multiple audiences in ways that go beyond official, print-based school writing.

When these students come to school, they experience a disconnect between their extracurricular digital writing and their school-based print-based writing, which is driven by a focus on preparing them for mandated writing tests, often five-paragraph expository essays. Or they use digital writing tools to complete traditional print-based writing assignments—for example, using a blog to write an essay on an assigned topic to be read just by a teacher. At the same time, they may still be using digital writing outside school primarily for social purposes, rather than using it to engage in academic learning. To address this disconnect between outside-school and in-school writing, teachers play an important role in helping students learn to use digital writing tools to foster learning.

As teachers engage students in digital writing, they recognize that in our networked society, effective digital writing involves the use of highly multimodal, linked, interactive texts. They also recognize that their students need to learn to use digital writing tools as personal learning networks to acquire knowledge and build social connections as future workers and citizens in a knowledge society. Simply introducing technology into classrooms—for example, by giving students their own laptops—does not necessarily improve students' writing (Warschauer, 2006). Teachers know that it is their pedagogy coupled with the technology that will improve students' writing.

As we worked with the many teachers featured in this book, we saw them engaging their students in uses of digital writing tools to create multimodal, connected, interactive texts. From observing these teachers' innovative work in the classroom, we noted some common strategies that reflect new ways of teaching writing and new conceptions of effective digital writing:

- *They help students perceive the purposes for using digital writing tools.* Understanding the use of any tool requires understanding the purposes that tool is designed to fulfill. A hammer is just a hammer. Its value is understood in terms of its purpose—that it can be used to drive in or remove nails. When teachers have students create blogs, wikis, or podcasts, they don't just use these tools for their own sake. They emphasize the *purposes* for using these tools—to search for material, record thoughts, formulate ideas, develop voice, collaborate with peers, revise texts, engage audiences, and reflect on their writing, composing practices we describe in chapter 1.

  By understanding how these tools fulfill certain purposes, students then perceive their value. Once students perceive the value of podcasting to share their audio performances of texts to audiences, they are then motivated to want to improve their podcasting ability. Because these purposes have to do with communicating with peers and audiences outside school as opposed to simply completing school assignments, the outside- versus inside-school disconnect is diminished as students then begin to use these tools in their everyday lives in multiple ways. As we argue in chapter 1, students then move from teacher-initiated writing to self-initiated writing because they want to write to communicate to their audiences.

- *They have their students use these tools to foster constructivist, project-based, collaborative learning.* The teachers in this book go beyond having students using digital tools as "information-giving" devices to using them to construct knowledge through collaborative work within larger projects (Boss & Krauss, 2008). They build on the idea of using informal digital writing-to-learn frequently associated with the uses of journal or free-writing to foster learning (Anson & Beach, 1995). For example, in studying an issue, their students use digital maps to identify and visually graph different positions on that issue to share with their class. Or their students use digital storytelling to portray their everyday lives in their neighborhoods.

- *They emphasize the social uses of these tools.* Although writing for social purposes has become a familiar emphasis in teaching writing, these teachers exploit the ways in which digital writing tools allow students to readily connect and interact with both immediate and global audiences as members of a larger "participatory culture" (Jenkins, 2006a). They have their students share blog posts to receive comments or engage in online discussions. Or they facilitate global connections by, for example, using the Spintheglobe wiki (http://spintheglobe.wikispaces.com) to have students in Australia and Alaska to share their experiences.

- *They encourage students to focus on visual design.* Although teachers have typically defined their job as teaching students to produce print texts, communication in the 21st century has shifted to use of multimodal texts that combine print, images, video, and audio. Knowing how to effectively create these texts requires knowledge of visual design to engage audiences.

- *They model uses of digital tools.* The teachers we observed continually demonstrated how they use digital writing tools for their own academic and social purposes. In doing so, they explicitly reflected on *how* they were using tools to achieve certain purposes, construct knowledge, and connect with audiences. Or they tapped expert peers to model tool use, enhancing these peers' sense of agency.

- *They foster metacognitive reflection on tool use.* Students develop their writing ability by learning to metacognitively reflect on their effectiveness in using these tools. They improve in their uses of blog posts by reflecting, for example, on their ability to include links in their posts as part of connecting to other audiences.

  As we note in chapter 9, teachers foster this reflection by providing students with descriptive feedback that give them a vocabulary and criteria for reflecting on their tool use. For example, in responding to students' uses of digital note taking, they identify instances in which students effectively employed specific descriptions of the event. Or they might have students use e-portfolios to perceive relationships between their texts and growth over time in their uses of tools.

- *They recognize that they can use digital tools to enhance students' engagement in learning and sense of agency.* When students often internalize labels based on test scores such as "struggling" writers or readers, they need alternative opportunities to be perceived as competent by others within and outside the school. When students use digital storytelling or video blog posts to display competence to their peers, they gain a sense of agency as effective communicators.

  In chapter 7, we describe the example of a 12th-grade student, Trish Devine, of Jefferson High School, Bloomington, Minnesota, who on her own self-initiative created a series of vlog (video blog) posts featuring herself reflecting about her responses to literature. Because her vlog posts were viewed by a lot of her peers, she was perceived by her peers as highly proficient in creating vlogs, which served to enhance her sense of agency. For us, Trish represents someone who became engaged with digital writing because it allowed her to display competence to her peers.

- *They continually engage in ongoing professional development.* These teachers were interested in learning new uses of technology tools by sharing ideas with colleagues; accessing online training, podcasts, blogs, and chat sites; and taking courses, workshops, and other professional development experiences we discuss in our final chapter.

All these characteristics evident in these teachers are mirrored in standards for teachers promoted by the International Society for Technology in Education (2008)—that teachers do the following:

- Use their knowledge of subject matter, teaching and learning, and technology to facilitate experiences that advance student learning, creativity, and innovation in both face-to-face and virtual environments

- Design, develop, and evaluate authentic learning experiences and assessments incorporating contemporary tools and resources to maximize content learning in context and to develop the knowledge, skills, and attitudes identified in the National Educational Technology Standards for Students

- Exhibit knowledge, skills, and work processes representative of an innovative professional in a global and digital society

- Understand local and global societal issues and responsibilities in an evolving digital culture and exhibit legal and ethical behavior in their professional practices

- Continuously improve their professional practice, model lifelong learning, and exhibit leadership in their school and professional community by promoting and demonstrating the effective use of digital tools and resources

Why We Believe in the Value of Digital Writing

In addition to being impressed with the ways in which teachers we observed are using digital writing tools, the authors of this book also witnessed firsthand how the uses of digital writing tools enhance our own students' engagement with writing as well as the depth of students' thinking and development of ideas within specific academic contexts.

Richard uses blogs and wikis in film and media studies classes to foster critical writing about film and media, as well as virtual learning environments such as Moodle and Ning in all his courses. Having used print-based dialogue journals for years (Anson & Beach, 1995) in teaching a media studies course at the University of Minnesota, Richard switched over to using student blogs in which the students respond to each other's posts as "blog partners." He found that his students were much more engaged with their blog posts than with journal writing entries not only because they could readily import images and video clips from the media but also because they are sharing their writing with all the other students in the class, something that was never the case with print journals.

Then Richard had students create chapters for a wikibook on media literacy (http://medialiteracy.pbwiki.com) that would be used in subsequent sections of the course as well as be available to a larger online audience. Because they perceived their wiki chapters as informing these audiences about media literacy, they were more motivated to write these chapters than if they were simply writing a final paper for the course.

An avid user of face-to-face peer conferences to help students improve drafts of their papers and develop important metacognitive writing skills, Chris, director of the Campus Writing and Speaking Program at North Carolina State University, has discovered many uses of Web 2.0 technologies for students to give and receive feedback on their writing. Recent innovations such as YackPack (http://www.yackpack.com), a Web-based voice response system that uses e-mail to announce the presence of new voice messages, and an online digital video exchange using such tools as Skype or podcasting offer exciting new ways for students and teachers to talk to each other about their work online. Chris's longtime use of reflection logs (Anson & Beach, 1995) is now significantly enhanced through online tools. In his work training teachers to use writing as a tool to foster learning across the curriculum (Anson, 2002; 2006), Chris has also developed activities for using Web 2.0 tools in a range of different subject matter areas. And as a member of the faculty in a new, cutting-edge Ph.D. program in Communication, Rhetoric, and Digital Media (http://www.chass.ncsu.edu/crdm/index.htm), he and his colleagues keep abreast of emerging technologies for potential use in educational institutions.

Lee-Ann has created online introductory college composition courses at the University of Minnesota that involve extensive use of online chat for developing ideas for writing and for providing peer feedback to drafts. She has also conducted extensive research on the value of peer feedback, resulting in her book, *Virtual Peer Review: Teaching and Learning About Writing in Online Environments* (Breuch, 2004). Based on her research, she has found that peers need training in how to provide concrete, reader-based feedback in virtual contexts in lieu of operating in face-to-face conferences. And in teaching her online composition courses, she has also had to grapple with issues of how one evaluates and assesses online writing based on the development of criteria specific to online writing.

Thom has been using digital writing for years in teaching courses on New Media, journalism, and digital literature. He is interested in how Web 2.0 writing tools represent a new way of communicating and constructing knowledge (Morris & Swiss, 2006; Swiss, 2001; Swiss & Herman, 2000). In his courses, he employs blogging as a means of helping students engage in multimodal writing associated with New Media communication. Thom also creates digital poetry (Swiss & Nakamura, 2002) that involves the extensive use of multimodal tools to mesh words, sounds, images, and video (http://www.uiowa.edu/~iwp/newmedia/gallery/thom_swiss.html). As past president of the Electronic Literature Association (http://eliterature.org), he has been actively engaged in promoting the use of Web 2.0 tools in creative writing classes.

We hope that in using the tools described in this book in their classrooms, the readers of this book will find that their students will be engaged in digital writing. If so, we ask that they share examples of such engagement on the book's wiki resource site: http://digitalwriting.pbwiki.com.

Acknowledgments

We would like to thank all the many teachers and students who contributed material to this book. Their work is a testimony to their engagement in digital writing.

We would also like to thank the reviewers of drafts of this book for their invaluable feedback and suggestions for revision: Andrea Bartlett, Barbara Ganley, Dawn Hogue, Sara Kajder, Michael Kamil, and Lisa Zawilinski.

We also thank Hiram Howard of Christopher-Gordon, for encouraging us to take up and continue work on this project. Finally, we would like to thank our editors, Jennifer Bengtson and Adam Shalvey, for all their good work in supporting this book.

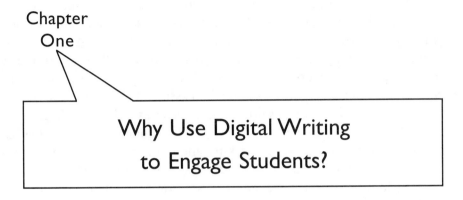

Chapter
One

Why Use Digital Writing to Engage Students?

Engagement in an Online Role-Play

In this book, we argue that digital writing through use of blogs, wikis, online discussion, digital storytelling, podcasts, e-zines, digital scrapbooks, or e-portfolios can serve to engage students in writing. This engagement was evident in an online role-play conducted in two sections of a 12th-grade college writing class taught by Elizabeth Boeser in fall 2007 at Jefferson High School, Bloomington, Minnesota (http://missboeser.googlepages.com/collegewriting). Elizabeth's students were reading the novel *Montana 1948* (Watson, 1993), which portrays family conflicts between a father, Frank Hayden, who is the local town sheriff; his brother, who is charged with raping the Native American maid; and the grandfather, who attempts to prevent one son from arresting the other son. The novel reflects the institutional racism of 1948 in eastern Montana that positioned Native Americans as second-class citizens, so that the rape of the maid was not considered to be a serious crime.

Elizabeth wanted her students to consider whether the institutional racism portrayed in the world of 1948 in the novel is operating in contemporary society. She therefore created an online role-play on a classroom blog focusing on the legal debates over the issue of the University of North Dakota's (UND) use of a "Fighting Sioux" mascot for that university's sports teams. She knew that this dispute over the mascot reflects the larger issue of the use of derogatory mascot names by many universities, which reifies negative media stereotypes of Native Americans. She also knew that this was a debatable issue—some people believe that the use of the mascot name does not in itself constitute a derogatory statement about Native Americans.

Because she wanted to help students learn persuasive writing, rather than simply conducting an oral debate, she decided to set up an online debate in which students would adopt roles and post written arguments in opposition to or in favor of use of the Fighting Sioux mascot as well as respond to each other's posts. She created a class blog using Blogger.com (http://roleplaymascots.blogspot.com). She then assigned roles based on the characters in the novel, as well as other related roles associated with the debate: the UND President, members of the Sioux tribe, students on the hockey team, the owner of the Washington Redskins, and so on. Students then used these roles to create bios to describe their roles. She also provided background reading about both the novel and the issue on her course website (http://missboeser.googlepages.com/montana1948), and she created a wiki (http://jhscollegewritingmontana.pbwiki.com) for students to collaboratively contribute information about the different characters in the novel and the issue. Students would later use material from this wiki to write a compare-and-contrast essay analyzing themes in the novel—for example, the conflicts related to race (White versus Native Americans), sex (males versus females), and class (rich versus poor) (http://jhscollegewritingmontana.pbwiki.com/Comparisons+and+Contrasts).

The students read background material on the legalities of the issue, which included the fact that the National Collegiate Athletic Association (NCAA) had issued a ruling barring UND from using this mascot that UND was challenging in court. A settlement was reached whereby within the next 3 years, UND had to seek approval from two of the major North Dakota Sioux tribes to use the mascot, or else it would no longer be used.

On the blog, students staked out their different positions. One student, Katie Nelson, assumed the role of the Native American novelist, Louise Erdrich, who frequently writes about the North Dakota Sioux Indians. She wrote that she:

> recently turned down an honorary degree from UND because of the mascot issue. I turned it down because I believe that having their mascot [be] a Sioux Indian is very disrespectful to the tribes. I think that changes need to be made in order to respect the tribes.

The character Gloria Hayden, Frank Hayden's wife in the novel, played by Maria Larson, posits:

> I agree with getting rid of the logo. I find it offensive to the Native American culture. I think the Sioux tribe should be celebrated and not be used as a mascot for a team called the Fighting Sioux. If people see this as a way to honor them, there are better ways. Native Americans have been through many hardships in their life and this should not be another burden for them to carry. There are different mascots the team can have. I am a firm believer in banning the mascot of the fighting Sioux.

Another student, Ellie Hannibal, assuming the role of a white female student at UND, voiced her support for keeping the mascot:

> I love going to the hockey games and hanging out with friends. I myself play on the North Dakota volleyball team. The teachers and academics are amazing here in North Dakota. The school is beautifully portrayed in the great city of Grand Forks. The students are friendly and welcoming. I am very proud of our school and I believe that our mascot should stay. It is a huge part of our state's history and I think it proudly represents the Sioux people in our community. GO FIGHTING SIOUX!

Students also provided comments on one another's posts. One student, Sarah Schofield, who was playing the role of Native American leader Clyde Bellecourt, used her comments to challenge the idea of retaining the mascot: "In comments I have been writing to other people, I have been trying to persuade them to think of other people because we are offended very much by this name." In a comment to the owner of the Washington Redskins, Winona Yepa, played by Shannon McKeown, noted:

> As a Native American woman, I am also very offended by the name "redskins." Perhaps your name should be changed to Washington "Whitetrash"; then perhaps you could see why I feel the way I do about the name. We are Native Americans, not redskins. I find it to be a very offensive name. At least NDSU has enough respect for Native Americans to address us properly as "Sioux"; the fighting part is debatable, but they don't refer to us as "redskins." We have names.

Participating in this debate for a week, both in class and at home, required students to respond to each others' arguments by creating counterarguments. In some cases, students changed their beliefs by participating in the role-play. Megan Ward noted that "the more I learn about how it's affecting people and why the nickname, mascot, and logo shouldn't be used . . . the more I think that it should be banned."

Students also found that conducting the role-play online allowed them to readily access all their peers' posts so that they could discern the different positions being voiced. As Megan noted:

> I liked seeing the sides of all different people and what they thought about the issue…I thought that it was a lot easier than what it might have been if we did it in person. We could share our opinions without maybe getting into a heated discussion that might have ended badly. I also liked that we had a bio that people read so they knew where we came from and why we thought the things we did.

Natalie Hazel valued the blog as encouraging students who often do not participate in face-to-face discussions to voice their opinions:

> I'm really glad that we did it on a blog because it gives people a chance to really voice their opinions. Especially people who don't say much in class. They can basically say whatever they want on their blog, because it's not actually them talking. It's their character. I would really like it if we could do it again for another book.

Katie Peterson remarked on the value of involving two different classes:

> I liked this role-play because it helped me change my mind on the issue. I think since we did this role-play with two different classes it was easy . . . also with the blog, it is easier to post links and have legitimate sources to back up your argument.

Students liked the fact that they could readily access related online information from the course website and elsewhere. Kyle Rusnacko noted that having online materials helped him in his role as the newspaper editor:

> It was easy to play devil's advocate because there was so much evidence that we read on both sides that I didn't feel like I was forfeiting my personal beliefs. I really liked the overall activity because there's so much research online that we could back up what we were doing with a lot of evidence. It was easy to make knowledgeable comments and get some background on the information.

The Value of Digital Writing

These students were highly engaged in writing in this online role-play. We attribute their engagement, the focus of this book, to Elizabeth's use of a blog and wiki, digital tools that afforded opportunities for students to do the following:

- read and respond to all of one another's writing from two different classes within a public arena, rather than a student simply handing in a written paper to a teacher as the sole audience

- Create an online persona involving different language uses and voices, as well as visual images, to represent their role

- Participate in a debate as a social conversation involving competing perspectives without the physical intimidation of face-to-face interactions

- Access and draw on online research for evidence to bolster their arguments

- Collaboratively share information and write papers using the wiki

Engagement in writing is critical to improving writing. Students are often not engaged in their writing in school, particularly because they perceive little purpose or value in completing work sheets or writing five-paragraph essays to prepare for standardized writing tests (Hillocks, 2002). Moreover, they spend little time writing in high school. One study found that 71% of high school seniors had written only three or fewer papers during their 2004 senior year. When these students went to college, they were often not prepared for the marked increase in the amount of writing they had to do; half of students at liberal arts colleges had to write at least five papers that were 5 to 19 pages in length during their first year in college (Center for Evaluation & Education Policy, 2005).

However, simply increasing the amount of writing in high school does not necessarily enhance students' engagement with writing. To be engaged in writing, students need to perceive some purpose and value in writing—that it can be used to influence and engage audiences, something that Elizabeth's students experienced. Nor does more writing result in better writing. Students are more likely to improve their writing when they learn to self-assess and revise their writing with appropriate reader response and feedback (Beach & Friedrich, 2006).

In this introductory chapter, we argue that use of Web 2.0 digital writing tools such as blogs, wikis, online chat, digital storytelling, and podcasts can help students improve their learning and writing ability (@ = Digital tools in teaching writing)[1]. We also argue that using these tools helps students learn crucial composing processes related to improving writing, such as generating, organizing, and mapping material; sharing and brainstorming ideas through online chat; collaboratively constructing and sharing knowledge; formulating arguments and ideas for online audiences; and providing and using feedback to revise texts in progress (Cushman, DeVoss, Grabill, Hart-Davidson, & Porter, 2005).

---

[1] As we explain at the end of this chapter, these symbols refer to terms used in a companion wiki to this book.

The user of Web 2.0 tools assumes an active role as both a participant in and contributor of information on the Web (O'Reilly, 2005). Richardson's (2006) description of the "Read/Write Web" (p. 3) involves both reading *and* composing on the Web (@ = Web 2.0 theory and practice). Rather than simply passively accessing information on websites, in creating and responding to blogs, wikis, podcasts, or chat sites, students are actively constructing and sharing their own knowledge (@ = Research on digital New Media/New Media research centers).

Henry Jenkins (2006a) has described this online social world as a "participatory culture" with the following properties (p. 3):

1. Low barriers to artistic expression and civic engagement

2. Strong support for creating and sharing one's creations with others

3. Some type of informal mentorship whereby what is known by the most experienced is passed along to novices

4. A belief by members that their contributions matter

5. A feeling among members of some degree of social connection with one another

Jenkins argues that engagement in this participatory culture enhances students' writing by providing students with immediate and worldwide audiences who value their writing. By submitting their narrative writing to online fan communities, students acquire feedback from other interested writers (Black, 2008). By participating in these online sites, students are learning to use written language to adopt different voices and perspectives based on their perceptions of the online audiences they are addressing (Lewis & Fabos, 2005).

Acquiring Digital Literacies Through Digital Writing

In using digital writing, students are acquiring what are known as digital literacies, associated with reading and creating digital texts. Given the importance of teaching students these digital literacies, the National Council of Teachers of English (NCTE, 2008) recommends that students engage in a number of activities related to digital writing:

- Developing proficiency with the tools of technology

- Building relationships with others to pose and solve problems collaboratively and cross-culturally

- Designing and sharing information for global communities to meet a variety of purposes

- Managing, analyzing, and synthesizing multiple streams of simultaneous information
- Creating, critiquing, analyzing, and evaluating multimedia texts
- Attending to the ethical responsibilities required by these complex environments

Combining Images, Video Clips, Audio, and Text to Create Multimodal Productions

Through use of digital writing, students are acquiring a number of digital literacies. In creating digital texts, students can readily combine images, video clips, audio, and text to create multimodal texts (Kress, 2003; Shipka, 2005) (@ = multimodal writing). In the role-play, Elizabeth's students could see an image of the mascot on the blog's front page. In creating their bios, they embedded images in the blog. In creating these multimodal texts, students are drawing on their high level of engagement with images and video. As Jeff Utecht (2007) notes:

> Morning after morning my middle school students come in and head to one website—YouTube. YouTube is the new entertainment center for teens, and I don't blame them. Spend some time there and you soon find the minutes flying by as you get deeper into viewing what people have created and contributed to this social-network. Where was this when I was in school? I remember having to run to the computer lab to make sure I got one of the copies of Oregon Trail . . . the original Oregon Trail! (p. 2)

Jeff recognized the need to tap into his students' engagement with these tools by having them create their own digital stories:

> Watching this day after day, I decided to harness this power of creativity and have my students create digital stories. Using the free Microsoft application, Photo Story 3, and the tutorials created by David Jakes, my students taught themselves how to use the program to create their stories for class. Then using the K12 group within YouTube that Miguel Guhlin created, the students uploaded the videos to share with a worldly audience. Students as creators contributing their new knowledge to the world. (p. 2)

To effectively combine images, video, audio, and text, students need to know how to select, edit, mesh, modify, or remix material in creative ways that will engage their audiences. Selecting digital texts involves collecting or appropriating material based on a certain topic, theme, or issue—for example, images in online magazine ads or sites such as Flirkr or Google Images. Once students collect this material, they can then edit and mesh this material to highlight certain patterns—for example, how some images of masculinity emphasize physical prowess while other images emphasize emotional bonding.

Creating these image collages then leads students to write about these perceived patterns in representations of masculinity to create text or audio that accompanies the images. In collecting digital texts, students can modify or remix images, video, audio, and text in ways that reframe the original meaning of these texts, as evident in "culture jamming" (Lankshear & Knobel, 2003) parodies on YouTube or Adbuster parodies of ads. In the role-play, students used images of University of North Dakota hockey fans to parody the obsession with hockey at that school.

Fostering Collaborative Interaction Between Writers and Readers

Another digital literacy involved in digital writing is the collaborative interaction between writers and readers. Gunther Kress (2007) notes that this interactivity between writer and reader shifts the direction of knowledge construction and authority from author to reader to a collaborative sharing of knowledge between author and reader:

> With the screen as a medium, the direction is always two-way—I can change the e-mail that has been sent to me or the text of the attachment that came with it. The possibilities of dissemination of my text-as-message are the same as those of the person who had sent me the message. This has entirely changed the "authority of authorship." (p. 30)

Because the reader now can readily appropriate and alter texts, the writer no longer can control how their reader will process those texts:

> In the "older" text, the reader was obliged by both the form of the text and convention to read the text in the order set out by the author. Now it is the reader's interest that fixes the order of reading. In that sense, all readers have become authors or designers of the texts with which they engage. This has its analogue in composing; a situation much lamented by teachers. When I am on the Internet, I may go where I please, constrained to some extent by the organization of choices in the architecture of websites. If I am thinking of composing a text, I can take the resources for that from anywhere—usually described and misunderstood as cut and paste and not as real writing or composition. (p. 30)

This shift toward a more interactive relationship between writer and reader means that students are more aware of potential audience response because they may be more likely to actually receive immediate audience response. A study of students' uses of digital tools finds that they enjoy creating digital texts because that work is immediately responded to by peers and larger online audiences (Olsen, 2008).

When Elizabeth's students posted their arguments to retain or remove the Fighting Sioux mascot, they knew that they would be receiving comments to their blog posts from opponents and proponents who challenged or supported their positions. They were therefore aware of writing within a rhetorical community in which their readers had a lot of power. As Elizabeth noted in reflecting on the activity:

> Because students are writing for and to each other in a centralized space, they then develop a sense of being members of a writing community who build off each other's ideas as members of a classroom community.

Students can also use digital writing tools such as wikis or Google Docs to collaboratively compose texts, something we describe in more detail in chapter 4. During and after the role-play, Elizabeth's students worked collaboratively to add material to the wiki about *Montana 1948* (Watson, 1993). They then worked in teams of two and three to write their compare-and-contrast essays about the novel. The wiki allowed them to work together on the same text without having to pass around a document, something that can be cumbersome for multiple authors.

One advantage of using wikis is that students in other or future sections of a course can then continue to add new material to a wiki. When Elizabeth teaches *Montana 1948* again in the future, other students can access the work of previous students and build on that work. Knowing that one is actually contributing to enhancing knowledge for one's present and future peer group can serve to motivate students' writing, which is reflected in people's willingness to voluntarily contribute to *Wikipedia*.

Using Hyperlinks to Connect Texts

Another important digital literacy involves the use of hyperlinks to connect texts. In writing blog posts, students are continually linking to other blog posts, texts, images, or video clips. In Richard's media studies class, students use blogs to analyze media or film texts (http://teachingmedialiteracy.pbwiki.com). In their blog posts, they can easily embed links to YouTube videos of movie trailers, advertisements, or clips from television shows. Rather than simply reading their peers' analysis of a video clip, the other students in the class can then also view these clips, leading them to post comments about their own perception of the clip.

Much early digital writing involved creating texts, particularly narratives, as hypertexts using tools such as Storyspace (http://www.eastgate.com/storyspace) (Landow, 2006). Hypertexts are organized around hyperlinks so that readers navigate through a text by clicking on optional links. For example, to navigate through Stuart Moulthrop's (1995) *Victory Garden* (http://www.eastgate.com/VG/VGStart.html), readers click on links to move from one event to another. Students also use more recently developed hypertext tools such as Hypertextopia (http://www.hypertextopia.com) to visually link ideas in their text as a continuation, illustration, or rebuttal of their positions.

All this raises the question of whether creating hypertextual links actually serves to enhance writing quality. Martine Braaksma, Gert Rijlaarsdam, and Tanja Janssen of the University of Amsterdam summarize the results of an ongoing research project that addresses this relationship between creating hypertexts and writing quality:

In our research, we examined the benefits of writing hypertextual writing about the topic of "good charities." We provided the students with documentation materials (e.g., newspaper articles, tables with results from research) about "good charities." So, there was no need for the students to gather information about "good charities" themselves. Furthermore, students did not start with writing their argumentative text immediately. Instead, they spent a large amount of time with practicing argumentation skills and with an exploration of the subject "good charities."

> The students liked the writing of the hypertexts. Furthermore, they responded positively to cooperation with other students, the provided documentation about "good charities," the making of the concept maps, the invention of an own "good cause," and the practical nature of the lesson series.
>
> In general, the hypertexts the students wrote were of a good quality (http://www.ilo.uva.nl/homepages/martine/hypertext_project.htm). Due to the clear technical instruction, all students were able to compose their argumentative text in hypertext form. Because we did not provide explicit instruction about the structure and (type of) links, the hypertexts were different in structure, which is, from our point of view, a good starting point for subsequent lessons. Some students wrote a quite long "linear-like" home page with "only" informative links in it (e.g., explanations of the work from nonprofit charitable organizations); other students also wrote a "linear-like" home page but used links to the arguments for their standpoint. Other students composed a more hierarchical hypertext containing a short home page with an introduction and the formulation of their standpoint and with links to subpages in which they worked out their arguments and conclusion.

The outcomes of a pilot study we performed indicated that hypertext writing may have positive effects on writing skills. In that study we observed that secondary school students (eighth and ninth grade) who performed hypertext-like tasks were more often engaged in planning and analyzing activities during writing than students who performed linear text-tasks. These planning and analyzing activities were positively related to text quality, both in the hypertext-tasks and in the linear text-tasks. Therefore, we concluded that writing hypertexts could stimulate the use of cognitive activities that were positively related to writing proficiency.

Subscribing to and Searching for Online Material

Another digital literacy involves accessing and subscribing to online material using digital tools such as RSS feeds. Blog writers employ RSS feeds to access and respond to one another's blog posts. Rather than having to wade through large numbers of blogs, they use an RSS feed reader such as Bloglines or Google Reader to subscribe to blogs that are then delivered to what amounts to a Bloglines or Google Reader post office. Readers can then quickly scan through post topics to find relevant material. As we explain in more detail in the next chapter, rather than having to continually search for material consistent with their interests, readers using RSS feeds can maintain an ongoing connection with these texts that builds a sense of community with other online writers.

A related digital literacy is the ability to search for relevant material using specific categories or key terms to access databases, something we discuss in more detail in the next chapter. Students need to learn not only to identify search categories but also to define the logical relationships these categories. In the online role-play, Elizabeth's students were continually accessing the online articles associated with the Fighting Sioux issue to find material to embed in their texts. To frame their arguments for or against the use of the Fighting Sioux mascot, they were searching for information using categories such as "mascot names," and "controversy," or "challenges" to find instances in which certain names such as the Washington Redskins or Florida State Seminoles had been challenged and the reasons for those challenges.

To help others find their own blog posts or online images or videos, students learn to use tags. For example, on Flickr or YouTube, students tag photos or videos as members of groups who create a "folksonomy" of tags or categories based on these shared interests—for example, pictures of 1950s cars. Tagging this material using relevant key terms requires students to infer the primary focus of their work related to their intended meaning. If they are keeping a blog about their soccer team's season, and their post is about their effective use of teamwork, they may then tag their post, "soccer," "teamwork," or "passing."

Editing, Formatting, and Customizing Texts

Another digital literacy that students acquire through use of digital writing involves the ability to edit, format, or customize digital texts to enhance audience readability and engagement. In contrast to print texts, digital texts can be easily customized through choices of templates, layouts, fonts, images, and formatting tools. Students can create their own unique look for blogs, scrapbooks, classroom newspapers, comic books, and so on through uses of images and templates. Because they perceive their texts as having an attractive format and appearance, they may then be more concerned with editing their texts, given the need to make them appear as published texts on the Web. Being able to customize their own texts—for example, selecting a template for their blog that reflects their own interests and personality—helps "students define themselves as individuals, not pupils who use a teacher-sanctioned tool to post work" (Glogowski, 2007, p. 10).

Purposes for Using Digital Writing Tools

Simply using digital writing tools such as blogs or wikis may not necessarily improve student writing. Students need to learn how to use digital writing tools to achieve certain purposes that drive their learning. Digital technology tools contain certain built-in information that allows people to use them as tools to fulfill certain purposes. Blogs are designed to connect to large audiences through use of RSS feeds. Wikis are designed to foster collaborative writing. Global positioning systems (GPS) contain geographical information that helps people to locate certain places. The iPhone allows people to interact with others and view videos at any time or place.

These digital tools mean that student learning is no longer limited to school space. Now that digital tools such as GPS, cell phones, or iPhones have become portable and ubiquitous, students have instant access to information, which reduces the limitations on when and where one can learn (Burbules, 2007). They foster interconnectedness, for one is in continual social contact with others, and they blur distinctions between work and play, public and private, accessing and creating information, and learning and entertainment.

These digital writing tools are not limited just to English language arts classes. In writing up a chemistry lab report as a blog posting in their science class, students can import and analyze video clips of chemical reactions. In a social studies class, they can keep digital field notes for an observational study. Digital writing tools fosters writing to learn in ways that encourages higher order, cross-disciplinary thinking. These digital writing tools can follow students across different subjects or different school years. Students can use the same blog or e-portfolio for different subjects, allowing different teachers to perceive how their students are writing in all their courses. As we discuss in chapter 10, students can then use these digital repositories of their writing to reflect on changes and development in their learning over time. The Teaching, Learning, and Technology site (http://www.tltgroup.org/resources/gx/Digital-WAC.htm) showcases assignments that foster higher order, cross-disciplinary thinking through the collection and synthesis of data, different kinds of reasoning, engaging audiences, collaborative writing, long-term development, and adopting different discipline-specific genres and voices. We also include examples of uses of digital writing in different subject-matter areas throughout the book. On the wiki site, we include further examples of digital writing across the curriculum (@ = Digital writing across the curriculum).

Fostering Student Development in the Use of Digital Writing Tools

Given the importance of learning how digital writing tools achieve certain purposes, we need to consider how students perceive their uses as more than simply completing writing assignments for teachers—now on blogs or wikis rather than in Word. Clay Burell (2008) warns that blogging can easily become "just another way to turn in homework. Blogging, like thinking, creativity, and other joys, turned into an aversive horror by the forces of schooliness" (p. 1).

In this book, we believe that one of the larger purposes of using digital writing tools is to encourage students to learn to voice their ideas on their own initiative, such as using a blog to rally support for a cause, instead of simply using it to complete a homework assignment.

Fostering student self-initiated digital writing occurs over a series of four phases defined in terms of whether the writing is teacher- or student-initiated or written primarily in a classroom or school context with adult-developed tools or in a peer and Web context. These two parameters are depicted in Figure 1-1. These phases are developmental; the initial three phases serve to model digital writing practices and literacies necessary to achieve students' self-initiated digital writing.

Phase I: Development begins with teacher-assigned writing, primarily for the teacher as audience in a classroom or school context—the process of using blogs for homework assignments for the teacher.

Phase II: This exploits the fact that digital writing shifts to composing not only for the teachers but also for peers and the larger Web audience. Students and these audiences then interact in what James Gee (2004) describes as "affinity spaces" built on common interests and the knowledge valued by a group. Through their

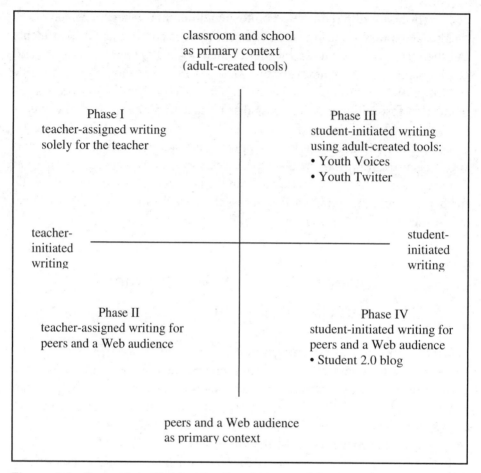

Figure 1-1. Parameters Shaping the Development of Students' Self-Initiated Digital Writing

participation in these affinity spaces, students know that they are contributing to and constructing "collective intelligence, turning the web into a kind of global brain . . . the blogosphere is the equivalent of constant mental chatter in the forebrain, the voice we hear in all of our heads" (O'Reilly, 2005, p. 14).

Writing for potential Web audiences transports the writing into a larger public arena, or what Konrad Glogowski (2006) describes as "third spaces" associated with out-of-school writing. In contrast to "first space" home and "second space" work or school spaces, third spaces are informal public spaces, such as restaurants, bars, parks, or malls, where people interact (Oldenburg, 2000). Within these third spaces that transcend the "forces of schooliness" (Burell, 2008, p. 1), students begin to adopt alternative or hybrid language styles that deviate from academic prose—for example, creating parodies of popular culture or official school discourses (West, 2008).

Glogowski (2006) argues that students need opportunities in school to use digital writing in relatively informal ways, similar to striking up conversations with peers or others in public. Students are then exposed to alternative perspectives and ideas that challenge their status quo thinking. He cites the example of an activity in which his students began writing about issues of genocide and human rights on their blogs. In doing so, they were still writing about these topics from their own individual perspectives. However, when they started reading and responding to their peers' posts, they began to perceive the value of links to others' posts to further their own thinking. Glogowski recounts this shift in their perspectives:

> Then, one day at the end of April, it all changed. They started linking to each other's work because they found other entries meaningful and relevant. No, I do not mean that they linked to entries that explored the same topics. No. They started linking to entries that helped them expand their own understanding of issues that they were struggling with. I began to see semantic relations.

Glogowski notes that as the students developed a shared interest in the topic of human rights, they "realized that the topics they had chosen brought them all closer together, through debate, through common research ideas, through links and correspondences that they created based on meaning, based on commonly shared research interests" (p. 3).

Phase III: Once students become comfortable writing for peers and Web audiences in a public third-space arena, they may then be more likely to engage in self-initiated writing. They no longer need teacher assignments to prompt their writing. At the same time, students, particularly in elementary and middle school, may still need support and modeling to encourage their self-initiated writing. This is where sites created by adults or teachers can be useful, such as Youth Voices (http://youthvoices.net) or Youth Twitter (http://www.youthtwitter.com), developed by Paul Allison of the New York City Writing Project to encourage student writing beyond school assignments. On these sites, Allison may still be a participant who encourages students to expand on their writing, but the writing is initiated by students. Similarly, students working on the LivingArchives.ca project in Nova Scotia, Canada—collecting and archiving artifacts from the early 1900s—were given a lot of autonomy in what and how they collected and exhibited their artifacts.

Phase IV: In the final phase, students initiate their own writing using their own tools—for example, student-run sites such as Student 2.0 blog (http://students2oh.org), which is only for students, or social networking sites such as Facebook. In this phase, students are no longer writing in response to an adult-sponsored assignment or project; they are writing because they want to write. In doing so, they are developing a sense of themselves as writers who perceive writing as a means of sharing their experiences or influencing others' actions. Sharing their writing encourages them to voice their subjective perspectives on their lives. Based on interviews with hundreds of adolescents about their uses of digital writing, Susannah Stern (2008) found that adolescents use blogs or social networking sites to share their feelings about their daily experiences. For example, one interviewee noted the following:

> My blog has helped me to center my feelings and realize that I need to take things one step at a time. It forces me to think about who I am, what I like, and who I want to be. I can think about one of the problems I am going to face, but writing about it allows me to work through the problem and start to look at solutions. (p. 102)

In this study, adolescents also used blogs to chronicle key events in their identity development. As one adolescent noted, "'My blog keeps tabs on me'" (p. 102). It is evident in the blog posts on Student 2.0.com that students are eager to share their critiques of current schooling or the political status quo practices, leading to the need to engage in collective action to address and change these practices.

The Importance of Phase IV Self-Initiated Writing

Self-initiated digital writing is important because it leads to increased writing. A Pew Internet and American Life Project study (Lenhart et al., 2008) found that 47% of adolescent bloggers write for personal reasons several times a week outside school, contrasted with 33% of nonblogging teens, with a quarter of these adolescent bloggers writing outside school on a daily basis. Also, 65% of adolescent bloggers perceive writing to be essential to their later success in life, whereas 53% of nonbloggers hold the same belief.

The teens in this study indicated that they enjoy self-initiated writing more than the writing they do for school; about half enjoy writing for personal reasons "a great deal," whereas 17% enjoy school writing with the same level of intensity—and these teens are more likely to participate in creative writing in school. When asked what motivates them to engage in self-initiated writing, they pointed to the importance of being responsible to their audiences by creating engaging writing. They also indicated that when they do writing in school, being able to choose their own topics and being able to publicly share their writing on the Web enhances their writing enjoyment. When asked what would improve their writing skills in school, 78% believed that teachers should employ more use of digital writing tools.

Given this developmental continuum toward students' self-initiated digital writing, most of the classroom activities in this book represent phase II and III activities, writing for peer and Web audiences in teacher-supported contexts, ideally leading students to engage in the phase IV self-initiated writing that the Pew study found leads to higher engagement with both digital and print writing. We do not perceive these phases as linear, but rather as recursive, for students may move back and forth among the phases depending on their assignments or rhetorical context.

A Preview of the Book

Not simply about Web 2.0 digital writing tools, this book is also about the uses of these tools to enhance students' engagement in writing (for other useful books on digital writing tools, see Barton & Cummings, 2008; Black, 2008; Green, Brown, & Robinson, 2008; Hendron, 2008; Hoechsmann & Low, 2008; Richardson, 2006; Solomon & Schrum, 2007; Warlick, 2007). We believe that these tools can be used to teach certain composing processes leading to enhanced engagement and improvement in writing. As outlined below, we have therefore organized this book uses of these different tools to teach specific composing processes.

Chapter 2: Using Digital Writing Tools for Collecting, Connecting, and Organizing Information

One key composing process involves learning how to collect, connect, and organize information typically associated with prewriting activities designed to develop material for use in drafting texts. To help students collect information, we discuss the uses of digital search tools to access information about their topics with search categories and RSS feeds to proactively "trap" sources for relevant information specific to a topic (Calishain, 2007). We then discuss how students can use digital note-taking or annotation tools to record their own perceptions and interpretations of information and the ideas they find in this information. To help students connect and organize information, we discuss how students can use digital mind-mapping tools to visually capture the links between key topics, terms, or ideas.

Chapter 3: Using, Creating, and Managing Digital Discussion Environments

Prewriting and writing activities are best facilitated through discussion, particularly for students who are extroverts on the Myers-Briggs personality inventory and prefer to talk out rather than write their ideas. Chapter 3 offers a number of strategies for engaging students in productive writing in online chat rooms and forums. Through online discussions, students can share ideas in their writing that help them to construct their voice, purpose, and audience.

Chapter 4: Fostering Collaborative Digital Writing

Collaboratively constructing knowledge through the use of wikis or Google Docs represents another important composing process. Wiki writing can invite participation from larger, online audiences; this is evident in Wikipedia, in which readers can contribute their own expertise. In creating their own wikis, students are sharing their ideas with not only their own immediate peers but also the larger public, motivating them to be concerned about the quality of their writing. Learning to write collaboratively helps students learn to work together in groups on projects through assessing and combining alternative perspectives.

Chapter 5: Navigating, Mixing, Creating: Digital Literature

Chapter 5 focuses on the ability to define the connections among texts, images, audio, and video that are involved in creating digital literature or storytelling. To help students make these connections, we discuss ways to provide them with examples of online digital poetry and storytelling, noting the uses of digital literacies involved in creating these texts. We also discuss ways of helping students to combine and remix texts in ways that create literary texts.

Chapter 6: Using Blogs in the Classroom

An especially important composing process—increasingly expected as students move into higher levels of their education—involves the ability to formulate arguments and ideas in a persuasive manner, such as the writing reflected in Elizabeth's online role-play. In chapter 6, we discuss the uses of blogs as a tool for social conversation for helping students formulate their arguments and ideas to both their teachers and peers, who then respond with comments. In responding with questions, reactions, statements, or counterarguments to the entries, the peers foster dialogic exploration of ideas and knowledge.

Chapter 7: Using Digital Audio Productions

Students are often more engaged in their writing if they can produce digital audio productions of their writing for audiences. To do so, students can create podcasts to record and publish their writing that can be readily accessed on iPods or MP3 players. In chapter 7, we describe the use of podcasting tools, as well as other audio production tools such as audio-video conferencing and

Ed.VoiceThread, for producing audio versions of one's writing. We also discuss the use of vlogs, or video blogs, for visually producing one's writing, as well as the uses of audio text-to-speech and speech-to-text tools for use in working with students with learning disabilities.

Chapter 8: Designing and Editing Digital Writing

Another critical composing process involves editing and formatting texts so that they are readable and easy to comprehend and engage audiences through visual rhetoric. As we discuss in chapter 8, editing and formatting texts involves knowing how to combine and vary fonts, images, layouts, templates, color, texts, and sound in ways that will engage audiences. For example, in creating their blog template, students need to know how to employ layout options for presenting information about their blog. In creating PowerPoints, students need to know how to utilize PowerPoint in order to involve audiences in their presentations.

Chapter 9: Using Digital Tools for Formative and Summative Evaluation of Writing

By learning how to "resee" their texts through major and minor revisions, students not only improve the quality of particular projects but also internalize the principles of effective composing. In chapter 9, we discuss the use of online peer feedback conferences and how to train students to formulate descriptive, reader-based feedback in an online context so that writers feel supportive and challenged. We also discuss ways of evaluating students' digital writing through formulating specific criteria for evaluating students' digital writing, criteria related to their ability to employ the specific digital literacies.

Chapter 10: Fostering Reflection Through E-portfolios

In the past, students employed paper portfolios to engage in reflection. As we discuss in chapter 10, they can now use blogs or wikis as e-portfolios to collect, link, and reflect on their writing, noting strengths and weaknesses in different types or genres of writing as well as ways to improve their writing.

Chapter 11: So Now What? Five Ways to Grow as a Digital Writing Teacher

Much of what we present in this book is relatively new to many teachers. This information involves continually learning and growing, including trying out the digital writing tools we discuss in this book for the first time. Our final chapter provides some suggestions on how to use online resources and engage in teacher reflection research to grow and develop as a teacher in using digital writing tools.

Challenges in Using Web 2.0 Tools

This book would be incomplete without a treatment of some of the challenges integrating Web 2.0 tools into the classroom. Before we launch into the advantages and possibilities of these tools in creating rich, forward-looking educational environments, we want to suggest some ways to overcome these challenges so that teachers can move ahead in using of digital tools in the classroom.

Technological Access and Use

Although schools have certainly improved in providing the hardware necessary for the use of these digital tools, issues of access remain a problem in many schools, particularly for schools in low-income areas that may lack the financial support for hardware and software, and for students who may lack broadband access in their homes (@ = Addressing access issues). Some schools still rely on the use of classroom labs, which are often booked up, because they do not have the capacity for students to use laptops in their classrooms. This suggests the need to encourage students to explore alternative ways to gain access—for example, by going to public libraries, which have now become popular places for adolescents to hang out after school.

Online Safety

In participating in social networking sites such as MySpace and Facebook, adolescents are often not aware of the potential risks of self-disclosure of personal information that can lead to unsafe or risky contacts with other adolescents or adults (@ = Avoiding digital dangers). To safeguard students, rather than simply block or restrict all access to Web 2.0 sites, teachers can discuss with them the ethical importance of taking personal responsibility for their online practices as public displays of behavior similar to those in any public space. As we reiterate throughout this book, this includes having students only use first names or pseudonyms, not disclosing their date of birth or other private information, requiring log-ins for school social networking sites, avoiding spam on blogs, and using online netiquette practices.

District Filtering and Blocking Policies

To address safety concerns, some districts have created filters or firewalls that block access to certain sites or software applications, often by contracting out to other companies to create these filters. Unfortunately, this can block access to useful Web 2.0 tools, in many cases, for arbitrary rather than educational reasons. As a result, students may not be able to use blogs, wikis, social-networking sites, or podcasts in the classroom. Teachers therefore need to take an active role in working with and educating school administrators and technology support staff to establish policies related to students' public postings of writing and access to legitimate education sites (Willard, 2007) (@ = Avoiding digital dangers).

Free-Speech Legal Aspects of Online Writing

In crafting a school's "acceptable use" policies, it is important to honor First Amendment provisions that protect students' freedom of speech related to what students can write about certain topics, or in certain ways, with impunity, consistent with the requirements of the Children's Internet Protection Act (CIPA) of 2000 (http://www.fcc.gov/cgb/consumerfacts/cipa.html) that are related to a school's acceptable-use policy.

Being Perceived as the Technology Expert

A major challenge facing teachers employing Web 2.0 tools is the assumption that unless they are an expert in the use of a certain tool, they should not use that tool in the classroom. Although it is certainly important to know why a tool is being used in the classroom, teachers should not necessarily avoid using a tool if they believe that they are not highly techno-savvy. In many cases, teachers can draw on the expertise of technology coordinators, media-center staff, colleagues, and even students to explain or demonstrate the uses of a certain tool.

By initially surveying or querying students about their experience with digital tools, teachers can ascertain the contributions they could make in sharing their experience with the classroom. For example, if some students have expertise in blogging, they can talk to the class about how and why they are engaged with blogging, sharing specific examples of their posts and comments. Treating students as experts serves to bolster their sense of status and agency in the classroom, enhancing their sense of membership in the classroom community.

Teachers can also learn much from online resources, something we discuss in chapter 11 (@ = Standards related to digital writing, @ = Online technology training modules, @ = National Writing Project sites).

We only briefly touch on these and others challenges involved in using Web 2.0 tools. We hope that our descriptions of various digital writing tools and examples of how they are being used effectively in the schools leads teachers to recognize the value of using digital writing tools in the classrooms despite these challenges.

The Wiki Resource Site: http://digitalwriting.pbwiki.com

Any book describing the latest new developments in Web 2.0 technology could be out of date quickly, given the rapid changing world of Web 2.0 technology. Because we are limited by space from including all these resources within this book for teachers' professional development, and because there will be new tools emerging after the publication of this book, we have created a wiki resource site, http://digitalwriting.pbwiki.com, which will be continually updated to include the latest in new Web 2.0 technology tools. This site includes additional information and resources not contained in this book: examples of teaching activities, students' digital writing, links to sites related to the topics in this book, and further reading. Consistent with the interactive Web 2.0 philosophy we espouse in this book, we hope that our readers will also contribute their own knowledge and experiences to this site by adding their own material and links, which are easy to add on a wiki.

To access information from and contribute to this site, just do the following:

1. On entering the site, go first to the side bar that lists the chapters in this book based on chapter topics. Clicking on a chapter topic opens up a list of subtopics within that chapter. Throughout this book, we include these topics through the use of "@ = Topic." For example, the (@ = Web 2.0 theory) that you have already encountered includes links about Web 2.0 theory. Because these "@" topics are listed in the same order on the wiki site as they appear in each chapter, we recommend that as readers read each chapter, they have that chapter link open on the wiki so that they can go to site references under that topic.

2. Click on the topics within each chapter to go to other pages, some of which contain further links to other pages.

3. For activities, student work, and links related to Richard's Teaching Digital Writing course for teachers, click on the CI5475/5330 link at the bottom of the side bar.

4. Add material to this site by contributing examples of teaching activities, students' digital writing, links, and readings that could be shared with other readers. To add material on a specific page, click on "edit page." You will then be asked to enter an "invite key," which is *digwriting.*

To add a URL link to a website, or an e-mail address, select the "Link" icon and select "URL." To create a new page or topic, select "WikiPage." In a new page, you can add more links or cut and paste in text such as a teaching unit or student writing—for which permission to share online has been granted by the student. To insert an image, click on "Insert Image."

5. We respectfully ask that you only add new material and do not delete material. By adding new material to this site, readers of this book are sharing their applications of digital writing in the classroom for the benefit of other readers, a manifestation of the ideal use of the "Read/Write Web" (Richardson, 2006).

We will continue to add new books and articles on digital writing to the "further reading" link for each chapter. We will also add books to a Digital Writing Teachers Shelfari group site (http://www.shelfari.com/groups/27518/about). Readers are welcome to add their own titles to the Shelfari group site.

Chapter
Two

Using Digital Writing Tools for Collecting, Connecting, and Organizing Information

In this chapter, we discuss the use of tools for collecting, connecting, and organi-zation information that students acquire online for use in their writing. One reason for the students' engagement with the Fighting Sioux role-play described in chapter 1 was that they could quickly find information and images online to create their biographical portrait for their characters or to bolster their argu-ments for or against retaining the University of North Dakota mascot. In reflect-ing on her experience with the role-play in an interview with Richard, Katie Nelson noted that:

> I really liked the role-play because there was so much research online that we could back up what we were doing with a lot of evidence if people referred to something. It was easy to make knowledgeable comments and get some background on the information.

Engaging in Online Searches

Consistent with the importance of prewriting to generate information for use in their writing, students need to know how to use digital tools to search for, access, and import online information from various databases or digital texts into their writing. Underlying the use of online information is the need for students to recognize the need to support their contentions with evidence or facts. After the students completed the Fighting Sioux role-play, they then worked collaboratively in groups of three to write compare-and-contrast essays about themes in *Montana, 1948* (Watson, 1993). In framing this assignment, the teacher, Elizabeth emphasized the importance of accessing and incorporating evidence from the novel and from outside sources (http://jhscollegewritingmontana.pbwiki.com/Comparisons+and+Contrasts):

> The best essays will include at least six documented (cited) examples from *Montana 1948* and at least three outside sources that are related to research. (You may use definitions from an online source like www.dictionary.com or a quote from an unrelated source like http://www.brainyquote.com, but they will not count as research.)

Framing a Purpose, Topic, or Question

Equally important in engaging in online searches is students' ability to frame a specific purpose, topic, or question that will guide their searches. If their purpose, topic, or question is too broad—for example, the effects of global warming on the environment—they may be overwhelmed with too many search results. If it is too narrow, they may generate insufficient results.

It is also important that students adopt an inquiry stance in which they develop their own questions about a topic or an issue driving their investigation. To frame their inquiry, students could list questions and then select those questions that most interest them (Beach & Myers, 2001) (@ = Inquiry-based learning). One useful tool for modeling inquiry-based questions or activities are Webquests—specific inquiry-based assignments that contain links for collecting information for completing specific activities (Dodge, 2006) (@ = WebQuest design).

In her compare-and-contrast essay prompt, Elizabeth specified the nature of the inquiry involved in analyzing the contrasting themes in the novel:

> Your paper will need a thesis. Looking at the general topic above, each group will need to present the topic and show how the contrasting elements suggested in parentheses relate to each other. You may want to show how the theme works in the world throughout history or in current events and use evidence from *Montana 1948* to support your claim. You can apply your topic to characters only in *Montana 1948*. You may want to show how your topic affects the outcome of events in the book. You could discuss how writers often use your topic as a theme in a book and use *Montana 1948* as a representative example of that idea. Some questions for your paper are supplied below to get you thinking about the topic: What does my topic mean (define the topic)? How does my topic apply to people in

> general? How have other authors presented this theme in their texts? How have teachers discussed these ideas in my classes? Which groups of people generally discuss, present, and/or defend issues related to my topic?

Students then wrote about the following themes: sex (males and females), race (whites and Native Americans), age (generations), class (wealth and poverty), power (control and submission), ethics (loyalty and betrayal), mortality (life and death), truth (lies and deceit), knowledge (innocence and wisdom), place (country and town), temperature and weather (heat and cold), and roles (hero and villain).

To frame their online searches, students selected specific keywords to access relevant information. Three students, Rachel Brummer, Claire Maccani, and Kyle Rusnacko, wrote their paper on the topic of "truth and lies." In an interview with Richard, Rachel noted that the novel revolves around characters deceiving each other:

> In the book, this kid's uncle was a rapist and he molested Native Americans. He deceived people with his character—he was charming . . . he was lying to the town with his character. The family never told anyone, to protect their reputation because they were a prominent family.

For writing their essay, the students were interested in what prompted these characters to deceive one another by not telling the truth. To frame their search, they posed the following questions: "What really prompted these people to lie? What situations were they covering up and how would their reputations be affected if people found out about these lies?"

Challenges in Engaging in Online Searches

In conducting online searches, students experience a number of difficulties. Students will often first turn to search engines such as Google, Yahoo Search, or Ask/Teoma, which simply scour the Web for frequently accessed or relevant sites. Although they may generate a lot of hits, these search sites may not be very relevant, leading students to choose limited or nonscholarly information unless they spend time sifting through many sites. Given the difficulties with search engines, librarians suggest that students are better off going directly to database collections of specific articles, documents, or materials associated with a specific topic or subject. In most cases, students can access these databases through their libraries' sites, such as InfoTrac Junior Edition, Academic Search Premier, Gale Group, CQ Researcher, or General Reference Center Gold.

Students may also browse unsystematically without any sense of purpose or direction related to addressing their topic or issue. As they are browsing, students need to critically reflect on the information they are acquiring so that they are purposefully making choices to select relevant links. "It's not just point and click. It's point, read, think, click" (Coiro, 2003, p. 3). Some of this unsystematic browsing is the result of not clearly identifying specific search categories or keywords. Students often have not formulated specific, relevant, mutually exclusive categories, so they then become lost in a sea of data.

They also may not know how to judge the value, sufficiency, relevancy, and validity of information they acquire. This requires self-monitoring and metacognitive awareness, which is a challenge for students with memory, attention-deficit, or spatial processing problems (McNabb, Thurber, Dibuz, McDermott, & Lee, 2006).

To help her students overcome these difficulties, Elizabeth modeled search strategies using a projector (@ = Search strategies); whiteboards can also be used for modeling search strategies (@ = Whiteboards). She described how she narrowed down her search by specifying certain key terms. She also discussed the need to select particular search tools to address particular questions or issues (@ = Search sites).

Elizabeth had students work with media center resource people, who assisted students in their searches using databases in the media center. To assist students in searching for material, librarians have created what are called "pathfinders," which provide students with directions on how and where to search for specific topics or to complete specific assignments (Valenza, 2005/2006) (@ = Pathfinders/research guides).

These pathfinders are designed to provide students with the same kind of support a librarian would provide in a face-to-face interaction with a student, although they don't substitute for such individual help. The pathfinders contain information about keywords to use for searching, databases (usually limited to library subscribers), links, blogs, wikis, or experts to e-mail. They also begin with an initial description of a topic or an issue that provides a context for students' research.

Once Rachel, Claire, and Kyle specified their questions for writing about why people lie, they then needed to search for relevant information, both in the novel and from outside sources, that would address their questions. To access online information on research for why people lie, they went to a number of different sites. In describing her search strategies, Rachel noted that she frequently begins with a Google search but then moves to more specific databases available in the school media center:

> I start with Google and then I look for articles that I find and then I read those and then I refine my search. Then I go to databases like Gale Group and CQ Researcher, and I go to a lot of university websites. There was one

at Cornell—I use that for Government; I have to write a paper on a Supreme Court case and I use that for a lot of law. I use a lot of advanced searches in databases; a lot of kids don't use them even though they are so helpful. They just go to Google, but it's not certified; but databases, they are.

For these searches, Rachel knows the importance of identifying specific keywords related to her questions: "I started out with 'why people lie' and then 'what is deception' and why do people deceive others"

From her search, she "found a lot of information about how people lie to protect their reputation . . . that people lie to protect themselves." She then made the statement we quoted on p. 27. Finally, she "tied the information that we found to the situation when the people lied—evidence for what happened in real life."

Evaluating Search Information

One of the central aspects of information literacy is the ability to judge the validity of information available on online sites (November, 2008). In contrast to information in peer-reviewed or edited journals, books, or news reports, there is often no editorial control over the information contained on many websites. Students may encounter websites or blogs created by groups with certain ideological agendas that present false information, as in the site http://www.martinlutherking.org, operated by white racists, that contains racist misinformation about Martin Luther King. Or they may go to Wikipedia to find what they assume to be authoritative information about certain topics. However, they need to know that because anyone can edit entries on that site, they should not rely solely on Wikipedia as their primary source, even through editors are continually reviewing and removing misinformation from that site.

Consequently, it is important to teach students to adopt a skeptical stance toward material on the Web by modeling critical analysis of problematic sites reported on monitoring sites, such as http://snopes.com or http://lijit.com, that identify misinformation on sites (@ = Evaluating websites). In analyzing Wikipedia entries, students can look at the revision histories on entries to note deletions and additions as well as Talk Pages for discussions of misinformation (Jenkins, 2007).

In modeling search strategies, teachers need to demonstrate practices of safe searching related to access to objectionable or pornographic sites, noting that if and when students encounter such sites in school, they need to avoid them (Willard, 2007) (@ = Safe surfing). Although school computers have filters that block access to the sites, students often find ways around the filters; there is also some concern about whether the filters block access to nonobjectionable information. Rather than our assuming that the problem can be solved simply by filtering content or censorship, it is important to take a proactive stance by addressing this issue as matter of student behavior and attitudes—that students need to take responsibility for their own behavior by adopting safe searching techniques.

Rachel was aware of the need to continually assess the value and relevancy of the data she was finding. She noted that "You get some weird stuff, but sometimes if you scroll down enough, you find something good." She noted the need to initially judge the scholarly nature of online material: "I read a little bit of it and if it's an article, then it'll be a little higher in ascendancy; if you get some really crazy, opinionated texts, those are fun to read but not helpful." For example, Rachel felt comfortable about including quotes on one site (http://www.bbc.co.uk/dna/h2g2/A996942) from Dr. John Busak, Professor of Psychiatry and Director of Neuropsychiatry at the University of New Delhi, because she believed the BBC site was a reputable one and that Dr. Busak was connected to a university. The research that Rachel draws on was directly related to her thesis that the Hayden family deceptions were part of a family culture:

> Investigations have shown that there are those who are genetically predisposed toward lying and deceit. . . . Those who come from chaotic and dysfunctional families have a greater tendency to lie than those who grew up in a caring household. Busak hypothesizes that children from such families lie to change or modify reality so as to make life more tolerable.

Digital Note-Taking Tools

As they gather information, students need to know how to take notes about that information through using digital writing or note-taking tools such as PC NoteTaker, Google NoteBook, FreeMind, KeyNote, Webnotes, or Journaler (@ = Digital notetaking). These tools allow students to type their notes and then copy and paste those notes into their drafts, and they show how to organize documents, image or video files, and URLs. Students can also add voice annotations to comment on texts, or create internal and external hyperlinks between their texts—for example, to connect definitions of key concepts.

In taking notes, students need to be able to translate information into their own words rather than just recopy text. Translating text into their own words leads them to integrate the information into their own cognitive schema or frameworks. Teachers can model this translation process by using Tablet PCs connected wirelessly to a projector to model collaborative note taking (@ = Tablet writing). Students can create notes simultaneously about a topic or text that can then be projected to their group on a large screen or whiteboard. Students can also use Tablet PCs to download lecture notes or PowerPoint presentations and then annotate this material for their peers and the teacher.

To share their notes of quotes and information from the novel, Rachel, Claire, and Kyle used a wiki so that they could each add and revise their own notes on the same site. They recorded quotes and summaries of events in the novel leading to identification of the lies operating in the novel. Their notes included the following description of Wesley's arrest of his brother, Frank, for the rape and murder of the Native American woman, Maria:

> Wes and Frank come home one afternoon and go down to the basement. Wes comes up alone shortly after, saying that he had imprisoned Frank in the basement (instead of sending him to jail—in order to protect the family name and keep the truth off the streets of Bentrock) "He's in the basement. God ---- it! Don't you get it? I've arrested him. He's down there now" [Watson, 1993, p. 109]. Wes arrests Frank and keeps him in the basement so the fact that Frank has been arrested doesn't get out and the reason that Frank has been arrested is kept a secret.

The students were then able to draw on their notes to generate this section of their final draft that ties this specific information back to their larger thesis that the Hayden family lied to protect their image in the town:

> In Bentrock, the Hayden name is prestigious. When Wes discovered Marie's murder at the hand of Frank, Wes decided to detain Frank in his basement instead of a jail cell. "He's in the basement. . . . Don't you get it? I've arrested him. He's down there now" [Watson, 1993, p. 109]. Wes imprisons Frank in his basement to protect the family name. He doesn't want the fact that Frank had been molesting his patients and had murdered Marie getting out to the town. David reflects on this matter by saying, "I imagined…someone peering out and seeing a Hayden and thinking not of power…but of perversion, scandal, family division, and decay. If the citizens of Bentrock didn't know yet that my father had arrested his own brother for sexually assaulting his patients and murdering Marie Little Soldier, they would soon enough. Then being a Hayden would mean having an identity I didn't want but could do nothing to disown or deny" [p. 127]. By locking Frank in his basement instead of a jail cell, Wes ensures that he can protect the family name for the time being. Wes is deceiving the public by maintaining the family's positive image in not releasing that his brother has been arrested for murder.

By using the wiki, they could then collaboratively share their search results and note taking, something we discuss in more detail in chapter 4 on wiki writing. In reflecting on writing about this paper in her final portfolio reflection, Kyle noted:

> Writing group papers is always difficult, especially when we did it for *Montana 1948*, but this one wasn't that bad. I thought it was a fun paper because we got to pick our book, pick our group, and pick the topic we wanted to write the paper on. I'd say that this was one of my favorite writing assignments that we did in this class.

Students can also annotate and share notes based on clippings of materials from websites—texts, images, and links using Google Notebook or Trailfire (a Firefox extension) (@ = Annotation software). For example, students can use Google Notebook to highlight and store clippings from related Web pages. They can select the content from a Web page, right-click on that content, and then select "Note this Google Notebook." Jen Budenski, a teacher in an alternative high school in Hopkins, Minnesota, describes her use of Google Notebook to clip, annotate, and store material from websites:

> Like many of my students, I went back and did my prewriting in the "assigned" way after I'd done it my own way, transferring my highlighted passages and marginalia into my Google Notebook. However, as I made the transfer, I discovered that Google Notebook replicates my analog notetaking fairly well. While I can't write directly on the text, I can write next to it. And I was able to clip, annotate, and store a goofy diagram in less than a second. In the old days, it would have taken me 15 minutes to sketch and label it or 5 cents and a walk to the library for a photocopy. I can then sort and categorize my notebook entries and drag them around the notebook page just like notecards. I didn't need to invent a complicated system of tracking sources for my bibliography—the source number goes in the upper right-hand corner of the note card and corresponds to the number on the bib card. If I clipped a section from the article, my Google Notebook automatically hyperlinked to the source. In my Google Notebook, I can organize my notes and simply export them into Google Docs.

Students can also collect data as a form of note taking by using online polls or surveys to capture their peers' perceptions on certain issues or topics (@ = Collect information through online polling or surveys). Students can use tools such as SurveyMonkey.com, Visu.com, or Poll Everywhere (http://www.polleverywhere.com) to create online polls or surveys. With Poll Everywhere, students can respond to questions using cell phone texting. Once students collect their poll results, they can use that data as notes for their reports.

Using RSS Feeds for Information Trapping

The search strategies we have described all require students to themselves search out information or texts. An alternative search strategy involves using RSS feeds (Hendron, 2008). RSS feeds are subscriptions to sites, blogs, wikis, or news outlets that feed information automatically to subscribers, what Tara Calishain (2007) describes as "information trapping." Rather than students' having to seek out information, the information is fed to them. When students go to a site or blog, they can subscribe to receive feeds from the site or blog by clicking on the RSS feed or orange button icon that appears. To organize these feeds, students can use "feed readers" or aggregators, such as Bloglines, Google Reader, RSSReader, SharpReader, My Yahoo, Newsburst, NetNewsWire (for Mac), or NewzCrawler (for PC), that automatically access and update feeds (@ = Creating RSS feeds).

Using Bloglines

One widely used feed aggregator is Bloglines. Students can install Bloglines on their computer at http://bloglines.com. They can then subscribe to feeds from blogs or news sites by clicking on the RSS feed or Bloglines icon on a blog or news site. These blogs or sites are then listed in a box in the left side of their Bloglines screen under "Feeds."

By clicking on "Feeds," on the upper left, they see a list of their subscribed feeds. By clicking on these subscriptions, they then see the specific texts in the right column. If they were to click on, for example, the Bud the Teacher blog, posts to that blog will appear on the right side.

To access feed URLs, students can click on the orange icons on sites, and Bloglines automatically opens up so that students can subscribe to that feed. They can also copy and paste a feed URL into the Add box on Bloglines. As part of installing Bloglines, students should add the "Easy Subscription Bookmarklet" to their toolbars. Then when they encounter a blog they want to add to their feed list, they can click on this bookmarklet and add the blog to their lists.

To share their lists of selected feeds in their folder(s) with others, they click on the option that allows the folder(s) to be public. When students make their folders public, teachers can determine what they are collecting in terms of relevancy and appropriateness and then provide comments on any of the feed material (Richardson, 2006).

Using Google Reader

Another free feed reader is Google Reader (http://www.google.com/reader). Once students set up an account with Google and install Google Reader, they can begin to subscribe to blog feeds; they can also add a Google Reader icon to their toolbar.

In Figure 2-1, the blogs are listed in the left column, and recently accessed feeds appear in the right column.

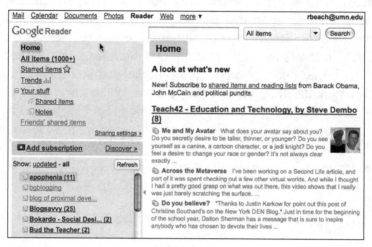

Figure 2-1. Adding Feeds to Google Reader

Students can add subscriptions by clicking on "Add Subscription" and then copy and paste in the blog's feed URL. Students can also star certain posts for reading at a later time. By clicking on "Shared Items," they can create their own list of blogs on a website or as code that they can insert on their blog.

One important aspect of RSS feeds is that if students are working collaboratively on the same topic, they can share their feeds on Google Reader with each other. Once they specify a keyword for their topics—for example, "obesity"—they go to Google Blog Search to create a feed for blog posts that use the word "obesity." They then go to the Subscribe box in Google Blog Search and copy the RSS feed link into the "Add Subscription" box. They can create a new folder named, for example, "obesity," to collect their feeds for sharing with each other.

Identifying and Searching for Information and Images Through Tagging

Tagging—using keywords or categories assigned to online material—is an especially useful tool to search for and organize material on the Web (@ = Tagging sites). For example, in writing a blog post about her high school cross-country skiing team, a student may tag that post with "cross-country skiing," "skiing," "winter sports," and so on. Then a reader can readily search for that topic using the keywords on the student's particular blog or millions of blogs on tagging sites such as Delicious.com, Diigo, Digg, or Furl.

Rather than rely on a predetermined category system such as the Dewey decimal system, users create their own categories relevant to the content they are creating. As millions of users apply tags to certain phenomena, they collaboratively define the meaning of the tags. For example, students can research the meaning of "horror" on Amazon.com as defined by Amazon.com users on its "most popular tags" page (Weinberger, 2007). As a social literacy practice, tagging reflects a bottom-up resistance to official category systems or taxonomies employed on search engines.

Tagging is particularly important in collecting and uploading material on image- and video-sharing sites such as Flickr and YouTube. Although it is possible to readily categorize the topics addressed in a text, it is more difficult to agree on categories associated with images or video. On the most active image-sharing site, Flickr, users tag photos based on "folksonomies," or categories used to label different images of videos.

Using Delicious.com

One of the most frequently used tagging sites is Delicious. Students can create their own free "my delicious" site for storing their tags on the Delicious site, then share those tags with peers. Once they have installed Delicious, they can click on the tag icon on their browser toolbar to tag a site with certain keywords. For example, as illustrated in Figure 2-2, to tag a Teachers Teaching Teachers podcast we clicked on "tag" to add information.

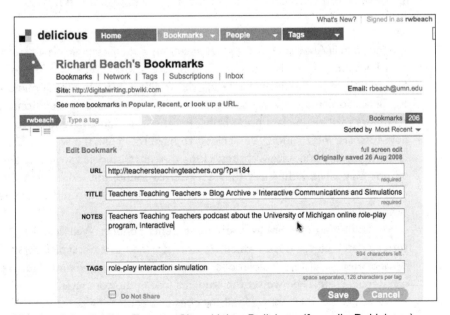

Figure 2-2. Adding Tags to Sites Using Delicious (formally Del.icio.us)

We then added a description of the site to "notes," and, based on the "recommended" and "popular" tags, we added tags, skipping a space after each tag. Once this site had been tagged, we could then click on the Delicious box and enter the tag "role-play" to find it listed with other sites with the same tag. Referring to the "popular tags" on the site, students can see other links that have been tagged according to "role-play." They can then focus on how other users are tagging items using similar tags, thereby providing a collective sense of the meaning of these tags as a bottom-up folksonomy associated with certain types of texts or images.

How does tagging serve to enhance students' writing? Because students can tag their own blog posts or wiki writing, tagging helps students identify the primary topics they are addressing in their writing in ways that would help them focus their writing on those topics. If students are writing collaborative essays, they can share their tag lists with their collaborators, serving as resources for each other. Adding tags to texts then helps to promote their writing to their readers. For example, for their blog posts, they may create a "tag cloud" that lists the different tags addressed in their posts, with more frequently addressed tags appearing in larger font size.

Using Delicious Tagging in a Literature Class

Tagging is a highly collaborative social activity in which users assist each other in sharing their tags. In their literature class at Edina High School, Edina, Minnesota, Anne Tholen and Kathleen West employ tagging in teaching a novel:

> Our goal as a class was to accumulate as much information as possible related to Julia Alvarez's novel, In the Time of the Butterflies, which is a fictionalized account of the lives of the Mirabal sisters, who were leaders in the Fourteenth of June Movement during the Trujillo regime in the Dominican Republic. Students were preparing to give speeches on their research to members of their in-class book clubs. Because we wanted students to be able to share information, we decided to have them use the website Delicious to tag and annotate websites. Using their tags, students would be able to not only review the sites they themselves found, but also access lists created by class members and other Delicious users who used the same tags.
>
> We explained tags briefly, and had students conduct Web searches on terms related to the novel, which we brainstormed as a class: dictatorship, Trujillo, Mirabal, sisters, revolutionaries, underground movements, Dominican Republic, etc. Then we set the students free in the computer lab. During the class period, they enjoyed tallying sites and comparing notes with their peers, and they created their own tags.

After students experimented with tagging websites, they completed an online survey that we created using Survey Monkey (http://www.surveymonkey.com/s.asp?u=270003742462). We wanted to get students' thoughts and reactions to the tagging process for school-related purposes, as well as for their own personal use.

Students had a largely positive response to the use of tags and the tagging process when conducting research. They commented on the ease of tagging, how it helped them organize websites in a thoughtful way that made their sources more organized, and noted a sense of enjoyment, engagement, and play while tagging during the research process.

Many students commented on the research process being made easier and more manageable by the tags. When asked if the tagging process was useful in the classroom, one student responded, "Yes. I do think this would be useful in the classroom because you would find information faster. You can look at other people's tags and cut your research time in half because it's been provided for you."

While all students talked about tags as being "fun" and "easy," many included a note of caution about the tags. Students understood that they were relying on the credibility of other people's tags and comments on websites when using the delicious tagging process. They likened it to Wikipedia and were uncomfortable relying on others' sources and tagging techniques for all their research purposes. One student wrote, "I think it's a good idea, but I'm worried that the sources tagged aren't very reliable and therefore promote incorrect information." Another student noted, "I think tags make the Internet much more accessible and manageable. However, I am unsure of the credibility of some of the tags. A search can become very broad." Even as students were aware of their reliance on others' tags and comments, they worked to make sure their own tags were helpful and accurate in description. One student said, "I think it's very helpful if you take the time to actually think about the notes you put about it and tag useful websites."

Despite students' appreciation and enjoyment of the tagging process for research purposes, few students said that they would use tagging for personal use. Students seemed tied to the idea of tagging as being an academic, classroom activity rather than one that could cross over into their personal lives. One student said, "If I was looking for information on a specific topic, this would be beneficial; however, I would use it mostly at school, though." When asked if she would use tagging outside school, another student replied, "To be honest, I can't say I would. It seems to help when working on school projects and homework, but I don't know what I'd use it for at home." It seems probable to assume that with more exposure to the tagging process, students would use tags for both academic and personal purposes.

Overall, student response to the tagging process was quite positive. They felt tagging helped them in the research process, was useful in keeping sources organized, and was something that they would use again for future research projects.

Collecting and Connecting Images and Video for Multimodal Presentations

In addition to collecting information, students are also collecting images, videos, audio, or artwork for creating blogs, wikis, digital storytelling, audio productions, scrapbooks, and so on. One study found that 39% of online adolescents post artwork, photos, stories, or videos online and 26% remix that material (Madden et al., 2007).

By collecting and connecting images and video, students can then produce multimodal reports—for example, a slideshow about their neighborhood. Drawing on the idea of the Cornell boxes as collections of disparate items, Geoff Sirc (2004) describes ways in which students in his writing classes function as curators who collect a range of different digital texts to create "box-logic" exhibits or "arcades projects" about different aspects of hip-hop culture (p. 112). His students begin by searching academic databases and sites related to the topic of hip-hop and rap. Students then take notes on the material they find. Sirc responds to these notes by posing inquiry questions about their topic or suggesting other links and resources. Then, by examining how museums present their physical and digital exhibits, students mount their own arcades project. They are then using digital writing as

> a compelling medium and genre with which to re-arrange textual material—both original and appropriated—in order to have those materials speak the student's own voice and concerns, allowing them to come up with something obscure, perhaps, yet promising illumination." (p. 113)

Sirc (2004) encourages his students to continually reflect on how these connections and combinations of texts serve as

> a vehicle of reverie, an object that would enrich the imagination of the viewer. The model of college writing, then, becomes the contemporary DVD—a compendium of "finished" text, commentary, selected features, interviews, alternative versions, sections initially deleted...our new classroom genre might best be called a diary journal, repository laboratory, picture gallery, museum, sanctuary, observatory, key...inviting us to see things in a light in which we do not know them, but which turns out to be almost that one in which we have hoped one day to see them bathed. (p. 146)

To collect these materials for such productions, students can search for noncopyrighted images from sites such as Flickr or Google Images. These and other sites contain millions of images with Creative Commons copyright licenses that allow for fair use by students in classrooms if students make an attribution to the producer, something we discuss in more detail in chapter 8 (Richardson, 2006) (@ = Online digital images).

Students can also search on YouTube and other sites (@ = Online digital video) for video clips to import into their writing (assuming that access to YouTube has not been blocked in a school; teachers can then bring in YouTube videos stored on their flash drives for sharing with students) (@ = Online digital video). They can add annotations to these videos using tools such as VideoANT (http://ant.umn.edu). Students can also find online audio material in the form of podcasts (@ = Online audio material).

Collecting Images and Videos in Richard's Class

To engage students in multimodal data collection in his digital writing class, Richard asked his students to collect images, video, and/or texts about a certain topic or issue (@ = Collecting texts activity). He asked them to frame an inquiry question, search for material that addressed that question, look for consistent relationships or patterns in the material that suggested certain groupings or categories, then reflect in a blog post about their findings. Noting patterns in their collections of images or videos led students to critically analyze their combined texts.

To model this process, Richard conducted his own search based on the question: "How are teachers represented in Hollywood films?" He went to YouTube to search for film trailer clips of teachers in Hollywood movies. Based on the clips he found, he inductively inferred consistent patterns in the ways that teachers were represented. He found that Hollywood teachers are often portrayed in ways that deviate from traditional pedagogical methods. For example, in *School of Rock*, the Jack Black character draws on rock music to engage and loosen up his upper-middle-class students. In *Freedom Writers*, Hilary Swank's character assumes the role of someone who fosters students' writing about the challenges of their everyday lives. In *History Boys*, a gay history teacher played by Richard Griffiths builds personal relationships with his private school students to motivate them to learn.

The students in the class then created and shared their own collections (http://digitalwriting.pbwiki.com/Box+Logic:+Collecting+texts+assignment+for+November+20). One student, Gina Nelson, analyzed representations of homelessness in the media, noting that the media often portray the homeless as drug addicts, panhandlers, or beggars living on the streets in urban areas. She included clips such as a trailer for *The Pursuit of Happyness* that portrays an employed male wearing a suit who is homeless, as well as material portraying rural families or children as homeless, noting that "after having watched *Pursuit of Happyness*, I became increasingly aware of my own judgments and bias about people who are homeless. Most of my preconceived notions of homelessness come from either the media or seeing men panhandling on the streets."

Another student, Nicole Kronzer, examined the portrayals of sisters in media, poetry, and literature. She found that sisters were portrayed in a binary way, either as "best friends," or as "enemies," with little alternative variation associated with her relationships with her own sisters.

Another student, Kasi Williamson, examined clips of representations of feminists. She found that feminists are portrayed as "loud," as evidenced in a comedy sketch, as "working against the institution of the family," and as "unpopular," given that people "don't believe that feminism is good or necessary." She then included some alternative examples of performance artists who challenge stereotypes about feminists.

In adopting an inquiry-based orientation, the students were more willing to use the images and videos they found to challenge their preconceptions. As Kasi noted:

> We often operate in environments where everyone sees things pretty much the same way that we do. By exploring Flickr, YouTube, and other user-generated content sites, it's possible to observe representations of views that are antithetical to our own and to see certain themes that may recur (and to turn off the sound, when we need to). I think it's okay to be critical of opposing views, but collecting them in "box-logic" style (collecting and sifting and selecting and absorbing and juxtaposing) can allow for new understanding. Observing such a collection can also shed light on the discursive barriers that might keep people from adopting viewpoints that could actually be beneficial to them.

Collecting and presenting digital images or videos also helps prepare students for creating digital storytelling productions, discussed in chapter 5, in which they combine these images or videos with texts, audio, and music.

Using Digital Mind Mapping for Connecting and Organizing Material

Having collected information, students also need to be able to connect and organize that information according to the logical relationships within that information. To do that, students can use digital mind-mapping tools such as Inspiration,

Bubbl.us, Curio 2.4, VUE, IHMC CmapTools, Spark-Space (3-D maps), Compendium, Gliffy, Visual Mind, Mind Genenius, Freemind, OpenMind, Kdissert, VYM (View Your Mind), and Mindmeister (@ = Digital mapping). These mind-mapping tools help students visually chart relationships among the topics and subtopics in circles or boxes and then draw lines between the circles or boxes to represent logical relationships between the topics and subtopics.

In using these mind-mapping tools, students begin with a box or circle in the middle and then create other boxes or circles containing related topics or items linked back to the central box. For example, in using Bubbl.us, students create boxes in which they type topics or ideas that they then link to other surrounding boxes. They can draw lines between boxes to visually chart how certain subtopics are related to each other and back to larger topics. For example, in participating in an online role-play, students could create "argument maps" that identify the different pro versus con arguments in a role-play (Marttunen & Laurinen, 2007) or create graphs to identify where certain roles fall on a pro-con continuum.

Using Inspiration

One of the most frequently used mapping tools in schools is a commercial tool, Inspiration, which allows students to create mind maps based on links between key topics (see the wiki resource site for links to tutorials). Inspiration provides students with two different ways of perceiving relationships between their concepts and ideas: a "Diagram" and an "Outline" perspective. From the "Diagram" perspective, students devise graphic organizers for their material. They start by creating a "Main Idea," which appears in an initial circle. They then create other related ideas around the main idea, drawing connections between those ideas and the main idea, as well as connections between the other related ideas.

To brainstorm ideas and further material, students can switch at any time to the RapidFire tool. They can then type in material associated with the indifferent topics, in some cases making links to visual icons or symbols. They can also import material from their own digital files or from an extensive collection of symbols, pictures, images, and digital clips including QuickTime movies and MP3 files. They can also distinguish among their ideas using different colors, fonts, and shapes.

Students can then perceive the material they develop on their maps by selecting "Outline View," which allows them to consider how they would organize their material for writing a paper according to a hierarchical outline with main topics and subtopics. In the Outline View, students can also hide subtopics so that they can perceive their overall main topics. They can also move material around if they want to rearrange their topics.

Using Inspiration for Writing About *Hamlet*

Michael Hasapopoulos describes his use of Inspiration for writing about *Hamlet* in his 12th-grade literature class, Armstrong High School, Robbinsdale, Minnesota:

> In my 12th-grade AP literature class, the students have been tackling the text that seems to be the ultimate challenge for readers—*Hamlet*. Needless to say, the classic revenge tragedy is regarded as Shakespeare's finest (if not most popular and produced) tragedy, and over the course of 6 years of teaching *Hamlet* to the advanced placement student, I have discovered that the challenges the play presents to students lie along two main lines: the myriad convolutions of plot and the myriad characters that come and go throughout the protagonist's experience. Over the course of shaping a curriculum for Hamlet that addresses student discussion, interaction with the text via journaling and student dramatic presentations, and soliloquy analysis, the challenges have persisted.
>
> Not one to accept academic defeat easily, I used some aspects of a previous curriculum devised for a research project on the use of technology in the high school classroom. Coincidentally (or perhaps not, due to this teacher's love of Shakespearean tragedy), the technology-based unit centered on *Macbeth*. For the *Macbeth* unit, students read, journaled, discussed, and tested entirely via the technology of the computer and of the Internet. I had created a website specifically for the class and the project, where students would go for assignments and readings and would download any activities involved with the play. Much of what we did as a class centered on student-directed searches and student-directed online discussions (via a specialized discussion site at http://www.proboards.com). The results of the study returned quite favorably, with the main conclusion that most of the students in our particular demographic had considerable technology savvy, which acted as a motivator to learn and interact with the text.
>
> I thought that this would be a good way in which to augment the students' journal assignment, which was to journal each act of Hamlet, focusing specifically on character development, use of language (literary and rhetorical terms), and a passage analysis (their choice). Here's the journal assignment:
>
>> Conduct your Act III journal using Inspiration. Remember to focus on character development and depth, plot nuances, language use (literary and rhetorical terms), and your passage analysis. You may use any kind of organizational structure that fits your fancy. I think it is a good way of breaking down, say, a soliloquy for passage analysis, analyzing character and character traits, breaking through to the subtext of character speech, commenting on literary devices and setting, etc. Be creative!

Students were able to use the Inspiration software to interact in any way they saw fit with the text; the software is particularly effective when isolating the requirements of the journal assignment: the character study, language analysis, passage analysis.

The software significantly aided in students' ability to place the text in a manageable format in which to break it down into patterns and to make interpretive leaps from the analysis. By having the information presented in one clear, colorful, creative manner, I believe, also aided in the engagement that students demonstrated in the assignment.

Using Digital Storage Tools for Organizing and Categorizing Information

As students collect or generate information and ideas, they need to store this material in files or folders based on emerging categories or topics. While students can certainly create folders in Word to store their material, a better alternative for storing large files is to use a digital storage tools such as Drop Box, Backpack, or Filemaker Pro (@ = Digital storage tools). Students can use Backpack (a free service) to store texts, lists, notes, photos, or files of up to five pages onto their own private, password-protected web page.

These storage tools can be used to revise students' categories or resort information, something that is more difficult to do with Word folders. Another advantage of using these tools is that students who are working collaboratively with others can readily share their material with peers so that they can all work together on the same material. And when students begin to create their electronic portfolios, as discussed in chapter 10, they can readily move their writing into their portfolios based on their categories.

Summary

In this chapter, we discussed the uses of informal digital writing tools for collecting, connecting, and organizing information, images, and videos using search tools, wikis, note taking and annotation, and mapping tools. We also noted the value of using "information trapping" (Calishain, 2007) tools such as feeds and tags for accessing relevant information. One benefit of digital tools is that students can collaboratively share their information and ideas, as illustrated by the students' writing about truth and deception in *Montana 1948* (Watson, 1993). Through uses of mapping, they can create visual representations of the relationships within the information. We want to emphasize that these processes are recursive—they can occur at any time during writing, even after drafting or editing, when students perceive the need to develop more material.

Using, Creating, and Managing
Digital Discussion Environments

In her 10th-grade English class at Cretin-Durham Hall High School in St. Paul, Minnesota, Theresa Haider used Moodle forums—the asynchronous discussion component of the Web courseware program Moodle—to foster a discussion of *The Kite Runner* (Hosseini, 2004). To illustrate how the students participated on the Moodle Forum, the discussion below includes some students' posts in response to Theresa's prompt regarding the relationship between two of the main characters in the novel, Amir and Hassan. In this novel, which takes place in Afghanistan during the Soviet invasion and the Taliban control, as well as in California, Amir recalls his experiences with Hassan, the son of the family's servant, with whom he had a close relationship. At one point, Hassan saves Amir from an attack by a local bully, Assef. Later, when Hassan tries to help protect Amir's kite, Assef rapes Hassan. Amir not only does not come to his defense, he also falsely blames Hassan for being a thief. After Amir escapes the Russian takeover of the country with his father, Baba, to go to California, he returns years later to learn that Hassan had been killed by the Taliban and that Hassan was his illegitimate half-brother.

Prompt: Explain the relationship between Amir and Hassan. How do you know that Hassan was an honorable boy? Was Amir as honorable? How do you know?

45

By adam anderson—Wednesday, February 28, 2007, 09:20 AM:

I agree with Adam about Hassan being an honorable person, but he is more of an honorable servant, and he'll do whatever Amir tells him to do. A friend probably wouldn't put up with all of the things that Amir makes Hassan do, but since Hassan is such a kind person, he puts up with everything that Amir does to him, like you said. I also agree that Amir needs to start taking responsibility for his actions and not making Hassan endure all of the blame for Amir's actions.

By Marcus Binns—Wednesday, February 28, 2007, 09:35 AM:

Amir and Hassan have a great relationship though they might not be friends they are real close. I think it would be hard for Hassan to be friends with Amir because he is his servant. In a way I would never want to be a friend of my owner because of jealousy. Hassan is an honorable guy because he listens and does whatever Amir asks if him. I would not consider Amir an honorable guy because he sometimes uses Hassan and doesn't man up and say it was he. I agree with Adam when he says Amir uses Hassan, though Hassan is the servant of Amir I still don't think its [sic] right that he has to be used. I also agree with Adam about how Amir needs to step up to the plate and take the blame for the things he makes Hassan do.

By jessica picha—Tuesday, March 6, 2007, 07:36 PM:

Hassan and Amir are really close, Hassan doesn't really have any true friends and Amir is the closest friend he may ever have. Amir has friends and he only plays with Hassan when there is no one else to play with. Hassan and Amir aren't friends and they aren't like brothers because brothers and friends are always there for you know matter what. I would not consider Amir to be an honorable guy because he never stands up for Hassan, he is to [sic] scared about what will happen to himself if he does stand up for him. I think Hassan is very honorable because he always seems to do what is right even if it will hurt himself. He is also always there for Amir even though Amir is never there for him.

I agree with Marcus when he says that it would be hard to be friends with Amir because of jealousy. Amir has almost everything: friends, a house, and goes to school. It would be hard to be friends with someone from a higher and more respected class.

By myke bangs—Tuesday, March 6, 2007, 08:38 PM:

Amir and Hassan seem to be friends, but not your typical friends. Amir seems to want to be friends with Hassan, but he treats him poorly. He never sticks up for Hassan. He is always letting Hassan take the blame for things especially throwing rocks at the dog. I wouldn't consider Amir to be honorable because he is always letting Amir take the blame and never owns up to his mistakes. I agree with Jessica when she says that she doesn't believe Amir is honorable because he doesn't stick up for Hassan.

In their analysis of the relationship between Amir and Hassan, the students consistently build on one another's opinions about Amir's lack of honor and loyalty in his relationship with Hassan. They restate their peers' positions and then formulate their own positions, in some cases extending the analysis with further evidence from the text.

As in any face-to-face classroom discussion, by asking students to respond to other posts, Theresa was encouraging them to build on one another's ideas and to develop some consensus within their group, enhancing their sense of the validity of their claims. When asked how and why she designed this forum, Theresa offered this explanation:

> Along with a one- to two-paragraph response to specific questions, I ask each student to respond to another classmate's response in three to four sentences. This takes some coordination because the students need to understand that they may need to go to Moodle a second or third time if their classmates are slow in putting up their initial answers to the question(s). It also promotes community in that each student is relying on all other students to help them complete the assignment. In the response to classmate(s), they need to refer to the person specifically, and they must refer to the content he or she wrote about. They can agree, disagree, or challenge what their classmates' write; however, most choose to agree with each other.

As Theresa notes, digital discussions can be productively used in the classroom as a way to create community among students, to check student understanding of assigned reading, and to review issues of expression and clarity in student writing. However, most important is the fact that Theresa's students were highly engaged in this online discussion of *The Kite Runner* (Hosseini, 2004), engagement that encouraged them to use writing to voice their opinions and develop arguments in defense of their interpretations. These reasons, along with others that we discuss in this chapter, demonstrate how digital discussions can strengthen both reading and writing practices.

What Are Digital Discussions?

In this chapter, we'll focus on ways to use digital discussion environments to enhance writing instruction and student engagement. By *digital discussion environments,* we mean Internet environments designed for conversation and collaboration. Other terms associated with digital discussion environments include *computer-supported learning environments, virtual learning environments, and online collaborative learning environments.* Web 2.0 tools such as blogs, wikis, Instant Messaging, and online forums or chats all support digital discussion environments, and so do tried-and-true discussion technologies such as e-mail listservs and online bulletin boards. Gaming environments offer yet another tool for digital discussions that incorporate visual and verbal elements.

These Web 2.0 environments may vary in terms of purpose, number of participants, software, and design, but they have several common elements: They are highly interactive, they require writing, and they encourage student-centered learning. For these reasons, students find digital discussions engaging and even fun. When used wisely by instructors, digital discussions can also help ground rhetorical concepts of audience, purpose, voice, and tone in interesting and engaging ways.

One reason for the appeal of online discussions is that students have grown accustomed to online social interaction on social networking sites such as MySpace, Facebook, or MyYearbook. In 2007, 71% visited these sites on a weekly basis, devoting an average of 9 hours a week to participating on these sites (National School Boards Association, 2007) (@ = Social networking sites). They are also accustomed to continually IMing their peers (@ = IMing tools). A Pew Internet and American Life Project study (Lenhart & Madden, 2007) found that 91% use these sites to maintain relationships with friends with whom they frequently socialize and 82% with friends with whom they do not socialize; 72% use these sites to make social plans. Much of this sharing involves writing private and public messages and comments to their peers—for example, on "walls" in Facebook, with 41% posting comments on a weekly basis and 50% of students talking specifically about completing schoolwork (National School Boards Association, 2007).

Students engaged in this social networking are also more likely to create online content: posting or remixing images or video, creating of or commenting on blogs, or maintaining a website (Lenhart & Madden, 2007). Schools have built on this online participation, with half of schools engaging in collaborative projects with other schools and about half engaged in online penpal programs (National School Boards Association, 2007). Schools also perceive value in online participation, with 76% of administrators expecting that social networking helps students improve their writing skills and their ability to express themselves through online communication.

In some cases, online bulletin boards or chat sites have a major influence on students' everyday lives. Based on a study of college sports fan bulletin boards, Matthew Pearson (2007) finds that potential college recruits and their families study these sports fan bulletin boards to ascertain the level of support for teams for a particular college. Knowing that their posts could influence such decisions, student contributors to these boards therefore take their writing seriously as having an influence on their team's future.

Unfortunately, social networking sites are often blocked in schools due to administrators' concerns about inappropriate online contact, despite the fact that 70% of students keep their profiles private and only 4% reported instances of conversations that made them uncomfortable (Lenhart & Madden, 2007).

There are multiple tools that can support digital discussion environments—so many that we could not possibly discuss them all. Instead, it may be helpful to describe digital discussions in terms of two broad categories: synchronous (real time) and asynchronous (delayed time).

Synchronous Online Discussions

Synchronous online discussions are described as *real-time discussions,* meaning that discussion participants are on the computer at the same time and are typing messages or speaking to one another via the Internet. When participants type messages to one another synchronously, the resulting discussion appears as an evolving written transcript, with contributions labeled according to participant names.

Synchronous discussions are supported by the Web; they can be closed or open discussions. Open discussions are often sponsored by Web-based providers such as Yahoo or AOL, whereas closed discussions must be set up by someone and are often a feature of a Web courseware program that houses multiple discussion or Web features, such as Blackboard, WebCT/Vista, Moodle, Tappedin.org, and free, open-source content management sites such as Drupal or Joomla, combine chat with blogs, links, calendars, and other tools all housed on the same one-stop site (@ = Virtual learning environments). One of the best free synchronous chat sites is Tappedin.org, which will e-mail transcripts of students discussions to teachers.

Synchronous discussions are an excellent way to connect people across time and distance; for example, synchronous discussions are often used for business meetings. People can then "meet" online, even though they might be sitting in different time zones around the world. Common forms of synchronous discussions include Instant Messaging, chat rooms, multi-user dimensions (MUDs) and MUDs, Object-Oriented (MOOs), and gaming environments.

It is often assumed that informal language employed in such chats—for example, acronyms in IMing—has little to do with and could actually have a negative influence on formal academic writing. However, in their research on young people's use of IMing, text messaging, and Facebook "wall" posts, Christina Haas and Pam Takayoshi (2008) find that this writing contains complex uses of linguistic features, constituting a new form of language communication. They also find that these young people can readily switch between informal and more formal language use associated with traditional academic writing. Students learn to vary their styles and appeals to suit the range of different audiences they are addressing (Lewis & Fabos, 2005).

Students often enjoy engaging in videoconferencing using tools such as iChat, using iSight Webcams to engage in synchronous discussions or interviews (@ = Videoconferencing).

As we discuss in chapter 7, students can use also cell phones or Skype to engage in interviews with people as part of conducting research projects. The increased use of the cell phone suggests the need to rethink the norms constituting valued written communication. As Guy Merchant (2007) notes,

> These examples of new genres of digital text suggest a need to re-conceptualise writing, and our approach to learning about writing, as well as our ideas about teaching and using writing in the classroom. They may well provide us with templates for a new interactive literacy that reaches well beyond the classroom walls. (p. 124)

The availability of these different digital discussion tools suggests the need for students to recognize differences between the practices involved in IMing or online chat and the practices involved in more formal school writing (Lewis & Fabos, 2005). Thus, teachers may want to have students discuss the conventions they employ in IMing or text messaging and compare those conventions with their more formal school writing.

Asynchronous Online Discussions

Asynchronous online discussions can best be described as *delayed-time discussions*, in which participants write separate messages at different times and send to one another via the Internet. The messages then are stored on a server, and participants must log onto that server through an e-mail account or a website password to retrieve their messages. The standard example of asynchronous discussions is e-mail. A person may send an e-mail message at whatever time is convenient for him or her, but because the recipient retrieves the message when he or she chooses, the recipient may not reply to that message instantly. Time lapses between discussion contributions, sometimes by hours, days, or even weeks (hence, "delayed time").

Asynchronous discussions appear as a kind of written transcript of conversational turns in an ongoing discussion. But depending on the technology, the turns can appear together in the same transcript (such as in blogs, which archive contributions in reverse chronological order); they can occur as separate messages, organized into categories or "threads" of discussion topics (as in discussion boards, e-mails, and listservs); or they can be separated by hypertext links (blogs and wikis allow for links to comments and outside websites). Other forms of asynchronous discussions include listservs (e-mail groups with distinct membership), discussion boards hosted by web courseware programs noted above (@ = Virtual learning environments), and online discussion groups such as Yahoo Groups or Google Groups (@ = Online discussion sites), blogs, and wikis.

There are a number of advantages of asynchronous online discussions (AD) over face-to-face (f-t-f) classroom discussions. In AD, students can participate at any time and at their own pace rather than being limited to classroom time. They are also less distracted by the nonverbal aspects and turn-taking demands of f-t-f discussions, so that they may be more comfortable participating in AD discussions. Furthermore, while one can be a member of an f-t-f discussion simply by being physically present but tuning out of the discussion, to be a member of an AD discussion, students need to follow the development of the discussion in order to contribute relevant posts. Because AD discussions are organized by topic threads, students can select a topic for commenting, something not present in f-t-f discussions.

How Do Online Discussions Improve Students' Writing?

Despite the advantages of online over f-t-f discussions, the question remains of whether participation in online discussions helps improve student writing by fostering a sense of voice or multiple voices, formulating convincing arguments, linking to others' ideas and information, and addressing their audience's interests and needs.

Through online discussions, students learn from one another by sharing and building upon each other's ideas. In other words, digital discussion environments support constructivist learning theories—the idea that knowledge is an active, experiential, and collaborative process. Conrad and Donaldson (2004) suggest that constructivist learning and online learning environments go hand-in-hand: "Activities that require student interaction and encourage a sharing of ideas promote a deeper level of thought" (p. 5). Many scholars, in fact, argue that online learning succeeds when it is engaging and represents constructivist learning assumptions (Adams, 2006). In this light, digital discussion environments are not only a useful activity but also perhaps a central activity for promoting engagement and strengthening community in a classroom. Lynne Sueoka, a teacher from Honolulu's Moanalua High School, reports that her goals for using digital tools are to "create students capable of initiating and directing their own learning, and share knowledge in a way that enriches and deepens what they learn" (Curtis, 2006, p. 25).

Another important reason to use digital discussions is that students *write to learn* as they compose messages and reflect on course material. Students can post summaries of class material; they can find related stories, articles, or links on a particular topic; they can respond to specific prompts created by the instructor; and they can discuss issues with other students. These and similar activities require students to think critically about course material and articulate their understanding of that material. Students consequently immerse themselves in writing, constantly composing and reading texts. Because students are continually engaged in online writing environments outside and inside the classroom, they are learning to use writing to be heard by others. As they practice this interactive writing, their writing can improve over time.

Digital discussion environments also help students understand audience and purpose more concretely. Because digital discussion environments are public, students understand that they have a ready audience of other students in class and the teacher. Gordon Brune, a fifth-grade teacher who uses blogs, reports: "My students no longer see themselves writing for a teacher or a bulletin board but for a real audience. Many times, my students have excitedly and incredulously stated things like, 'Man, people all the way from China are reading my stuff!'" (Curtis, 2006, p. 25). Digital discussion environments can include students from other schools—even other countries—thus broadening awareness of multiple layers of audience in writing tasks. The implications of a real audience are powerful: Students may have more motivation to write and may take more time thinking about and preparing their messages. This stronger sense of audience can help students craft messages with sharper focus and purpose than traditional paper-based assignments.

Planning Digital Discussion Environments

Of course, digital tools themselves do not create powerful learning experiences; it is what teachers do with these tools that make them effective. This idea has been expressed in the popular mantra *pedagogy must drive technology*, which means that it is important to first articulate goals for using technology and not let tools drive choices and actions. Clearly articulating goals serves to justify uses of technology in the classroom and explain how and what students are learning as a result of technology integration.

In the remainder of this chapter, we will discuss several pedagogical goals for using digital discussions (@ = Strategies for fostering online discussions). These include:

- Developing and creating a learning community
- Stimulating critical thinking
- Exploring, constructing, and maintaining online identities
- Reflecting on course material
- Engaging students in productive collaboration and response

Of course, these are but a few pedagogical goals that might drive digital discussion environments, and they are not necessarily mutually exclusive. In fact, integrating digital discussion environments might include overlapping goals. For example, Grisham and Wolsey (2006) articulate the multiple goals they had for using threaded discussion groups:

> We wanted to build group coherence among students. We wanted to share information about the readings with them and have them share information with one another. We wanted students to process ideas about the reading. We envisioned that we might do some tutoring online, refine students' communication skills, and also provide feedback to students. (p. 652)

The important thing is to let specific goals guide student activities in terms of the specific kinds of reading or writing practices that are valued in a classroom.

In addition to articulating overall goals for using online discussion, it is important to scaffold digital discussions in specific ways that help students build writing and critical thinking skills. For example, Conrad and Donaldson (2004) articulate one scaffolding strategy called "phases of engagement" in which they suggest four gradual phases of increased engagement. They suggest that in phase 1, the student plays the role of "newcomer" and the instructor plays the role of "social negotiator." The goal of phase 1 is to simply help students become comfortable in the virtual environment. In phase 2, students play the role of "cooperator" and teachers play the role of "structural engineer." In this phase, the "instructor forms dyads of learners and provides activities that require critical thinking, reflection, and sharing of ideas" (29). Phases 3 and 4 require increased participation from students: Phase 3 requires students to collaborate more fully, such as through team exercises, and phase 4 requires students to initiate exercises in the class and take leadership roles. The "phases of engagement" approach can be a useful guide for teachers planning to integrate digital discussions purposefully. It promotes the idea that online instruction thrives when we purposefully involve students in their learning.

Another way to scaffold discussions is to offer several different forms of online discussion in an online environment, keeping in mind that different technologies work best for different activities. To illustrate, Grady and Davis (2005) suggest the following strategies for scaffolding online: (a) developing personal home pages for students as a way to initiate discussion and interaction; (b) establish a class listserv and personal e-mail as a way for instructors to make announcements and connect with students (and for students to make their presence known as well); (c) schedule synchronous chats weekly for 1 hour to supplement course material and assignments and use a planned agenda and discussion moderator for chats; (d) create online discussion boards organized according to discussion topic, to further discussion on ideas mentioned in other forums (pp. 116–118). Offering multiple discussion forums may reinforce concepts and give students the chance to reflect in a variety of meaningful ways.

Given the range of synchronous and asynchronous tools for digital discussion, as well as overall strategies such as scaffolding and creating pedagogical goals, the remainder of this chapter discusses and provides examples of the aforementioned goal-driven approaches for using synchronous and asynchronous technologies to support and sustain digital discussion environments.

Developing and Creating a Learning Community

Developing the sense of a learning community online takes time and practice. Students need time and practice with a digital discussion environment in order to feel more comfortable as a participant. It is often useful to begin with synchronous chats to help students adjust to the online environment. Many students are familiar with chats already (at least in social contexts). In addition, synchronous chats bring a sense of fun and engagement, and students sometimes feel more relaxed contributing to these chats because they can be informal and experiment with language as a way to foster online social relationships.

Although using synchronous chats to engage students in online discussions can be a useful, creative exercise, there are some precautions to consider, particularly in using public chat sites. Considerable concern has been expressed about people posing or passing for someone they are not on chat sites to establish relationships or solicit sex (Burbules & Callister, 2000). Given the anonymity of the Web, people can use pretend identities for the purpose of attracting others in an attempt to create actual live-world relationships (Donath, 1996). To avoid these concerns, we recommend using chat sites that are password protected, where participation is limited to students and teacher, or where participants require teacher permission to join the site.

Underlying a constructivist approach to learning is the idea that students use online forums to construct knowledge to contribute and explore information and ideas a social activity, leading them to construct new knowledge. This is most likely to occur in creating expectations for online participation. Alison Black (2005, p. 20) employs the following expectations for her students' online discussions:

- Specific guidelines, checklists, and rubrics regarding acceptable responses
- Modeling of what constitutes a "reflective piece"
- Well-designed open-ended questions and topics to provide a context for the discussion and to help students stay centered (I have students create them, and I approve them, usually editing or adding something)
- Requirement of specific connections made to the readings (In this way, I am able to get students to pay attention to important people and ideas noted in the text and journal articles)
- Private notes to students who are inappropriate or off topic with their talk
- Summary or wrap-up of the discussion by the instructor or students
- Accountability (I assign one-quarter to one-fifth of students' total grade to their responses online)

To reduce her own workload in facilitating and evaluating online discussions, Black expects her students to assume major responsibilities for selecting topics related to readings, formulating questions, facilitating the discussion, and providing summaries of what is learned. She also assesses students based on their ability to respond to questions as well as the number of their contributions.

In the following discussion, students from Sara's Williamson's literature class at Westonka High School, Mound, Minnesota, are engaged in an evening chat on Tappedin.org (http://tappedin.org). Sara notes that in her students' exchanges, verbal "fooling around…actually helps to foster a chat environment that is more open and fun, and thus more engaging overall." The following is an excerpt from the beginning of an evening chat.

Oklahoma:	yes the java download worked
Pennsylvania:	thnax mrs w
Ohio:	ok enough pennsylvania lets talk
Pennsylvania:	lol
Hawaii:	ha
Hawaii:	thems be fightin words
Ohio:	yup
Wyoming:	Sry I am late

Oklahoma:	sweet, we should do this often, i like doing this at home
Sara:	Okay, okay, KENNEL.
Ohio:	get out your late
Wyoming:	frowns
Kansas:	lol ur silly
Hawaii:	ha...mrs. W...new Q

In this exchange, students are just logging on and getting oriented to the online space. One student, "Oklahoma," downloads Java to prepare for the chat. Other students enter the chat room and join the conversation, which is very informal, and full of chat abbreviations like "Sry" for sorry, "lol" for "laughing out loud." Within a few entries, however, the students begin to focus, as the student "Hawaii" prompts the teacher for the next discussion question: "mrs. W. . . new Q." Through engaging in this online verbal play, students are establishing social connections critical to forming a sense of community. In an interview with Sara, one student contrasted face-to-face classroom discussions with their online discussions:

Jim (student):	Um, I really think that those out-of-class in-the-evening online discussions...those were really fun...I had fun doing those. I seemed really loose and it was a comfortable environment because we were at our house—I don't know if that makes you think better or what, but there were a lot of different, like, good answers on those, like ones you wouldn't see in class.
Sara:	So, you think it was because people were more relaxed that they were then able to think more clearly about what the book is actually saying?
Jim:	Yeah, and they can be more themselves and say what they really think.

Many scholars agree that helping students become comfortable in an online environment is a critical first step in using any digital discussion environment. For example, using a chat to create community falls very much in line with phase 1 of Conrad and Donaldson's (2004) "phases of engagement" approach. The goal of phase 1 is simply to help students get to know one another in the online space. Activities they recommend for this phase are "icebreakers, individual introductions, discussions concerning community issues such as Netiquette rules in a virtual lounge" (p. 29).

Stimulating Critical Thinking

To push the idea of a learning community further, we can consider the pedagogical goal of stimulating critical thinking. At the beginning of this chapter, we saw one example of how Theresa Haider used an asynchronous discussion prompt to stimulate critical thinking about required reading. She asked students to select a discussion question and address it, while also considering other classmates' responses. The result was a threaded online discussion in which students responded not just to the question at hand but also to one another's comments, broadening and deepening the conversation with each new point that was raised.

Synchronous discussion tools can also be used for this purpose, and to illustrate, we turn back to the class example with the instructor, Sara. In the following discussion, Sara uses the chat function of Tappedin.org with her same students for a different purpose. Here, she exemplifies phase 2 of Conrad and Donaldson's (2004) approach by modeling how to frame questions to help students think critically. In this case, students are discussing Jon Krakauer's (2007) *Into the Wild*, a story that recounts the experiences of Christopher McCandless, a college graduate, who attempted to survive on his own in the Alaska wilds only to starve to death. In the excerpt below, Sara poses a question related to explaining McCandless's motives: "Why would anyone be so extreme in throwing off society and the material world?" This question leads some students to focus on the larger world as "fake." Through posing questions like these, Sara is modeling the inquiry process in exploring a person's motivation, leading her students to expand their thinking. Also, unlike in the opening chat, which was more social in nature, students respond directly to the question at hand, putting their thoughts into words.

Sara:	Why would anyone be so extreme in throwing off society and the material world?
Oklahoma:	in life people need to make there [sic] own decisions, or their life wont be fully complete he wouldn't have been able to feel complete without this journey, it was a life journey, he was finding himself, how can you live life not knowing who you are, he needed this trip
Ohio:	i think that if you really want something your [sic] not going to look at all the consequences your [sic] gunna just do it
Oklahoma:	because the material world is fake
Oklahoma:	he hated that

Wyoming:	Maybe they werent happy with their life so they decided to go and try something new.
Kansas:	thats a good? I dont get it
Montana:	but was it worth dying over?
Pennsylvania:	because he probably wants to adventure a new life that's extreme
Wyoming:	He didnt mean to die
Montana:	i understand, but he DID

Sara's example can be applied to many different digital discussion formats. The key ingredient in stimulating critical thinking is the teacher's interaction with students, specifically keeping them on task and pushing them to explore ideas and concepts further.

Reflecting on Course Material

Another common pedagogical goal associated with the use of digital discussions is reflecting on course material. For this goal, asynchronous discussion tools are a great choice. One of the benefits of using asynchronous discussions, as opposed to synchronous, is that the delayed-time nature of asynchronous technologies allows students more time to reflect on course material. In this way, asynchronous discussions can be used for creative, reflective assignments and can be tailored to help students adapt to digital discussion environments. For example, to introduce students to a digital discussion environment (Conrad and Donaldson, 2004, phase 1), students can start by posting messages and responding to other students as a way to become familiar with the online space. The following includes a specific example of a phase 1 asynchronous exercise.

Favorite Place on Earth

Use bulletin board technology and have students write about their favorite (physical) place on earth. Have students put the name of the place in the subject line of their message. In the content of the message, have students write one paragraph in which they describe this place and explain why they like it. Then, have students reply to at least one other student in class about that student's favorite place. A simple exercise such as this could accomplish many goals: it introduces students to the discussion environment; it encourages them to respond to other students in the environment; it requires them to craft a coherent paragraph; and it requires them to use descriptive language.

Reflective discussion activities could also be designed at a phase 2 level of engagement, in which a reflective activity is still structured by the teacher but requires more effort from the student. Alison Black (2005) explains: "A reflective response involves critical thinking and focuses on what students in the classroom may have learned" (p. 6). Asynchronous discussions could be created to have students talk about readings, answer thought-provoking questions about course material, or even explore related topics and bring those back to the class discussion. In her study of "e-lit groups," or electronic literacy group discussions, Dena Beeghly (2005) reports that students wrote short responses about assigned literature readings and then used those responses to stimulate discussion. Beeghly found that using asynchronous discussions allowed students to have more time to think about their responses to readings, thus stimulating critical thinking while also creating a learning community (p. 16).

As these studies show, asynchronous technologies have been used for reflective purposes, often to create a kind of discussion forum. These activities are fairly easy to set up. Using bulletin board or forum tools found in tools such as Moodle, Ning, WebCT/Vista, or Blackboard, students are given a specific prompt on a topic or an issue, requiring them to post entries on a specific topic and to respond to another student's entry. Most online discussion tools accommodate the structuring of online discussions, particularly multiple postings, which can be organized by topic, person, or date.

One useful discussion tool, Moodle Forums, includes a number of user-friendly features that foster productive discussion by multiple students. Using Moodle, students can subscribe to a forum, which displays their pictures or avatars with each posting; participate in discussions based on specific topics, dates, or readings; post to this forum at any time, as well as reply to the posts; add attachments and links to the posts; receive e-mail copies of posts; edit posts within a limited time period (30–60 minutes) before they are e-mailed to users; and receive ratings on their posts either by only the teacher or by both teacher and peers.

One example of the use of Moodle for sharing discussions and course content on different sites throughout the world is the PiccleForum (Pedagogy for Inter-Cultural Critical Literacy Education) (http://piccle.edu.psu.edu), operated by Jamie Myers at Pennsylvania State University. PiccleForum seeks to foster sharing of how students' different cultural perspectives shape their responses to texts and the media. Teachers can create their own course on this site as well as view discussions and access resources from other teachers' courses.

FanFiction Sites

Students can participate in sites such as FanFiction.net (http://www.fanfiction.net) in which writers create spin-off stories of well-known TV shows or movies.

Writers post their stories, much like a blog entry, and anyone logging onto the site can post comments and critiques of their stories. FanFiction provides a tangible readership and social support network for aspiring writers. Rebecca Black (2008) comments on the power of sites such as FanFiction.net as a discussion site:

> Many fan fiction and help sites also feature a range of meta-discussion on elements of fan fiction—related topics that are relevant to and in many ways mirror school-based composition topics and practices, such as peer review, giving constructive feedback, editing, proofreading, effective plot development, robust characterization, and constructing effective rhetorical structures, to name just a few. (p. 42)

Cross-Cultural or International Exchanges

Collaborative online discussions can take the form of cross-cultural or international exchanges in which students from different schools are writing to and for each other. Teachers from classes in different schools or schools in different countries could take turns providing discussion prompts. As students respond, they can read replies from students in both classes. For example, the Youth Wiki site (http://youthwiki.wikispaces.com) developed by Paul Allison involves students from schools all over the world sharing their place-based experiences in their local communities. Students can also participate in sites such as http://PolarHusky.com, which offers a dynamic curriculum that chronicles the journeys of explorers in different locations around the world, such as a trek across the Arctic. Explorers write about their journeys or send videos, and students can write to explorers, asking questions or offering comments and observations about the explorations. Discussions that occur in environments like these involve students around the world, providing students with an understanding of how writing is a critical vehicle for communication.

Students can also engage in online writing with students throughout the world using tools such as ePals. ePals is a site with 5 million students and teachers from 191 countries that includes e-mail and blogs, as well as ePals Mentoring for students to interact with local community experts. These tools include multilingual translations tools so that students can interact with other students on a global basis (@ = ePals).

ePal writing can be particularly valuable when students are working with others from different countries so that students learn about their lives in different social and cultural contexts. For example, a class in Spanish in the United States can link to a class in English in Mexico. Students in each class must write in the native language of the other class. Because their exchanges are meaningful, based on personal interaction, storytelling, descriptions of their lives and activities, and the like, learning takes on a functional dimension not present when students are practicing a foreign language in an interpersonal void.

There are also many free sites that arrange links between individual students or whole classes. The Mixxer (http://www.language-exchanges.org), for example, allows teachers or learners to locate a language partner for electronic exchanges. Each partner is a native speaker of the language the other partner is learning. The partners meet online using Skype to give each other a context for discussion and practice and to help each other learn. Another site, Hands Across the World (http://hatw.net/), a free international penpal service, employs Facebook-like profiles, pictures, and Skype to facilitate communication. Its goal is to promote international friendship, but it is an excellent site for arranging foreign-language exchange as well.

At Cary Academy, Cary, North Carolina, eighth-grade students collaborated with students at the same level enrolled in a school in Vienna, Austria (Cary Academy, 2003). After exchanging ePal letters electronically for 2 years, the groups decided to conduct an international project together. Each group researched both Vienna and New York City at the turn of the century, during the period 1880–1910. They wrote several articles in their native languages about their research in the genre of newspaper reports and then formatted them to look like they had appeared in either *The New York Times* or the Austrian equivalent in Vienna, the *Viener Tablat*. For example, students created mock *New York Times* articles with headlines such as "Roosevelt Wins! Roosevelt Sweeps Opposition Away." Articles on New York addressed politics, science, technology (e.g., "Pleasure Railways, a New Fad for New York?"), architecture, literature, music, fashion, theater, and gossip (e.g., "Carnegie Living the Big Life"). Articles on Vienna included similar categories ("The Unexpected Death of [architect] Joseph Maria Olbrich"; "Blood Is Not the Same as Blood" (a report on the discovery of coagulation by Karl Landsteiner); and "Farm Boy From the Woods to Poet: Peter Rosegger." After the students had created the drafts of their texts, they swapped them electronically between the two school groups. Each class then translated the texts written by the other class into their own language from the language they were learning. The resulting website includes all the mocked-up newspaper articles on both cities in both English and German (http://project1.caryacademy.org/turnofcentury/).

Using Online Games to Teach Writing

Students can also participate in gaming environments that correspond well with Conrad and Donaldson's (2004) phase 3 level of engagement, which shifts the focus away from the teacher and toward student involvement and collaboration. Gaming environments involve technologies such as MUDs, MOOs, or massively multiplayer online role-playing games (MMORPGs), as well as virtual reality worlds (@ = MOO and Second Life sites).

These forms of synchronous discussion are digital writing spaces that invite students to adopt avatar roles and formulate strategies for navigating worlds, as in Everquest, Lineage II, Civilization III, SimCity, Second Life, or Lively. Students can also participate in (MUVES) such as the PalacePlanet (Thomas, 2004), in which students draw on popular culture to adopt roles; River City, in which students cope with medical diseases in a city; and Quest Atlantis, in which students, ages 9–12, engage in quests to 11 different worlds (@ = Games/simulations).

Learning literacy practices associated with adopting avatar roles involves becoming new members of a virtual social community, something that can be a challenge for students. These games provide students with support to help them discern the rules and develop virtual characters as they move through a series of steps or challenges in order to succeed in the game (Gee, 2003; Shaffer, 2005). Video games are therefore designed to support novice players in ways that minimize risks or failures and that reward success. Gee argues that through participation in games, children and adolescents also engage in critical learning of how they are manipulated by games as design spaces and how they can, in turn, manipulate the game for their own ends. Because players may be working together online as members of an affinity group, they are learning that knowledge is distributed to different players and that tools are designed to achieve certain goals. As players acquire experience with the game, they assume the role of insider producer and teacher of knowledge, as well as an active agent in altering the game itself. (For links to MMORPGs, visit http://massivemultiplayer.com/, http://gameogre.com/freemmorpgs.htm, and http://gameogre.com/strategygames.htm).

Games or online simulations such as the Fighting Sioux online role-play described in chapter 1 can be developed to create a social context for writing based on a situation involving a problem, a conflict, an issue, a challenge, or a crisis that requires some action. Students assume various roles in which they engage in writing associated with addressing a situation. For example, in an introductory journalism course at the University of Minnesota, Professor Kathleen Hansen used a modified version of the computer game "Neverwinter Nights" to engage students in newspaper writing (Berger, 2005/2006). Because this game comes with a game-building tool set, Hansen and her colleague, Nora Paul, modified the game to create a small city world in which students assumed the role of a newspaper reporter writing a story about a train derailment that resulted in a spill of anhydrous ammonia. Students can research their story by accessing a news library of documents and links, as well as characters who can be interviewed. Students keep notes in a notebook and then generate a final news story based on the information they gather.

There are also role-play sites in which students employ collaborative writing by adopting roles and strategies consistent with the rhetorical demands of the situation. For example, to help students learn to use digital writing tools, the Writing in Digital Environments (WIDE) Research Center at Michigan State University created an online game, Ink (http://writing.msu.edu:16080/ink/). In this game, students are participating in a fictional government and city council that involves extensive writing over a long period. Playing the game requires students to engage in chat and produce various texts associated with particular rhetorical contexts and game like situations. For example, as they enter the game, a student receives the following writing prompt:

> Welcome to Ink. This is a great place. But we have a problem right now, and I'm hoping you can help. Our neighborhood isn't doing well. We need to get a group of people together to address this problem. Can you help us? We need to design a flier that will motivate people to come to a meeting where we can talk about this problem. We need to draft a resolution that we can circulate to those who show up. We also need a brochure that explains why other citizens should vote for our proposal. And we're going to need a white paper to explain to City Council the principles that inform our proposal. We've got a lot of work to do. Can you help us?

As in any game, students progress through different levels on various "thematic paths." To advance on a path, students provide their journal entries to other veteran players who then judge whether the entries meet the requirements for succeeding on that particular path based on criteria having to do with convincing audiences, particularly voters, of the validity of their positions. As part of the game, students also reflect on their writing and experiences in the game. Their teachers then receive reports on students' participation in the game, as well as copies of the students' writing produced in the game.

Given the fact that many students are engaged in playing video games, students can also write guides on how to play certain games. Brock Dubbels had his ninth-grade students at Roosevelt High School, Minneapolis, Minnesota, create "walk-throughs"—summary guides in their blogs for how to play video games, an example of "shared expertise" describe in chapter 1:

> A writing assignment that has inspired my students to write much more than they normally do is the walk-through. Just consider it a travel journal, where the travelers, in this case my students, are traveling through the world of a video game. They are asked to note all the important elements of the game world, the purpose, and strategies for success, excitement, and subtle treasures and secret doors. The key element is that students are positioned to observe and describe, so details and elements of the video

1. Play the game through, then play it again; but now you have taken some notes and mapped out what to do and where to look for secret doors and treasure.

2. Make a summary of each level that is about 15 sentences long, with hints and previews.

3. Create headings and new entries for each level and subheadings for stations on each level. You are basically narrating a map and where to look and what to do.

Tips:

- Use screen shots or artwork of the game on the Web.

- Try to predict where people will get stuck during the game and provide strategies for this.

- Describe where cool stuff is hidden.

- Try to find everything in the game, what it does, and how to use it.

- Give examples and, if possible, record footage of your game play and narrate what you are doing and why.

game are necessary for the creation of the walk-through.

Video games are built upon many of the same elements as textbooks, short stories, and novels. They therefore provide an opportunity to develop awareness and practice using ideas like character, plot, setting, cause and effect, tone, theme, and even conventions. Although the conventions in a game are often expressed in multiple modalities in the form of print, audio, and image, they also include puzzles, interface, and interaction, and this may provide the student with more accessible portal stories and an opportunity to develop higher level comprehension skills. This can be a real asset when you have a class with both successful readers and students who struggle to decode.

In order to make a game walk-through, my students take notes as they go through the game and look for elements from a list of literary terms and organizational elements from expository text structures. As they play, observe, and note, they eventually take their notes and describe what they have experienced and compose it on a blog as technical writing to help others get through the game.

They search the Web, use screen capture techniques, and even use cameras to capture images and video of game play to describe on their blog.

What I have found through using this new genre is that my students jump right in and start without the normal complaints about having a writing assignment. As they get further into it, I have them evaluate the game using a rubric, in which they rate the point of view and awareness of audience, voice and consistency, images, point of view and purpose, soundtrack

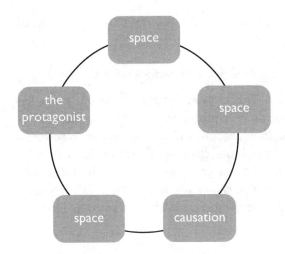

and emotion, economy, dramatic question, engagement, complexity, rules, and usability. They begin to develop and refine their writing to fit the criteria of the rubric.

The trick is showing them how to add images and create multimedia around their text, and this gives them another aspect to describe to inform, extending length and depth of their description and explanations.

Even my most reluctant students eventually join in. They see the fun my academically motivated and middle-of-the road students are having, and they start. They are always very surprised when we take each little entry out of the blogs and connect them in an essay to see that they have written more than they ever have in their lives. It is here that they begin to see the wisdom of writing in chunks like paragraphs and learn about transitions, headings, supporting details, when they begin to put it all together in an essay. Here is one student, Casadi Rasmuson, describing the game, Sly Cooper:

Sly Cooper is a thief and has the police following him. Although he steals, he mostly steals from criminals. So what he is doing is something like Robin Hood, but without giving to the poor. Along the way he also put the criminals in front of the police so they are sent to jail. He is sending people to jail that need to be put away, and he gets back what is his which is o.k., but the stealing is not so good. And it should not give any one justification on stealing.

You start on top of the police headquarters, with Bentley talking to Sly through the Binocucom. Then you move Sly to the water tower (follow the coins). Then Sly and Bentley talk some more. Go up to the blue sparkles and hit the circle button to sneak around the tower. Jump on the antennas to the roof. Hit the air vent open and walk through. Jump down the hole and hit the alarm. Then go into the hall and take two lefts to Carmelita's office. The door is locked so go through the window and sneak along the ledge into her office. When inside smash everything and collect the coins. Go to vault and enter the code that Bentley tells you. Go out the fire escape. Carmelita will see you. Run down the fire escape, and across the packing lot in to the van. And the level is done. When you collect 100 coins you get a lucky charm that allows you to tack one hit. You can have a maximum of two lucky charms.

In rating the Point of View and Awareness of Audience, for Casadi:

> Sly Cooper gets a 4. The game is for every one but more for younger people so the game is pretty easy to get a handle on. The game tells you how to do the actions you need to be able to perform, but a challenge is finding all the clues on a level (which would be almost imposable if you did not get a lay out of the hideouts connected to the Binocucom that shows you where the clues are hiding). And as you get farther in to the game you are able to do more things as you unlock vaults.

One of the reasons for Brock's students' engagement in writing their game walk-throughs is that they have a strong sense of purpose and audience because they are providing their peers with directions for how to play a game.

Managing Digital Discussion Environments

Use of digital discussions requires a lot of careful management to address issues such as the following: Does one student dominate digital discussion? Do some entries include inappropriate language? Are some students avoiding the digital discussion environment? As we think further on a continuum of engagement in digital discussion environments, we can consider ways to move to phase 4 of engagement, which encourages students to take leadership roles in class. The previous gaming examples illustrate some ways that students can take leadership roles in class discussions through sharing their expertise on playing games. Other activities can encourage student leadership as well. One example is the "question of the day" activity. In this activity, each student is assigned to write a question of the day. On their assigned days, this student posts a message on a discussion board with his or her question. Then students post a reply to that question and read and respond to one another's replies. The student who created the question reads everyone's postings and replies with a summary of the various ideas included in the posts. The "question of the day" exercise allows students to take a leadership role and greater investment in class discussions.

It is important that discussion questions posted by the student or teacher be open-ended. In describing her use of questions for the *The Kite Runner* (Hosseini, 2004) discussion, Theresa noted that:

> I give students a choice of 3–6 questions for each discussion, so there is bound to be at least one question that appeals to each student. The questions I use are open-ended, higher order–thinking questions designed to elicit responses that demonstrate the student has been keeping up with the reading as well as their opinion of the reading.

It is also important to set specific expectations about deadlines for completing posts and/or having peers reply to posts. To ensure that students actually receive a reply to their posts, an important incentive for posting, students could be assigned as specific partners who will respond to their peer's posts within a certain period. It is also useful to draw on student posts as the basis for face-to-face classroom discussions or further analysis.

Another management issue in digital discussions involves politeness, or "netiquette," in online environments (@ = Online netiquette and safety). This issue arises when students use acronyms, abbreviations, or symbols to shortcut communication. Such conventions might be acceptable and familiar to many students—but most likely, this is not true for all students.

Politeness could also emerge as an issue when students "hog the floor" or dominate digital discussions or when students use inappropriate language. These issues are more prevalent in a chat environment than in an asynchronous environment, when participation might rely on such things as typing speed. To address these challenges, teachers can act as a discussion leader or assign a student facilitator who leads conversation with discussion questions. Another strategy is to monitor turn taking through visual symbols that create etiquette online. For example, Craig Smith (2006) proposes that chat participants use simple symbols to indicate turn taking: (a) an exclamation point [!] or a question mark [?] to indicate when someone wants to make a contribution or raise a question, like the equivalent of raising a hand in discussion; and (b) three forward slash marks [///] to indicate the end of a contribution. Smith suggests that participants follow these rules and wait to see participant contributions unfold before jumping in the discussion. In analyzing his students' use of these symbols, Smith found that participants believed that the technique worked well to manage discussion and create a more coherent conversation.

Another issue has to do with students' access outside school. Before committing to digital discussion environments, students could be polled about their access to technology outside the classroom. Questions might include: (a) What forms of online discussion have you used? (b) What are your favorite forms of discussion? (c) Which online discussions do you use in school? (d) Which online discussion do you use outside school?

Such a poll might reveal that some students have access to a broadband Internet connection at home or at a local library or that they participate in other personal digital discussion environments on a regular basis, information that can be used to recommend or provide different ways to access the classroom online discussions.

Evaluating Online Discussions

Students' online discussions can be evaluated using a set of criteria or rubrics having to do with both the quantity and quality of contributions. Students could be evaluated not only on the number of posts and replies but also on the extent to which they elaborate on their posts by providing reasons or evidence for their positions or interpretations. One problem with students' online chat is that, as modeled for them on radio talk shows, students may believe that simply voicing an opinion is sufficient to convince audiences. To evaluate quality of contributions, teachers can focus on the extent to which they provide supporting reasons or evidence for their opinions. In evaluating her ninth-grade students discussions on Moodle in her social studies class at South View Middle School in Edina, Minnesota, Gina Nelson notes the following:

> In regards to my students' posts and replies, I have simply given completion points for answering a question. I have tried to be more diligent in reading my students' comments and debates and have come up with a 5-4-3 grading scale: "5" for excellent, thoughtful, at least three reasons or explanations; "4" for good, could provide more justification, two reasons or explanations; and "3" for fair and needs more thought. This seems to be working for simple discussion posts. Honestly, I focus more on the process, thought-formation, and interaction online than the correct answers. My goals with Moodle have been to foster and encourage discussion and debates outside class, allowing students to develop a voice online.

It is also important to focus on change over time in students' participation, providing positive feedback to students when they demonstrate increased participation. Students can also self-assess their participation in terms of quantity and quality, leading them to provide reasons for their degree of participation and development of their ideas.

Summary

In this chapter, we posit that digital discussion environments encourage students to practice writing, to build community, and to enhance learning. We have reviewed various synchronous and asynchronous technologies that can support digital discussion environments, and we have suggested strategies for scaffolding discussions and helping students participate through reflection and increased critical thinking. These digital discussions can then continue when they begin to consider how to engage in collaborative writing using wikis, the subject of our next chapter.

Chapter Four

Fostering Collaborative Digital Writing

In the last two chapters, we described ways in which students can use various digital writing tools for generating material and conducting online discussions. In this chapter, we discuss how students can use digital writing tools such as wikis and Google Docs to work together to create collaboratively written texts. Collaboration is an important skill to learn in preparation for working with others in schools and the workplace. It is often the case that having students work collaboratively on their writing results in higher quality writing than when students are writing by themselves.

Why Use Collaborative Digital Writing Tools?

Unfortunately, much of writing instruction in schools assumes that writing is a solo act. Students are assigned to write a paper on a topic based on what is assumed to be their *own* knowledge, research, and work, based on the belief that students are prone to plagiarize others' ideas assumed not to be their *own* work.

This model of the solo student writer fails to recognize that knowledge is constructed through a collaborative sharing of ideas. It also ignores the fact that people in academia or the workplace often work collaboratively on writing reports. Building on shared perspectives that transcend an individual's perspectives results in higher quality writing than is the case with an individual's own writing. In working collaboratively with others, students also learn how to negotiate differences among opinions, ideas, and perspectives.

However, collaborative writing can be challenging. In the competitive world of schools, students are not accustomed to sharing responsibility and authority with peers through achieving consensus and interdependence. They may also simply have difficulty working with others. Students in one study (Brunk-Chavez & Miller, 2007) noted difficulties in collaborative wiki writing in groups because of the following:

- Students do not believe that knowledge is socially constructed.
- They dislike groups in which there is a leader and followers.
- They distrust their peers as having less knowledge or writing ability than their teacher.
- They believe that they are not capable of helping their peers.
- They perceive little value in shared talk to improve their writing.
- They disagree with their peers' beliefs, leading to struggles in sharing ideas.
- They respond negatively to poorly designed collaborative groups and assignments.
- They become frustrated with peers who do not contribute.

Students may also have difficulty determining who is responsible for contributing what material to their writing. Unless students have a clear understanding of who is responsible for contributing what material, they experience frustrations with some members of their group not making adequate contributions, leading to resentment that some members are not contributing as much as other members.

Digital Collaborative Writing Tools

Despite these challenges, we believe that digital collaborative writing tools, such as wikis or Google Docs, can assist students in engaging in productive collaborative writing. Although most of this chapter focuses on the use of wikis, the following are some alternative digital writing tools that could be used to foster collaborative writing.

Listservs

One tool that can be used to foster sharing of material is the listserv. Listservs or shared e-mail postings can be used to automatically send material to everyone in a class, group, or community, and then responses to those postings are shared with everyone. Students can choose whether to respond to postings, but when they make a post, they know that everyone will receive the post. Listservs can also be used to communicate with students' parents, providing them with information about assignments. Parents are more likely to receive this information than to access a classroom or school website or blog. Or, as noted in the last chapter, students can engage in shared e-mail projects in different classes, schools, or countries through projects such as ePals (http://www.epals.com) (@ = Listservs).

Word

When working collaboratively on the same Word text, students can use the "Comment" and "Track Changes" features to perceive the changes made in one another's drafts and see who made those changes. Or students could use CoWord (http://cooffice.ntu.edu.sg/coword), which converts Word into a collaborative version. However, Word becomes more cumbersome if a group of three or four students is working collaboratively on the same text, which suggests the need for other collaborative writing tools discussed in this chapter.

Web-Based Composing Tools

Students can also use any number of different free Web-based tools such as Google Docs (http://docs.google.com/), Writeboard (http://www.writeboard.com/), Zohowriter (http://www.zohowriter.com/login.sas), or AjaxWrite (http://www.ajaxlaunch.com/ajaxwrite/), for collaboratively composing on a website. One highly visual workspace is Thinkature (http://thinkature.com), which allows students to engage in collaborative chat within specific cards that represent certain topics that can be moved around the screen to map relationships among topics (@ = Collaborative writing tools).

One advantage of these Web-based tools is that students have to access the same documents online to collaboratively write, revise, store, and publish documents on the Web. These tools are less difficult to learn to use than wikis because they employ familiar word-processing formatting.

Google Docs is emerging as the most frequently used of these tools. On Google Docs, students can upload Word, RTF, or text documents Google Docs and then convert them to HTML for collaborative writing and editing. They can also store their documents on a secure site, and access to documents is controlled. Students can then publish their text or download documents as Word, RTF, PDF, zip, or HTML files.

To compose on Google Docs, students create a Google account and then go to the site, where they can create a document. They can invite their peers to collaborate with them by e-mailing them; their names will appear next to the file name as collaborators. To create and revise text, they employ the editing options on the tool bar; there is also a spell-check tool. However, the somewhat limited formatting options means that students will need to do sophisticated formatting after they have converted their file to another format such as Word.

Students can use Google Docs to compose their texts offline—while not being connected to the Web—using Google Gears (http://gears.google.com), an open source extension that enables Google Docs to be used offline. Students can then work on their writing when they are not connected to the Web, and changes are stored on their computer. Once they connect back to the Web, these changes are added to the shared text.

Students can promote their documents as websites as well as export their documents to a wiki or blog. By clicking on "Revisions," students can perceive changes in the text, just as they would with "Track Changes" in Word (Spinuzzi, 2007). Students periodically click on "Save" to save their changes, using different file names after major revisions. When their peers go to Google Docs, they see the different versions of their document listed as files. Teachers then access these different versions to determine the nature and extent of the students' revisions. Because each student's writing appears in a different color, the teachers can also determine variations in students' contributions as part of their collaboration. To foster peer feedback during drafting, peers and teachers can add comments to foster revision. Spinuzzi has his students add him as a collaborator so that he can give feedback as students are writing (@ = Collaborative writing activities).

Online Meeting and Conferencing Tools

Students can employ online video conferencing or IMing and chat tools for collaboration with one another outside their classroom or with students in other schools or countries—tools such as Google Talk (http://www.google.com/talk), Gizmo (http://www.gizmoproject.com), Skype (http://www.skype.com), Yahoo Messenger (http://messenger.yahoo.com/chat.php), PalTalk (http://www.paltalk.com), YackPack (http://www.yackpack.net), Twitter (http://twitter.com), and others listed on the wiki (@ = IMing/Twitter). For engaging in online video collaborative brainstorming sessions, students could use iChat, Adobe Breeze, or Agora (http://agora.lancs.ac.uk), described in chapter 7. Students can use Google Groups (http://www.google.com/googlegroups) to create a website that serves as a Usenet bulletin board search for sharing discussions and posting links to group members.

Collaborative Fiction and Role-Play Sites

Students can also access collaborative fiction writing sites such as FanFiction.net in which they contribute to one another's fiction or engage in online role-play activities (@ = Collaborative fiction/role-play). One example of a collaborative fiction-writing and role-playing site is the New Worlds Project (http://rpgnewworlds.net), which is based on a science-fiction world in which participants grapple with issues of peace in the midst of a world war in 2051. Within this site is a creative writing project in which participants collaborate on stories about their experiences in the world war.

In her creative writing class at Champlin Park High School, Champlin, Minnesota, Nicole Kronzer created a wiki for her students to write a collaborative short story (http://champlincw.pbwiki.com). The students first brainstormed ideas for their story, considering, for example, the Holocaust, a school shooting, or a murder mystery, but then settled on a story about a wedding (see Figure 4-1).

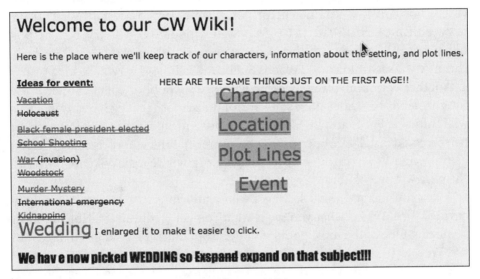

Figure 4-1. Brainstorming Story Ideas on a Wiki

Using Wikis for Collaborative Writing and Learning

One of the most powerful collaborative writing tools is a wiki—a website that allows designated users to create and edit online texts. Wikis are an invention of Wart Cunningham, who in 1995 wanted to create Web pages that would be readily revised by a number of different users (Leuf & Cunningham, 2001). With wikis, students can easily revise the same text simultaneously at any time simply by accessing their wiki site. Because many different writers can collaboratively construct the same texts, some organizations, companies, schools, and groups have found that they provide an efficient means of collaboratively creating documents by more than just two or three people (@ = Using wikis in the classroom).

Although blogs involve more individual student effort, wikis involve collective student effort in which students are mutually constructing knowledge through contributing their own information as well as revising and adding to others' information. Wiki writing therefore lends itself particularly well to writing reports, joint essays, reference guides, directories, manuals, glossaries, resource guides, or anything in a bibliographic format in which students contribute their own particular expertise to a collaborative text (Barton, 2004).

Setting Up and Using a Wiki in the Classroom

There are a lot of different wiki platforms available for use in the classroom: PBWiki (http://pbwiki.com), WikiSpaces (http://www.wikispaces.com), JotSpot (http://jot.com), wetpaint (http://www.wetpaint.com), EditMe (http://www.edit.me), StikiPad (http://www.stikipad.com), TikiWiki (http://tikiwiki.org), UseMod (http://www.usemod.com/cgi-bin/wiki.pl), and Seedwiki (http://www.seedwiki.com) (Woods & Thoeny, 2007) (@ = Wiki hosting).

Another option involves checking with one's school or college to see if the Internet service provider (ISP) software for the school or college already includes wiki software. For example, Moodle has a built-in wiki. Or a technical support person could install free open-source software onto the school or college server, using Media Wiki (http://www.mediawiki.org/wiki/MediaWiki) or PmWiki (http://www.pmwiki.org).

A key consideration in selecting a wiki platform is ease of use, particularly having WYSIWYG ("what you see is what you get") editing available on most platforms. One of the most popular of these options is PBWiki given its ease of use. We selected this platform for this book's resource site because of its ease of use. Wikispaces and Wetpaint are also popular wiki platforms, given their appealing layout formats and ease of use.

Editing Wikis

Having selected a certain wiki platform, it is important to model ways of using wiki features (@ = Creating wikis). Students experience wikis in either read or edit mode. When they read a wiki, they are perusing the text as they would any Web page. However, if they want to edit or revise the text, they switch to edit mode by clicking on the edit link or button—for example, on Wikipedia, by selecting the "edit this page" option.

In some cases, there are no restrictions on editing a page. In other cases, to edit a page on a wiki with restrictive access, students will need to have an account and a password. The reason that it is important to have a password for a wiki is to prevent spammers from automatically accessing and altering a wiki site. For a classroom wiki, it is therefore important to limit editing access to only the students in the course while allowing anyone to read their wikis.

To edit this book's wiki, find the specific topic listed on the side bar and go a specific page. To add links or material, click on "Edit page" and enter in the "invite key," which for our wiki is "digwriting." This then creates the edit box with the following menu of editing options shown in Figure 4-2 (note: the more recent 2.0 version of PBWiki has a different template).

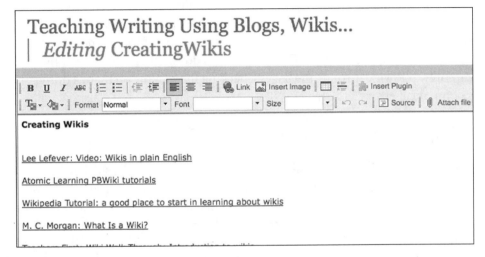

Figure 4-2. Editing Options for PBWiki

In the upper left corner are options for creating bold, underline, and italics, as well as strike-through. Clicking on "Link" opens up a box with a pull-down menu that allows for insertion of a hotlink, wikipage, or e-mail address. Clicking on "Insert Plugin," leads to options to insert items under Productivity (Calendar, Google Gadgets, Address link, Stock chart), PBwiki magic (Equation, HTML, Recent Changes, Recent Visitors, Table of Contents, Number of Visitors), Video (YouTube video), Photos (Bubbleshare slideshow, Slide photoshow), and Chat (chat room). Students can change the font color, size, and type, as well as view the original source code by clicking on "Source" and attaching files. Once a page has been edited, click on the "Save" button at the bottom to save the changes that were made for that page.

Wikis also include a history feature that displays each revised version of a page with the revisions displayed in different colors. To model these revisions, refer students to screencasts of wiki revision (@ = Screencasts: wiki revision). For example, in one screencast (http://ia300212.us.archive.org/1/items/PaulAllisonLatinoPrideAStoryofCollaboraiveWritingonaWiki/LatinoPrideBoth.swf), Paul Allison of the New York City Writing Project describes his students' revisions of their writing about Latino Pride in which the students are writing about their identities as Dominicans or Puerto Ricans.

You can use this feature to demonstrate the value of revision by showing students how subsequent revisions improved a text. In using a wiki site (http://studyingsocietiesatjhk.pbwiki.com) with his social studies middle school students, Clarence Fisher (2007), shows students different versions of the same text on a class projector and has them discuss how and why the revisions they made improved their writing. He subscribes his wiki to his Bloglines using RSS feeds so that he can receive notices of revisions; he then gives student credit for making certain revisions in texts. Fisher finds that "some kids are not fact checkers and spelling editors. These kids are more often contributing pieces of new information about a topic to a page. Other kids are adding little that is new, but are carefully following through the pages, checking the spelling on them, editing for grammatical errors, etc." (p. 2).

Creating Sidebars and Links Between Pages

In setting up a wiki, an essential component is the side bar. The sidebar serves as a table of contents that lists the topics covered in the wiki and that appears on all pages. On our resource wiki, because the list of chapters in the sidebar is present on any page, readers can readily move to a chapter by clicking on that chapter.

In creating the side bar, students can use the topics listed to organize or scaffold their content, which is particularly useful for dividing up responsibilities for writing within a group. Then, as they alter their organization or add new topics, they can revise their topic list.

Another important feature of some wikis such as Wikipedia is the use of hotlinked key terms or concepts, often described as "wikiwords," used to create links between pages. On a wiki, clicking on different key terms or concepts serves to create another page in a wiki for writing about that particular term or concept. In contrast to reading a text in a linear, chronological order, readers therefore read a wiki text according to links between key terms or concepts that serve to connect a network of pages. As Mike Morgan (2005) noted, "On a wiki, we don't write in just words, sentences, paragraph, parts, but collect those units into topics and arrange those topics in various ways."

Classroom and School Wiki Activities

Wikis can also serve as a central portal for sharing work or resources related to a specific class or school (@ = Classroom-school wikis). One teacher who makes extensive use of wiki sharing among classes and schools is Vicki Davis, a teacher and technology administrator at Westwood Schools in Camilla, Georgia. Davis (2006) argues that her school wiki (http://westwood.wikispaces.com) serves as a focal point for student work so that students and teachers, as well as other adult readers, can all share perceptions of topics in her courses. Davis notes the following:

> The Wiki serves as a virtual hub of all classroom activities. It is a place where classroom instruction, team projects, and all online content can be posted and shared by everyone in the class. It keeps the dissemination of hyperlinks, online projects, and results simple for students (and the teacher.) Often in-class projects move from discussion to the wiki. In the Westwood classroom, the wiki is considered a place to post facts. Blogs are taught as the place for personal opinion and expression. This helps students discern the appropriate place for their information. (p. 2)

This means that the wiki becomes a one-stop site for students to acquire and share information. Davis has students create study wikis at the end of the semester to review what they learned from their readings, notes, and other materials in a course. One group of students created a "study-hall" wiki (http://studyhall.wikispaces.com) on which they posted information about ways to study for and complete projects in their class. Davis uses wikis to assess students on final open-book exams in which students have access to one another's writing. Rather than finding instances of plagiarism of others' work, she found that access to others' work enhanced the quality of students' work.

To share writing among different schools in different parts of the worked for her 10th-grade computer class, Davis worked with Julie Lindsay's 11th-grade computer class at the International School Dhaka (ISD) in Bangladesh on what they described as the Flat Classroom Project (http://flatclassroomproject.wikispaces.com), based on shared wiki writing about Thomas Friedman's book *The World Is Flat*. Because these students were sharing their writing from the perspective of being in two different parts of the world, they could discuss the role of technology in fostering a "flat world" related to increased globalization. As evident in the Youth Wiki (http://youthwiki.wikispaces.com) developed by Paul Allison (2006), wikis work well for these cross-cultural exchanges because students can readily locate links to topics, issues, or schools on the side bar. In another wiki developed by Allison, the High School Online Collaborative Writing wiki (http://schools.wikia.com/wiki/Main_Page), students in four local high schools collaborated to write different versions of the opening scene of *MacBeth*. For other examples of students' wiki writing, see @ = Student wiki writing.

Wikis are useful for organizing group projects or joint teacher planning. Jaimee Bohning, a Minneapolis teacher, employed a wiki to organize her LearningWorks School Year Program, which involved 26 teachers—high school and college students working in teams of three or four—teaching 92 middle school students on alternative Saturdays. The teachers, who attend schools in different parts of the state, used the wiki (http://learningworks.pbwiki.com) (Figure 4-3) to collaboratively create their lesson plans.

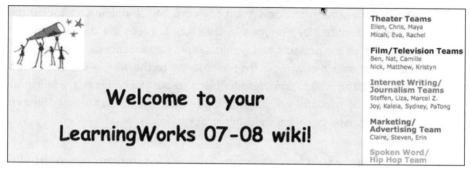

Figure 4-3. LearningWorks Planning Wiki

Team members then shared and revised their teaching plans, and Jaimee provided them with suggestions and feedback:

> Hey y'all! I looked at your lesson plan—looks great! Great job! Check it out—I made all my comments in red highlights and also provided you with a page to give you structure for the research portion of your class. I look forward to hearing your ideas and feedback. Keep up the great work!

In addition to using the online discussion tools described in chapter 3, students can also use wikis for synchronous discussions of literature. In one classroom wiki, Mrs. Huff's Classroom Wiki (http://huffenglish.pbwiki.com/) (Figure 4-4) uses the wiki to foster discussions of literature. In the discussion that follows, students respond to questions that she posted on her 10th-grade honors literature class wiki.

Because they are not limited by chronological time, these students can enter the discussion at any time or place, in some cases even going back and revising some of their initial comments or adding new comments.

In his college poetry classes, Mark Phillipson employs wikis in which specific words or lines in a poem are linked to commentaries and other sites to other poems. In his Romantic poetry course, he asked students to create linkable websites for specific lines in the poems they were studying, as well as essays and commentaries on each others' analyses that were posted on the course wiki (http://ssad.bowdoin.edu:8668/space/snipsnap-index). Students could also use a wiki to create a "Choose Your Own Adventure" type story containing optional pages representing different options for a story to develop (Hendron, 2008).

Students could also use wikis to create book review or study guides for

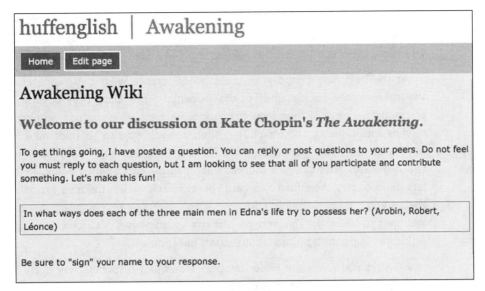

Figure 4.4 Mrs. Huff's Classroom Wiki

their peers for use in future classes studying certain books. Students in Elizabeth Boeser's college writing course created wikis for their books (http://missboeser.googlepages.com/bookwikis). They created pages with information about authors, setting, characters, vocabulary, study guide questions and answers, a reading schedule, a book review, links to research about the novel, and individual reactions and reflections.

Using Wikis to Improve Reading Ability and Literary Interpretations

We believe that wikis can be used to improve students' reading ability, particularly middle or junior high students who, as struggling readers, are often intimidated by texts. When they encounter a wiki, these students may be less intimidated than if they are reading a print text because they know that they can revise or change a wiki text. As a result, they are responding to a wiki text not only as readers, but also as writers who are thinking about how they might revise or improve the text.

Knowing that they can revise a text requires their ability to infer a writer's intended meaning in order to make the appropriate revisions that build on that intended meaning. In working with his junior high students, Andrew Rummel, West Junior High School, Minnetonka, Minnesota, describes how he uses wiki writing not only to help students share their writing but also to improve their reading skills:

I look at wikis as a new type of text. It is a community text that can evolve in a way that a traditional paper isn't able to. In my seventh grade language arts class, the students use the wiki to explore a few different subjects.

At the beginning of the year, the students create wikis that represent the interests and backgrounds of the students in our class. They begin by selecting an aspect of their lives that is interesting, such as fashion, gaming, reading, music, movies, or travel. They then develop ways to get information from each other about this interest. As they interview each other online and in person, they present the information they find. Then the wiki first lets them display the information in hypertext. This allows them to express their findings through multimedia production, including text, images, sound, and links to websites. This first part of the assignment facilitates a number of interesting conversations about these questions:

How do you represent other people's views in a respectful way even if you disagree with their tastes or opinions?

How do you clearly present information on a website?

How do you best balance images, sound, links to other sources, and text?

Because they have created wikis, it allows them to read and respond to the discoveries about the class as a group of people with a rich base of interests, experiences, and knowledge. They have the opportunity to expand on the topics and comment on the writers' representations of their responses.

At the same time, in contemplating revisions in others' texts, students need to be respectful of others work so that they are not altering or deleting work in ways that change their peers' intended meanings. Rummel encouraged his students to reflect on the problems with altering their peers' work by having them reflect on the following questions:

How do you change text created by another person in a way that still validates the work he or she has done?

How do you add to another person's creation in order to expand on the topic in a way that holds true to his or her vision and organization?

What rules of conduct apply to people working in this context?

Rummel notes how his students learn to respect each other's work:

Later in the year, the seventh graders used a wiki in their unit on mythology. In the past, the students would research a topic, and each class period, the groups would basically find the same information. The wiki format changes this. I teach four different blocks of seventh-grade language arts, and the students in different blocks select from the same cultures. As they work, the students are creating one wiki for their culture's mythology. As they work, they are reading what three other groups have found, so they are required to dig deeper into the research to discover different resources. The wiki allows the students to both report what they find and add to what others have found. The nature of the wiki leads us to many different discussions.

How can you edit a classmate's work without being offensive?

How can you add work cohesively into a page created by others?

How do you present information that contradicts what others have found?

Because they need to agree as a group how to present the contradicting information, they need to both examine their sources and defend the validity of their information.

The wiki serves as an evolving text that allows the students to return to it and evaluate the information for clarity and validity in the context of a growing understanding of the subject. The students have the opportunity to continually change the organization and content of their pages based on discoveries made along the way.

Wikis can also be used to enhance students' collaborative development of literary interpretations. As we noted in the last chapter, Theresa's students were using the Moodle forum tool to share their interpretations of *The Kite Runner* (Hosseini, 2004) in preparation for some collaborative writing using the Moodle wiki (@ = Theresa Haider's wiki writing on *The Kite Runner*). Theresa describes how she set up, facilitated, and evaluated her students' wiki writing about *The Kite Runner*:

My goal with the wiki assignment was not just related to technology use, but also to getting my students to see connections between real-world topics (like the Muslim religion) and the novel we were reading. I try to teach my students how to become better readers because many of them do not consider themselves to be readers at all. It seems that poor readers think there is a secret to being a good reader, when in reality it's that good readers got that way because they inquired about what they were reading, questioned it, or already knew something about it, and in the end, the more they knew, the better they were at understanding the text. In turn, this leads to becoming a better reader.

As part of the unit I teach on *The Kite Runner* by Khaled Hosseini (2004), I wanted my students to work collaboratively and research various topics they could then teach to their classmates. Our school recently started using Moodle, and I had been using it to list assignments and documents for my course. I had also used it as a mode for online discussion via the forum option in Moodle. I decided that the wiki assignment option in Moodle would be a current medium through which they could demonstrate their knowledge, teach their classmates, and maybe have some fun.

Before beginning the unit, I created an assignment that asked students to include eight aspects on their wikis: the title of their topic, names of group members, a thesis statement, a four- to five-paragraph summary of their topic with links to outside sources which they have determined to be reliable, a paragraph explaining the connection between the topic and the book, images related to the topic, three higher order–thinking questions that could be used on a quiz, and a list of references:

> A wiki is a website that allows multiple users to create text, add pictures, etc. You will be using wikis as a way to educate your classmates on a topic related to the book *The Kite Runner*. You will be writing a "chapter" of a book that can help others understand more about Afghanistan. The topics for the wiki are predetermined, but each group (no more than four people per group) may choose their own topic. Each topic can only be taken by one group, and wiki due dates will vary based on when your topic fits with what we're reading. The wiki will be able to be modified by you and your group mates.

Students spent three days in the classroom working on their wikis before the first presentation. There was a weekend in between the classroom work time and the first presentations. I suggest more preworking time be given if possible. Students had to communicate with each other before they left for the weekend about who would be working on the wiki and when so that each group member didn't try editing it at the same time. In-class time continued for about 2 days each of the next 2 weeks of class. By this time students were more comfortable with the wiki and they knew more about their topics so class time could be spent on other activities for the unit.

Before working on the wikis and beginning the presentations, I explained the grading rubric to students based on criteria having to do with layout, content, links, interest, and copyright. Students had to juggle creating an eye-pleasing page while also addressing the content in a logical, thorough way. Likewise, they needed to focus on choosing links that would effectively add to their page, and they had to adhere to citation and copyright rules.

For the presentation aspect, students were graded on content, delivery (eye contact, posture, speaking ability), preparedness, time limit and use of wiki in the presentation. Again, each category was graded based on a 10 point grading scale.

After the first presentations, the class gave constructive criticism about the presentation. I reminded the class that the first groups had significantly less time to prepare, so the things we were addressing for improvement were directly related to the reality that they didn't have time to understand their topics better. I also gave the first groups extra time to make their wikis complete. Roughly, they had a week longer to work after their presentations.

One of the groups, consisting of Lauren Monson, Mallory Shimpach, and Jessica Picha, worked on their report, entitled "The History and Culture of Afghanistan" (@ = Theresa Haider's wiki writing project on *The Kite Runner*). Theresa describes their work:

> The girls included a variety of content on their page including a basic synopsis of Afghanistan's history and some interesting cultural facts. They would individually log into the wiki and post their content while also reviewing one another's work. The content they posted is what I wanted them to focus on in order to give their classmates a better idea of what Afghanistan is and was like during the different periods that *The Kite Runner* took place. The presentation of this wiki occurred during the first 2 weeks of reading the book because I wanted this particular content to be a foundation from which all students continued to learn about Afghanistan.
>
> Since the girls gathered information relating to religion, education, and food, these descriptions would have been natural places for them to explain how these cultural aspects of Afghanistan relate to the book. Instead, there is only one short paragraph at the beginning of the wiki that generally makes connections to the book:
>
> > The book *The Kite Runner* by Khaled Hosseini takes us through the life of an Afghanistan citizen. This wiki will help you understand what events Amir is going through. It will also help you understand what is happening in relation to actual historical events.
>
> I felt that a paragraph stating the connection between the topic and the book was essential because often, when presenting information relating to a course or book, students don't see the direct connections. Since this group presented so early and had less time to prepare their wiki, the paragraph connection they made to *The Kite Runner* works. The entire book also continues to make mention of many of the aspects they included in their

wiki, so only a student who is not reading the book would not recognize how this content relates to the book. Other topics, like the Taliban, for example, were more complex, and many students did not understand how the Taliban fit into the book. In these cases, it was essential that the wiki groups wrote detailed descriptions of the connection beyond just "the Taliban took over when Amir was young" or something similarly general.

Creating Course Wikibooks

Another important use for wikis is the creation of course wikibooks, which function as evolving textbooks for a course, particularly given the increased costs of traditional print texts (@ = Wikibooks). Once a class creates a course wikibook, students in future classes or sections of that course can continue to add new material to that wikibook. These wikibooks can be organized according to chapters devoted to specific topics studied in a course. For example, Matt Barton's first-year composition students at St. Cloud State University, Minnesota collaboratively created a *Rhetoric and Composition Wikibook* (http://en.wikibooks.org/wiki/Rhetoric_and_Composition) that includes different aspects of learning to write in college: the composing process, different types of writing, editing, writing in different disciplinary areas, and so on. These students were motivated to share their experiences in first-year college writing courses because they knew that other students would benefit from insights on how to grapple with the challenges of learning to write in college.

In Richard's media literacy course, students contribute material for a course wikibook devoted to critical analyses of various types of media texts (http://teachingmedialiteracy.pbwiki.com). Throughout this course, students work collaboratively in pairs as blog partners responding to each other's blog posts. These blog partners then work collaboratively on creating final projects to post on the wikibook. Each new section of this class adds material to the work of previous sections, creating a repository of work for students to draw on.

Teachers also use wikis to share teaching ideas and resources. For example, the Wikiweb (http://wikiweb.org/index.php/Main_Page) contains lessons posted by teachers; Wesley Frey's wiki (teachdigital.pbwiki.com) and Will Richardson's Weblogged-ed Wiki (http://weblogged.wikispaces.com) contains a host of teaching ideas for using Web 2.0 tools.

Learning to Create and Navigate Wiki Links

There are a number of challenges in creating wikis. In creating links between pages in wikis, students need to provide readers with clear navigational support so that readers do not become lost within a morass of linked pages. Reading wikis can be difficult because readers may not know which links to select to move to another page (Dobson, 2005). Once they begin linking between different texts, they may lose track of where they are going and not know how to return to their original starting points.

Based on a study of her students' navigation of wiki texts, Theresa Dobson (2005) equates her students' difficulties in knowing how to navigate a wiki with the experience of going to a museum in which they selectively attend to certain works and not others based on their particular interests. Students may then not have a clear sense of where they are in the museum just as they may not know where they are going in a wiki text.

At the same time, Dobson found that her students experienced pleasure in getting lost in the text through creating their own multiple paths. The fact that they had the freedom to move through a text based on their own interests and needs served to actively engage them as readers who are constructing their own meaning of the text. Recognizing the challenges of navigating links between pages led Dobson's students as writers to provide clear directions and cues for their readers on how to navigate their own wikis.

To help students think about their uses of links between pages as well as links to other websites, images, or video clips, students could go through a wiki site and identify different reasons for including links to another page, website, image, or clip, reasons that may include switching to another topic that requires a new wiki page, creating another episode or event in a narrative, or providing an illustrative example or visual representation of a concept or idea.

Simultaneous Editing of Wikis

Students simultaneously working together in a class on the same wiki page will not be able to all edit and save the same wiki page at the same time. To avoid this challenge, it is useful to have students create their own different pages that they can then work on without having to be concerned about simultaneous editing and saving of the same pages.

Learning Collaboration Strategies

Another challenge in creating wikis has to with learning how to effectively collaborate with peers. Any form of collaborative writing can be difficult. Group members may not know how to work together effectively or may not all contribute with the same degree of effort. It is therefore important that teachers help students develop strategies for working collaboratively.

One useful collaboration strategy is to have students mutually decide what each member of a team will contribute to a wiki and how best to make that collaboration. To assist her students in writing essays about *Montana 1948* (Watson, 1993) using a wiki (http://jhscollegewritingmontana.pbwiki.com),

Elizabeth had her student groups initially define what and how each member would contribute.

In an interview with Richard, Katie Nelson described her strategy for collaborating with another student on their paper on knowledge and wisdom in the novel. She noted that:

> We wrote notes to each other about what I thought the paper was about and I bolded the stuff that was important because if we're writing two different papers, it's not the same. It was hard because we never saw each other…but he was a smart guy so he knew where I was going. We made the outline very detailed and then we divided up who was doing what paragraphs.

Katie identified some of the affordances in a wiki that fostered their collaboration:

> It was easier to organize. I learn better when things are visual. This way was very clear—who you could click on. You can also easily delete something and adjust it; it's very flexible as far as multiple authors and multiple things that you're trying to do at once because it wasn't just a paper; it was organizing notes, and reading the book and collecting information; so it's multifaceted in meeting our needs.

In describing his collaboration with two other students on a paper about power in *Montana 1948* (Watson, 1993), Josh Hiben described their processes of collaboration:

> It was cool to have a couple of people from different classes that I didn't really know too well to see what they got out of it and their perspectives; we mailed blogs and wikis back and forth and we came to a compromise as to what we wanted and I learned twice as much as I wanted because of their perspectives.
>
> We created a thesis together and we all OK'd it. We decided who did what paragraphs. Over the span of a week we did paragraphs and then I did the intro and I said you guys do the conclusions. If everyone does their part, it works out. You definitely have to be organized; you have to get people together and they have to be motivated. I learned more because I got different perspectives. I would have written a similar paper, but it would have one with a biased perspective of what I thought about it, but getting their perspectives led to different conclusions.

In describing their wiki writing, some students noted that in some groups there were disparities in how much individuals contributed to the wiki, leading some to argue for the option of selecting their own group members. However, one advantage of assigning group members is that less able writers can be assigned to work with stronger writers, while insisting that all group members contribute equally to the writing.

Using Wikipedia to Examine the Challenges of Using Wikis

Another challenge in using wikis is that because wikis that can be edited by others, in some cases, those revisions can include misinformation or even defamation of a site. This challenge is most evident in the development of Wikipedia, the world's largest and most accessed encyclopedia. A third of all adult Internet users seek out Wikipedia; it is the most frequently used site on the Web (Rainie & Trancer, 2007) (@ = Wikipedia).

Wikipedia represents a bottom-up, open-source effort by millions of contributors. As of February 2007, 5.77 million volunteers have contributed to the 6.4 million articles and 250 million edits (Wilkinson & Huberman, 2007). The fact that so many people are willing to share their knowledge for no other reason than the need to contribute to the larger good of society reflects a democratization of knowledge production given the belief that "learning is nothing unless it's a contribution to others," rather than the "individualized and privatized" current transmission and testing system (Willinksy, 2006, p. 18).

In Wikipedia, if misinformation or invalid information is posted, typically it is generally quickly removed or revised by others. It is also the case that the validity of information reported in articles varies according to the number of contributors who are editing that article (Wilkinson & Huberman, 2007). If a larger number of people are editing an article, the more these people are cross-checking the validity of the information. In contrast, if only one or two people who lack expertise on a topic are contributing an article about that topic, then it is more likely that the article may contain misinformation.

Critics of Wikipedia note that because there are no editors or expert contributors, it is difficult to determine the definitive nature or validity of information or ideas in various entries. Thus, it is argued, if students cite information from Wikipedia in their papers, they may be citing unreliable misinformation (Shareski & Winkler, 2005/2006).

As of summer 2006, Wikipedia changed its policy so that certain entries can no longer be edited by any user (Hafner, 2006). And they have increased the use of editing to ensure the accuracy of the information in its entries. Then, beginning in March 2007, in response to instances of fraudulent contributors, Wikipedia required that contributors identifying themselves as experts, while they will still remain as anonymous contributors, must provide evidence of their qualifications (Mackey, 2007).

It is important for students to discuss these issues of validity and editorial oversight related to their own uses of Wikipedia (Jenkins, 2007). Students certainly need to realize that because the Wikipedia is a collaborative enterprise in which different people may contribute different, even conflicting, information, they should consider it as a highly useful, often initial source of information, but not consider it to be the final, definitive source of information.

Students could also write their own Wikipedia entries, for example, about their school, hometown, or topics that interest them. Andreas Brockhaus and Martha Groom (2007), University of Washington–Bothell, had their students contribute entries on the topic of globalization and the environment. Students had to learn the standards for linking to and citing sources and other Wikipedia entries, as well as how to provide peer feedback based on these standards. Some of the students' entries were deleted, which provided them with an awareness of the Wikipedia review process.

All this suggests that in using Wikipedia or in creating their own wikis, students need to do the following:

- Determine the extent to which an entry uses and cites authoritative sources or references

- Note the extent to which research studies are cited as authoritative sources

- Note the recency or currency of sources cited

- Compare what they find on Wikipedia with information from other alternative sources, noting differences in the number and type of references

- Note the degree to which alternative perspectives are included in discussions of controversial topics

Issues of Privacy of Information in Using Wikis: The FERPA Law

In creating a wiki (as well as blogs) as a public site that can be accessed by people outside their classroom, teachers need to be aware of legal issues associated with public disclosure of private information about students to protect their confidentiality. This is particularly the case for publicly sharing any evaluation of their work. For specific information, see @ = Family Educational Rights and Privacy Act.

Summary

In this chapter, we discuss the use of a range of digital writing tools, particularly wikis, to engage students in collaborative writing. Given the focus on individual writing in schools, collaborative writing can be challenging but rewarding, because students are engaged in mutual construction of knowledge for their peers and larger online audiences. Learning to work collaboratively to develop knowledge and ideas is essential preparation for learning how to effectively work with others to construct knowledge.

Chapter Five

Navigating, Mixing, Creating: Digital Literature

Jason Nelson's student Tanisha knows that people are collectors, hoarders of objects and memories of objects as well as of experiences. A red stain on the carpet, a dented fender, a favorite doll, or a vacation with family—all are (or contain) signs of the lives we have lived, and each possibly offers a hint about future experiences. Tanisha's teacher has told the class that our brains are like filing cabinets and that writers dig these objects and memories out of storage to make poems and stories of them.

For this assignment, Tanisha has been asked by Jason to design a digital image map of objects that are important to her. Then she will create a story or poem that grows out of the "hot spots" on her digital map. The assignment is meant to help students see the connections between print work in a creative mode and digital work in the same mode as they create.

Jason first had his students search through their homes, cars, lives, or local thrift store to find objects or collections of objects that tell or inspire a story or poem. Students then picked three objects and photographed or scanned them from as many angles as possible (and in various settings). Then, using either a pen for prints or an image manipulation program for scans, students highlighted areas on the images that could be hot spots: visually identifiable spaces that had some significance to them, points from which their poem or story would develop.

Students then chose one of these hot spots and created an overarching narrative that served as a framework for their creation. From their photographs or scans, they identified one that served as the front or main page from which all the hot spots would be linked. For example, if they chose a neighbor's balding, twelve-year-old Persian cat, they used a large image of the whole cat. They then created links from this large image to their specific hot spots. They wrote about these images from different perspectives—for example, descriptions from both the back and the front of the cat. The students then expanded on their writing and inserted this work into their various image maps to create a digital story or poem.

Why Focus on Digital Literature?

One of the most powerful aspects of digital writing tools is their ability to readily link, alter, combine, or remix texts to create new digital literary forms that differ from print literature. Learning to understand and create these digital literature texts requires a new set of literacy practices. Given the centrality of literature in the school curriculum, it is therefore important that students acquire these practices so that they can interpret these new forms and also use these practices to create their own texts.

In this chapter, we define and discuss hyperlinks, mixing and appropriating digital texts as part of creating digital literature and storytelling.

Learning to Use Hyperlinks in Hypertexts

As we noted in chapter 1, a primary literacy practice in digital writing is the ability to use hyperlinks in creating hypertexts. The use of hyperlinks challenges the traditional emphasis on producing unified, coherent texts based on a definitive, single perspective. To counter this single-perspective effect, Bolter and Grusin (2000) advocate teaching a "rhetoric of expectations and arrivals" (p. 10). In using hyperlinks, students need to determine whether those links provide audiences with relevant, useful information to make it worth sending their audiences off to another text and how their audiences should respond to arriving at these other texts. Otherwise, they could include so many links that their audiences do not know where these links will take them (Dobson, 2005).

As we noted with creating and navigating pages in wikis in the last chapter, students also need to consider how their audience processes links in reading hypertexts in ways that differ from reading linear print texts (@ = Hypertext theory). Gunther Kress (2003) notes that readers process print texts by reading in a linear, left-to-right manner. With hypertexts, this linear approach no longer works. Rather than reading line after line on a printed page in a linear manner to acquire information, readers are seeking out information relevant to their needs and purposes for reading. They are therefore scanning a Web page to find those images, buttons, and texts on the screen, evaluate the relevance of each, make judgments about their usefulness, and then click on those items that seem likely to take them on the most appropriate path for their purposes. As Kress notes:

> The new task is that of applying principles of relevance to a page which is (relatively) open in its organization, and consequently offers a range of possible reading paths, perhaps infinitely many. The task of the reader in the first case is to observe and follow a given order, and within that order to engage in interpretation. . . . The task of the reader of the new page, and of the screens which are its models, is to establish the order through principles of relevance of the reader's making, and to construct meaning from that. (p. 162)

From responding to websites, students learn the skills involved in reading for relevant information on a site. They know how to quickly scan sites to locate relevant information, cues, or links. For example, in reading blogs, they know where to look on a blog page to find biographical information, links to other blogs, archives, internal and external links, and RSS feeds.

Learning these ways of reading hypertext then transfers to constructing hypertext as writers. For example, in creating a digital story or poem, they know that they can use multiple links and paths that are not limited to chronological order. Rather, as with Jason's assignment, they can create a digital story or poem that allows readers to navigate it in any number of different directions.

However, some students coming to hypertexts for the first time may experience some reservations. It can be difficult to accept the idea that a text that doesn't have to have a single definitive form. They may also be reluctant to take on responsibility for shaping the form of a text through navigational choices.

In analyzing her students' responses to hyperlinked digital literature, Ingrid Daemmrich (2007) found that while some of her students were frustrated by become lost in hyperlinks and text fragments, those students who recognized that hypertexts gave them more control over constructing meaning were more engaged with hypertexts, noting that "'We can play at being authors'" or "'Hypertext storytelling makes us aware that we are the storytellers'" (p. 427).

Different Types of Hyperlinks

To engage audiences in responding to their digital stories or poems, students can employ the following types of hyperlinks. Students may make links between their current text and other texts—other poems or stories, or characters' thoughts and feelings within a story or poem. Or they may create links between their text and images, video clips, sounds, or music—for example, adding images or music to their poem.

In using these different types of links, students need to decide whether to add a link and what kind of link to add to inform or engage their audiences. They then need to be able to formulate their purposes for using these links based on the following questions:

> What do you want your audiences to learn from your text?
>
> What may be some purposes they bring to your text—what do they want to find in reading your text?
>
> What are some paths that you have created to help them achieve their purposes?
>
> What cues, icons, links, prompts, or directions will you use to help them select the right path to find what they are looking for?

Combining and Remixing Digital Texts to Create Multimodal Texts

As we've discussed, in addition to collecting, generating, and organizing information about certain topics or issues, students are also combining or remixing digital texts themselves—images, clips, poems, websites, reports—for use in constructing their own texts. The idea of combining or mixing texts in writing classes emanates from multigenre writing in the 1990s (Romano, 2000). In multigenre writing, students combine different text genres—poems, essays, autobiographical recollections, flyers, and ads, as well as images or photos, to create texts based on combining these genres or images.

While much of composition instruction in the past has focused on the idea of creating *original* texts, writing in digital spaces shifts that focus to one of playing with, juxtaposing, manipulating, altering, and rearranging *existing* texts to create *new* texts. As reflected in postmodern art, film, architecture, and music, this represents a shift in attitude about the meaning and nature of texts and the concept of "original" work. Johndan Johnson-Eilola (2004) argues that in a postmodern era, "texts no longer function as discrete objects, but as contingent, fragmented objects in circulation, as elements in constantly configured and shifting networks" (p. 208). This challenges traditional legal copyright notions of "original" texts because texts in digital spaces represent combinations and rearrangements of multiple texts produced by others, something we discuss in other chapters related to issues of plagiarism in digital spaces.

The idea of combining and remixing texts draws on a long history of writers such as Shakespeare who drew on others' material to write his own plays (Jenkins, 2006b). It also draws on hip-hop notions of sampling and remixing of digital texts (Rice, 2004; Sirc, 2004). Students can remix photos using tools such as Photoshop, combine different songs or music videos (Animemusicvideos.org), create remixes of novels and movies (fanfiction.net), or create AdBusters-inspired spoofs of ads (@ = Remixing texts).

In remixing, students draw on and "borrow" others' work, something that may not be viewed as orginal work. Henry Jenkins (2006b) expresses a strong concern about the demand in school for original work that implies that such borrowing of texts is problematic, when borrowing and reworking texts actually fosters critical thinking through what he describes as "textual poaching." He cites the example of My Pop Studio.com, a site for early adolescent females that involves students in remixing images, texts, and music from celebrity magazines, reality television, and popular music in ways that foster critical analysis of media representation of females. On this site, through reworking and altering texts, students are asked to reflect critically about the alternative meanings they create related to popular culture images of adolescent females.

In hip-hop theory, combining texts involves what is known as mixing, a process based on a DJ's combining different sounds from records in their performances (Mahiri, 2006). By mixing digital texts together, students create new texts with new meanings. Jeff Rice (2004) also finds instances of rearranging and combing texts in the practice of "scratching" records in hip-hop culture and suggestings ways of interrogating beliefs and assumptions through rearranging texts. In his composition classes, Rice has students engage in "cut-ups" to alter the meanings of texts. Students take newspaper articles, speeches, ads, or television commercials and cut them up or edit them on a video editor into parts and create a new text, leading them to reflect on how the new text conveys a meaning different from that of the original text.

In remixing texts, students are also engaging in "culture-jamming" (Lankshear & Knobel, 2003), associated with adopting a critical stance on the original meaning of texts. In creating Adbuster-like parodies, students are critiquing the intended positive meanings of ads through altering the ad images and language.

The Centrality of Digital Images and Video

Digital images or video are central to creating digital stories and poems. Using digital cameras, students can easily create their own images or video for inclusion in their stories or poems (Schoonmaker, 2007). In working in a high school class of 16 female students of color entitled "Sistahs," Kelly Wissman (2008) involved students in using photography and poetry to create Web-based visual autobiographies for sharing with others. (www.urbanedjournal.org/archive/Issue3/notes/notes0006.html). Rather than perceiving photography as simply a means to represent reality, Wissman's students used photography as a social practice to portray their identities in the social contexts of their lives. As she notes:

> Envisioning photography as a social practice recognizes that the images produced are not simply a transparent recording of reality; rather, the images encapsulate a particular framing of that reality that is highly intentional and unique to the individual photographer. Envisioning photography as a social practice also entails considering the social context in which images are produced and received and considering the shaping influence of those contexts on the images and interpretations of those images. (p. 14)

In one activity, students created self-portraits in a certain pose or setting that conveyed their social identities, the subject of their poems. In doing so, they were often countering deficit stereotypical media representations of students of color by portraying their strengths and values. One African-American student, Geneva, situated herself outside her house with her sister poking her head out the front door. This image led her to begin her poem, "What do you see when you look at me? This is what I see, I see a young African American girl wearing long braids like my African ancestors did. Eyes that I use to see if someone is good or not so good" (p. 32).

While images can stimulate poetry, poetry can also serve to evoke certain images. In writing the poem "14 Reasons Why," a tribute to the novelist June Jordan, Korina Kocson created a digital video consisting of images she associated with the poem—for example, images of leaders such as Angela Davis and Che Guevara, who challenged the status quo (cie.asu.edu/volume8/number5/index.html). Photos can serve to evoke written scripts for organizing a digital story. For example, two adolescent females who decided to make a digital story, "Big Sitters," about their friendship, drew on pictures of themselves to create a nine-page script (Pleasants, 2007).

Photos can lead to adding music or audio evoked by images. For example, four African-American eighth-grade females constructed a multimodal PowerPoint presentation that portrayed different images of poverty and homelessness in their community (Mahiri, 2006). They wrote material based on their perceptions of homeless people in their neighborhood, including some digital photos. To add music to their photos, they went to some singers' sites, including www.aaliyah.com and www.kirkfranklin.us, where they found some background music such as the song "I CARE 4 U" by Aaliyah as well as gospel music, which, as one student noted, "'leaves you with a spiritual feeling'" (p. 59).

In contrast to the grim realities of their images of homelessness, adding the gospel music provided a more positive set of meanings suggesting the potential for change.

Digital Literature: Remixing and Appropriating: "Bad Writers Borrow; Good Writers Steal"

We've all heard this maxim. But who said it? A few documents on the Web that borrow this line claim that the following writers *might* have said it: T. S. Eliot, Oscar Wilde, or Mark Twain. We want to make two points here, one rooted in the implications of the quote itself, the other on its unverified and diverse attributions. Our first point is that writing that "appropriates" has a long and interesting history. Our second point is that the unstable attribution of the quote is a good example of how information and knowledge "floats," especially in the age of the Web. That is, a lot of writing (like a lot of music), produced or reproduced in digital formats, has been stripped of those particular signifiers that can give a piece a certain kind of authenticity and authority. Without branding, often without a named author, and emanating from sources that themselves have no particular credibility, media files can become free-floating works, uploaded to peer-to-peer distribution systems and traveling in circles that they would not normally reach in the pre-Web world, raising issues of copyright, fair use, and plagiarism (@ = Copyright/fair use/plagiarism issues).

What is appropriation? To appropriate something involves taking possession of it. In the visual arts, the term often refers to the use of borrowed elements in the creation of new work. The borrowed elements may include images, forms, or styles from history or from popular culture, or materials and techniques from non-art contexts. The term also refers to quoting the work of another artist in creating a new work. The new work may or may not alter the original. For example, quoting previous works is a common practice in symphonic music; it was considered an honor for a composer to be quoted in another composer's piece.

Artists such as Roy Lichtenstein, Claes Oldenburg, and Andy Warhol appropriated images from popular culture and both images and techniques from commercial art. These artists fully engaged with the ephemera of mass-produced culture, embracing expendability and distancing themselves from the evidence of an artist's hand. Henry Jenkins (2006a) writes about appropriation and education:

> art emerges through the artist's engagement with previous cultural materials. Artists build on, take inspiration from, appropriate and transform other artist's [sic] work: they do so by tapping into a cultural tradition or deploying the conventions of a particular genre... Despite the pervasiveness of these cultural practices, school arts and creative writing programs often remain hostile to overt signs of repurposed content, emphasizing the ideal of the autonomous artist. (p. 16)

Appropriation in a College Creative Writing Course

In Thom's college creative writing course, students were engaged in appropriation across genres and modes. Students were told that the class would offer possibilities for creative writing while examining traditional notions of authorship, the artist, and notions that are increasingly complicated by contemporary practices such as file sharing, sampling, and digital replication. During the term, the rich history of forgery, frauds, hoaxes, avatars, and impersonations across writing and the arts was traced, and students employed appropriation as a compositional method for writing in new media.

Students were asked to read, write, and "create" each week. The Web, spam, file sharing, and chat rooms were employed as objects of study and as sources for writing material. Readings were chosen to present conceptual frameworks and to offer fresh ideas for creative writing projects the students might undertake during the term.

Students learned about appropriation, its history, its contexts, and its possibilities for writing in new media. As writers, students learned how to take possession of another's material and reuse it in a context different from its original one in order to examine issues concerning originality or to reveal meaning not previously seen in the original.

Later in the term, students were encouraged to develop projects using Flash, Photoshop, iMovie, and other multimedia software. Here are three early-in-the-term assignments:

- Let's start low-tech and think about appropriation as collage. Taking a magazine of your choice, cut out as many images as you like. Using the same magazine, cut out as many words, phrases, and sentences as you like. Now *make* something with them: a physical object that employs at least some of the images and language you chose. You only have a week, so you won't be building anything too elaborate, but whatever you make should somehow work with the language and images you chose. Finally, write a few paragraphs about what you did and why.

- Design a Web page, blog, or wiki (or a number of linked pages) that incorporates the following: lines from poems (professional or amateur) that you find on the Web, images you find on the Web, links you find on the Web, and sounds you find on the Web. The design of the page, however, should be your own. Write a few paragraphs about what you did and why.

- Locate, in digital form, an official document that has social power over some aspect of your life: a state law, a marriage contract, or a work or school policy. Take any written part or parts of the document and connect them, in any manner you choose, with other found digital language from a different genre of writing. Create a Web page, blog, or wiki using this language to create a text that now has different meanings because you have placed it in a different context. By "repurposing" the language and possibly adding images or sound, you are creating a new context for the contents of both originals. Can you help us see meanings not previously seen in the originals?

In these assignments, it is process rather than product that plays a central role in what the instructor wants students to learn about new media writing. More important, however, the assignments work with and foster the dimensions of practice that are key to digital writing. Students are invited to experiment with appropriated language, sounds, and images to remake and recirculate these resources. They are also acquiring practices associated with visual literacies—the ability to attend to how they are using the visual to communicate their ideas (@ = Visual literacy). In one student's project, for instance, canonized poetry lyrics were juxtaposed with magazine copy for madeup ads and made to look like a brochure, thus allowing the student to cross modes and genres to create new meaning.

Responding to and Writing Digital Literature

What is digital literature? In the broadest sense, digital literature includes all writing that is produced in digital form. This would include everything from the reproduction of Shakespeare's plays on the Web to Sylvia Plath's poems reproduced for reading on newly developed electronic devices. It would also include Stephen King's novel *The Plant*, which was downloaded from the Internet and paid for by readers in installments.

More narrowly, as we have noted earlier, another category of digital literature is hypertext—literature meant to be read on a computer screen characterized by multiple links from pages or sections, multilinear structures, and recursive loops. Software programs specifically designed for literary hypertext became available in the 1990s, and the Storyspace program was key in the development of early notable works of electronic literature, including Stuart Moulthrop's *Victory Garden*. (For a teacher-narrated story about how Storyspace has been used in high school, see "Linday's Story" (www.eastgate.com/storyspace/art/Taylor.html)).

Teachers have been teaching students how to write hypertext literature for some years now using Storyspace (http://www.eastgate.com/Storyspace.html), Web development tools such as Dreamweaver, or a tool such as StoryMaker (storybox.co.uk/sm.php), designed for creating digital stories. Students can also compose digital poetry using The Erica T. Carter site (http://etc.wharton.upenn.edu/MysticWritingPad.aspx), a program that lets students compose poems with the help of a "poetry engine" that arranges or scrambles and then assembles a poem.

Before having students create their own hypertext creative work, they should first look at some literary hypertexts at the Electronic Literature Organization site (http://eliterature.org), a nonprofit organization established in 1999 to promote and facilitate the writing, publishing, and reading of electronic literature. The wiki site also contains examples of digital literature and articles about digital literature (@ = Digital literature).

Digital Poetry

One example of a digital poetry site, designed by Jason Nelson and programmer Rory Hering, the Poetry Cube (www.secrettechnology.com/poem_cube/poem_cube.html), allows users and poets to enter a 16-line poem and to experience how the lines are automatically placed within multilayered sections. Readers use buttons to move in and out, recombining the poems by turning the Cube upward, downward, and inward. The cube was built to act as a bridge between the print and digital worlds.

The digital poem "Blind Side of a Secret" (www.hyperrhiz.net/issue04/swiss/swf.html) written by Thom, features two characters. One is a male who is at his therapist's office, where he is removing tissues in the middle of the image as he is talking to the therapist (see Figure 5-1).

Figure 5-1. Blind Side of a Secret

The other character is a woman, presumably his girlfriend, who is sharing her experience driving around the city and on the bridge pictured in the background. With music playing, and as color and images morph on the screen, audiences engage with this text by clicking on images, which, when it turns yellow, creates some dialogue. For example, when readers click on the tissue box, they hear, "Sitting in a shrink's overheated office next to a box of Kleenex" and "What was the story she wanted to tell?" When readers click on the female character, they hear: "She hated to be on the blind side of a secret." Then they hear, "She said, I got into my car and followed the steering wheel as it led me back to the shadowed lanes and under the reddening sun as I crossed the long bridge home and the sky started burning," and "She had come home early a bit drunk and tried to sit on the edge of the bed when he was trying to sleep."

A key feature of "Blind Side of a Secret" is the appearance of the woman's face—at times she appears to be sleeping and at other times she is awake; these shifts convey her character as an embodied figure that evokes certain audience responses. In navigating this poem, readers therefore assume an active role in determining the mans and the woman's different perspectives on the events and each other as an aesthetic experience.

As a poet, Thom began his own collaborative, Web-based work with visual and sound artists several years ago, working mostly in Macromedia Flash (@ = Digital video). For example, a Flash-based animation software was used by programmer/artist Motomichi Nakamura to create *Hey Now* (Swiss & Nakamura, 2002), a collaboration that had its roots in conceptual art. The artists began by experimenting with the idea of "wrapping" language. Following the work of Christo and Jeanne-Claude, contemporary artists well-known for wrapping artifacts, buildings, and landmarks with fabric, Thom and Motomichi were interested in what "wrapped language" might look and sound like. Christo's "The Pont Neuf Wrapped, Paris 1975–85," for example, draped the famous French bridge in fabric and was widely regarded as a fascinating experience for its viewers—wrapping and unwrapping objects hides and then re-reveals the familiar, allowing us to see objects in a new light (@ = Digital literature).

In the case of the Swiss-Nakamura composition, the poem is hidden and revealed by animated characters, who whisper jibberish before speaking verses of a cut-up poem. Just as audiences were taken aback by a 24-mile fence of fabric (in the case of the Christo's *Running*

Figure 5-2. *Hey Now,* a New Media Poem

Fence, Sonoma & Marin Counties Coast 1972–76), they may be startled by the agency of a pacing man on the screen of *Hey Now*, who, when clicked by the viewer, kicks the head of a cartoon figure who whispers like an alien before launching into the next sounded and imaged section of the poem. Readers of new media poems are often challenged to make sense of synthesis, but it's an opportunity to broaden our own interpretations and to look critically at how language is shaped by new media.

The hypermedia work *The Ballad of Sand and Harry Soot* by Stephanie Strickland (1999) (http://www.wordcircuits.com/gallery/sandsoot/) brings together a unique poetic text with images of digital artworks originating in a variety of disciplines to create a web of relations with limitless potential for diverging and converging series of readings. The linear unfolding of the ballad in the print version serves to keep the reader on track. The reader can still perform imaginative leaps, but only in the realm of Sand and Soot, who emerge as the central characters in their literary ballad. In the poem, the center of the narrative is destabilized as links within the ballad and links to images provided by various contributors from a variety of disciplines create multiple reading tracks within the work.

It is important to note that students do not need to employ tools such as Flash to create digital poems. They can use something as simple as PowerPoint or Keynote, as well as iMovie or Windows Movie Maker, to create digital poetry. For example, Kori Ashton, a 12th-grade student in an English class taught by Jennifer Budenski in a high school in the Hopkins, Minnesota, school district, used iMovie to create a poem about her home country of Honduras (http://jenbudenski.vox.com/library/video/6a00e398a591e2000200e398a701360003.html). Kori, who was

Figure 5-3. *The Ballad of Sand and Harry Soot,* a new media poem, by Stephanie Strickland, 1999

adopted when she was 6 months old by an American family, combines the following poem with images of the mountains and rivers of her home country, along with pictures of herself and her American mother at different times in their lives:

In My Country There Is a Mountain, by Kori Ashton

In my country there is a mountain

In my country there is a river

Come with me

Night climbs up the mountain

Hunger goes down to the river

Come with me

Who are those that suffer? I do not know but there are my people

Come with me

I do not know but they call to me and say to me:

"We suffer"

Come with me

And they say to me, "Your people, your luckless people,

between the mountain and the river, they do not want

to struggle alone, they are waiting for you, friend."

Oh, you, the one I love little one red grain of wheat

Oh, tu, la que yo amo, pequena, grano rojo de trigo

the struggle will be hard,

life with me hard,

but you will come with me

Figure 5-4. Kori's Video Poem

In describing Kori's writing, Budenski (2007) notes that:

> In her video interpretation of "In My Country There Is a Mountain," she demonstrated advanced literacy and critical thinking skills....While the order of ideas in the poem was clearly already established, Kori chose to foreshadow her ending epiphany about the voices of her two mothers by inserting a photograph of herself under the text "I do not know, but they call to me" and a photograph of Honduran children under "We suffer." By visually interpreting this shift in the poem, Kori demonstrated both her perceptive reading of its mood and the decision-making behind the coherence of her own visual text. As she neared the end of her video, she faced the complicated decision of how to represent her two mothers' voices.... Some time later, she showed me what she had decided upon—two converging lines of text, one English moving left to right (carrying her forward?) and one Spanish moving right to left (looking back?). Finally, she broke the final stanza of the poem into its three lines corresponding to three chronological photographs of her with her adoptive mother. I told her "this is the smartest reading I've ever seen you do." Kori edited for two days, and still when I see her show this film to others, she has her finger poised on the touch pad touse the pause button to get the timing of the text just right. (p. 191).

In a unit on writing digital poetry, Nicole Kronzer, whose creative writing class at Champlin Park High School, Champlin, Minnesota, we referred to in the last chapter, began her unit by having students identify different characteristics of digital poetry—audience participation; the use of audio, music, or sound effects; the movement of text; and the nonlinear experience. Students then explored the idea of visual and audio metaphors for use in creating their poems and created their poems using PowerPoint slide shows. For example, Emily Pierskalla created a digital poem in which the words, *me, soul,* and *body* move around and across different PowerPoint slides, as illustrated in Figure 5-5.

In the poem, these words move around in ways that explore definitions of identity. The "me" as one's identity is defined by the relationship of the "soul" and one's "body." On one slide, rather than "me = soul + body," the slide reads "me = soul – body," suggesting that the soul is distinct from one's body. By playing with the visual combinations of words, Emily is inviting her audiences to reflect on the shifting relationships among one's identity, soul, and body.

As with all digital writing, students like to have audiences for their work. Students could broaden their audiences by creating student-run online literary magazines including submissions from both their own school and elsewhere that contain poems, stories, essays, videos, artwork, and photography from students all over the country who are on the Youth Twitter Network.

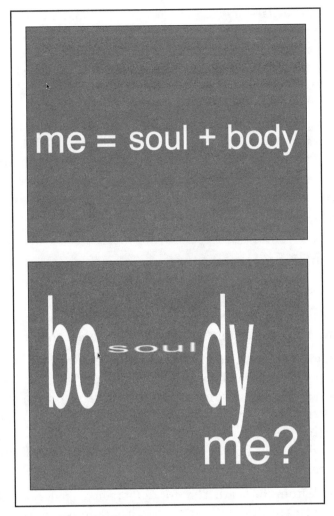

Figure 5-5. Digital Poem

Digital Storytelling

Another type of digital literature is digital storytelling, a movement that began by groups such as the San Francisco Bay Area–based Center for Digital Storytelling (www.storycenter.org) (@ = Digital storytelling). Typically, digital stories are 2- to 5-minute-long digital videos that combine a narrated piece of personal writing, photographic images, and a musical soundtrack. Students can scan photographed hand-drawn images into a computer, using a digital camcorder, importing music, recording voices, and composing and editing their stories using iMovie or Windows Media Maker (@ = digital video/digital images).

In his book on digital storytelling, Jason Ohler (2007) recommends preparing students for digital storytelling by studying the use of tensions and conflicts to understand story development. Story development revolves around a "story core" (p. 72) associated with characters' change or growth in coping with challenges, leading to transformation in characters' lives. Having formulated the idea for a story core, students then create a story map (p. 79) that fleshes out the events in a story, leading to a storyboard or script for a digital video production.

The Center for Digital Storytelling provides guidelines and elements, which we've adapted below into a list. Other genres can be substituted for "story" so that students can create essays, poems, and letters, instead of only creating narratives. For example, students could create comics or graphic novels, a popular genre with adolescents (@ = Comics and graphic novels).

The Elements of a Digital Story

Like any good story, a digital story benefits from the following:

1. Making a clear and specific point. Focus on telling a story simply. If you have a lot to tell, it might be best told in more than one story.

2. Asking a dramatic question (and maybe answering it in a surprising way). Conflict drives storytelling. We wonder who did it, who will get the boy or girl, or if the hero will win the fight. Set up a conflict and have readers to ask themselves the dramatic question. That keeps them reading your story, and if you answer it in an unexpected way—the antihero gets the girl or boy, or the butler didn't do it—they'll enjoy it even more.

3. Speak from the heart. The stories that affect readers are stories that affect writers. If something has touched or moved or challenged you, that's emotional engagement that your readers would like to hear about.

4. Telling your story in your own voice. Digital storytelling offers an enhancement over the written word: Readers can also be listeners and hear parts of your story recorded and replayed in your own voice.

5. Setting it to music. Ever watch a movie without a musical soundtrack? The emotional cues for what the audience should be feeling are missing. Music makes suspense more chilling, love more romantic, tender moments more poignant. Help your readers understand your story by adding music.

6. Wise editing. Your story doesn't need thousands of words and hundreds of images. The right few words and the right few images create a more powerful impact than too much to listen to and too many visuals.

One digital storytelling program for middle and high school students is the D.U.S.T.Y. after-school program located in Oakland, California (http://www.oaklanddusty.org/index.php). In this program, students create digital storytelling that often draws on their everyday lives and provides them with a sense of agency as authors. For example, one student, Randy, created "Lyfe-N-Rhyme" (http://www.oaklanddusty.org/videos.php), described by Hull and Katz (2007):

> Randy narrates the movie, performing his original poem/rap to the beat of a Miles Davis tune playing softly in the background. He illustrates, complements, or otherwise accompanies the words and the message of his poem/rap, along with the Miles Davis melody, with approximately 80 images. Most of these images are photographs taken by Randy of Oakland neighborhoods and residents, while others he found on the Internet, and a few screens consist solely of typed words. The pace and rhythm of the piece varies, as does Randy's speaking voice, in keeping with the background melody and the message. (p. 56)

They note that Randy is continually appropriating material as an artist:

> This movie is about Randy, and in it he enacts several senses of self, including talented artist. He enacts himself as artist, not just directly through his artful use of poetic and aesthetic techniques, but by implicitly connecting himself with works of art and African-American icons, past and present…removing them from their particular historical contexts, and recenters them, recontextualizing them in his own creative universe of this digital story and his own social world of Oakland, California. (p. 58)

Evaluation of Digital Storytelling

To evaluate students' digital storytelling, teachers could provide students with criteria or a rubric (see Kevin Hodgson's rubric: www.umass.edu/wmwp/DigitalStorytelling/Rubric%20Assessment.htm). These criteria could focus on:

- Story development through well-integrated uses of images, video, audio, and text
- Fostering audience engagement and reflection through appropriate pacing and editing
- Use of variation in pacing, tempo, and editing speed to engage audiences
- Effective use of music choices and voice-over appropriate to the content
- Selective use of video versus still images
- Quality of self-narration that employs an authentic, conversational style and pauses

Peers, mentors, or teachers can also help students develop their digital storytelling by posing questions about emerging storylines and characters. In a digital storytelling program at the Las Redes Fifth Dimension After School Program in Los Angeles, undergraduate tutors provided scaffolding and questions in working with elementary-age students to create their stories (Nixon, 2008). As one student was creating a story about animals at a zoo, she exchanged a series on online letters with her undergraduate tutor, who encouraged her to imagine herself as a zookeeper, to think about the responsibilities she would have as a zookeeper, and to relate these responsibilities to what she already does to take care of her pet dog. The student then used these questions to develop her story about how she takes care of her pet dog and what she'll do with animals as a zookeeper, an illustration of how digital stories can emerge through joint activity.

Some Notes on Copyright

The advent of the Web raised copyright issues that have only been exacerbated by the Web's development and the types of software and uses discussed in this chapter (@ = Copyright/fair use/plariarism issues). Unfortunately, students often upload copyrighted material without obtaining permission from owners, unless, as we previously noted, those owners have granted Creative Commons copyright permission to use their material.

The following are some guidelines to provide students in determining whether or not they are violating copyright with the classroom context governed by fair use of copyrighted material. The fair use of a copyrighted work for purposes such as criticism, comment, news reporting, teaching (including multiple copies of excerpts), scholarship, or research is not an infringement of copyright.

In determining whether the use made of a work in any particular case is a fair use, consider the following:

- The purpose and character of the use, including whether such use is of a commercial nature or is for nonprofit educational purposes
- The nature of the copyrighted work
- The amount and substantiality of the portion used in relation to the copyrighted work as a whole
- The effect of the use upon the potential market for or value of the copyrighted work

Briefly, these indicate the following:

1. The use must not attempt to "supersede the objects" of the original but rather be educational or critical.

2. The less of the original that is used in relation to the whole, the more likely that use is fair, although the importance of the specific portion is also considered.

3. The use must not infringe on the copyright owner's ability to exploit the her original work (for instance, by acting as a direct market substitute for the original work), though not through criticism or parody.

Text

Brief attributed quotations of copyrighted text used to illustrate a point, establish context, or attribute a point of view or idea may be used under fair use.

Image

There are a few blanket categories. The basic rule seems to be to use them "in good faith," opting for use of creative common images.

Audio Clips

Brief song clips (under 30 seconds) may be used. Spoken-word audio clips of historical events, such as speeches by public figures, may be used when attributed to the speaker.

Summary

Students need opportunities to engage in responding to and creating digital literature, so that they can learn to appreciate forms of new digital hypertext media that require different ways of reading and composing than with linear print literature. In responding to digital poems and stories, students can begin to articulate reading practices and features, leading them to production and analysis of digital literature, particularly in terms of combining and remixing digital text, images, video, audio, and music to construct digital literature.

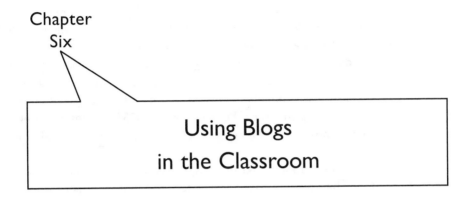

Chapter
Six

Using Blogs
in the Classroom

In her American Literature class at Edina High School in Minnesota, Kathleen West was frustrated with her classroom discussions of literature. Many of her students were not sharing their responses, and when they did, they just offered cursory interpretations, disconnected from other students' ideas. She recognized that the usual teacher-led classroom discussion just wasn't working. She decided to set up a blog as an optional tool to foster more engaged interaction between students:

> I hoped that blogging would change the dynamics of our large-group interactions in positive ways. On their blogs, students would not necessarily be referring to a teacher-generated question based on a particular reading assignment. Instead, they could feel free to offer thoughts and opinions on different sections of the book in their asynchronous electronic conversations, which would level the playing field in terms of ability and motivation to complete reading assignments.

Kathleen took her students to the computer lab once a week to spend time writing their blogs:

> When I directed the kids to create Weblogs using Blogger, I hoped that encouraging them to post and comment on personal Web pages would change our discussions about literature for the better. Instead of asking

students to explore the passages and ideas I thought were most interesting about *The Crucible* and *The Great Gatsby*, students were encouraged to explore the facets of the texts that excited them.

To get us started, I set up a blog on Blogger where I posted my own thoughts and questions about class texts, as well as photos and links. I used one of Blogger's many available templates, which I edited to include a link to each student's blog. This way, classmates could easily find each other. Although I didn't want to limit creativity or prescribe content for students, I did want to encourage participation, so I set up minimum writing requirements: During each computer lab session, students had to publish one post and add comments on three other student blogs. If 55 minutes wasn't enough time to accomplish this, the blogs could easily be accessed from home.

By using blogs for discussing literature, Kathleen's students were much more engaged than they had been in their face-to-face discussions. Instead of simply answering Kathleen's questions, now the students were driving the discussion with their own questions, formulating and extending their responses in a student-led dialogue.

In writing to Kathleen's class blog, students were mutually sharing their responses to literature. Kristina's post elicited two responses from her peers, which in turn encouraged her to make some further responses to *The Great Gatsby* (Fitzgerald, 1992):

> *Kim:*   I don't really think that being on separate islands meant that Gatsby and Daisy were doomed not to get together. Gatsby moved across from her on purpose.

> *Kristina:* He did? Where did it say that? And did Fitzgerald say why he wanted to be across the bay from her? I think it would make more sense if they lived on the same island, since he was doing everything he could to get close to her.

> *Axeman:*   Thank you for your thoughts [KH], and I have a question for you; How does Gatsby know it's her light? He would have had to sneak around her house and find out that she has a green dock light which is on 24/7. Isn't that kind of creepy?

> *Kristina:* I don't think that he would even have needed to know that it was specifically her dock where the light resided, because the symbolic significance would still be there. I think that the point was that the light was on the other egg where she lived and in that way, by seeing it he could feel closer to her.

Composition teachers such as Kathleen have increasingly turned to blogs to foster writing in their composition courses, particularly given the fact that 30% of students have their own blogs and 1 in 6 online students indicate that they've posted to their blogs at least weekly (National School Boards Association, 2007). Thirty-five percent of online female adolescents are engaged in blogging, compared to 20% of online male adolescents. Contrary to expectations, 35% of adolescents living in low-income households compared to 24% of adolescents living in high-income family households are more likely to blog (Madden et al., 2007).

While blogging was initially often associated with journalists, pundits, and political candidates to comment about political or social events for large, public audiences (@ = News blogs), as more people began to use blogs, they were increasingly employed as a tool for recording their personal experiences to an audience of their friends and family. A study by Universal McCann (2006) found that for young people, the most popular blogs were those written for family and friends, followed by personal diary blogs, news blogs, photo blogs, and film or music blogs. In another study of 135 college student bloggers at the University of Minnesota, most students kept blogs primarily as a tool for staying in touch with peers on campus or family members (Scaletta, 2006). When asked to indicate how often they post entries on certain topics, the most frequent three topics were "information about your day-to-day life," "thoughts and reflections on your academic or professional interests," and "venting of strong feelings or emotions" (p. 25).

Given their personal uses of blogging, blogging students in the composition class, could reflect on their use of rhetorical strategies and sense of audience Anne Beaton of Robbinsdale Armstrong High School, Robbinsdale, Minnesota, shares her experience of integrating a blog into her 11th-grade AP composition class (http://beatonenglish.blogspot.com/):

> I use the blog in my Advanced Placement English 11 course at Robbinsdale Armstrong High School, which prepares juniors to take the AP Language and Composition exam. We spend the majority of our time looking at the *way* in which something was written, focusing on the rhetorical devices and strategies employed by the author in addition to audience, tone, and purpose. Students read an assortment of nonfiction texts and write a fair number of papers as they transition from learning the material, to identifying the material in professional writing, to incorporating the material into their own writing. Additionally, students practice for the exam by taking sample AP written and multiple choice tests from previous years.
>
> For me, a blog is not about the bells and whistles. I have snooped around the Web enough to realize that my blog is very basic—I have not even filled in my personal profile. What matters to me is that I have created a space

outside my classroom where my students can look more carefully at an issue from class, discuss a text, or (their favorite) chat with one another while writing a paper.

Once school started, I had high hopes that I would make the blog an integral part of my curriculum; it might be a place to post weekly homework discussions or a method to get my students to beef up their vocabulary. I had yet to discover what form the blog would take in my class. What I did not expect is that the blog truly became a part of the class only once my students took ownership of the space.

Initially, I set up the blog as a way to help students learn a new concept I was introducing in class. I marched everyone into the computer lab to view the site, where they were greeted with an assignment about connotation and denotation—complete with a description, steps to follow, and a link. I instructed each student to post a comment to the thread and read their classmates' posts. My first venture was a success; however I felt that my students were essentially experiencing a typical classroom task via a blog—an electronic substitute.

I tried next to supplement student learning by opening a thread and requiring that students post their favorite new vocabulary word. As with my first thread, each student only posted once. There was no real reason to engage in any sort of dialogue. My students were only doing what was required of them, and the blog seemed contrived and was not enriching their learning experience in the least.

At winter break, I sent my students home with Anne Fadiman's *The Spirit Catches You and You Fall Down* and I opened up one more thread encouraging students to post any questions they had about the book as they were reading. Posting on the blog was optional, and by the end of winter break, there were five—including two of my own. After such a weak response, I was ready to sever all ties with my blog for good, but I kept the thread alive by explaining to my students that if they were interested they could post any questions they had while writing their *Spirit* essays over the weekend. I mentioned that I would check in occasionally to help with any answers.

By the following Monday, there were 29 posts—8 of them mine. Since the first draft of their paper was due the next day, I reminded students about the blog and suggested that (if interested) they jump into the discourse. Late that night I checked in on the blog and was floored to read that there were 154 posts! I scrolled through and read with fascination a record of my students' activity as they questioned, answered, griped, empathized and commiserated, all while constructing an understanding of their paper topics. The thread narrates an evening during which students demonstrated a collective grasp of the material and a genuine care toward fellow class-mates.

Some posted comments directly related to the rhetorical devices we had been studying in class and were met with an immediate and careful reply:

> So I'm noticing that Fadiman uses a lot more parallel structure when she's talking about the Hmong history. Any ideas on what effect this has? By James, at 5:52 PM

> james: i think the use of parallel structure when talking about Hmong history emphasizes the fact that everything to the Hmong is con-nected. example: if ur sick, the cause may be because of something you did in this life or a past life. to them, every action means some-thing and it makes sense to use parallel structure to get that across. thats just my thoughts.

> have you seen any examples of Fadiman's voice when looking at Hmong history? :) By anna, at 5:58 PM

Later into the evening, weary students spurred each other to write all the way through to the four-page requirement. Their verbal sparring offered others a humorous break:

> Thanks, Elliot. As for you, you've got the easy modes. Unless you've squeezed dry every single aspect of each and every point you've made in your paper, you should still be able to add more, (more examples from the text, more elaboration on points that haven't been beaten to death, or a more thorough intro/conclusion). Joe 8:28 pm

> Trust me joe, many ideas have been beaten dead, looked over, and severely beaten again, just in case. It's just that I'm trying to focus in on the main purpose of the novel (depicting cultural collision...i hope) and not run off on the smaller points. Elliot 8:33 pm

> ok joe and elliot...ur comments are so funny....whenever i start hating this paper i just come look at them and laugh! keep up the good work! By anna, at 8:42 PM

It appeared that once blogging was no longer an assignment, the blog itself created a sense of community where students were free to exchange ideas and anxieties, protest and receive feedback without fear of reprisal or a lower grade. The scholarly (and sometimes wacky) exchange convinced me to continue to incorporate the use of blogs in my curriculum.

When I first thought to use a blog in my classroom, I had hoped to create a space where my students could interact beyond our four walls. After some trial and error, I have stumbled upon a method of blogging that works for *this* group of students. Most recently, one student requested that I start a new thread for their upcoming synthesis paper. I have, and as of 10 pm tonight with our first draft due tomorrow, there have been 45 posts—none of them mine. Rather than require all students to artificially post and respond, it has worked best to offer a blog as a resource to those who seek further interaction with their classmates.

Employing Blogging as Social Conversation

We believe that blogging serves a primary role in improving students' writing by providing them with a social purpose for writing to peer audiences within a classroom community, consistent with phase 2 described in chapter 1. Rather than perceiving blogs as another form of journal writing to a teacher (phase I writing), it is important to perceive them as a tool for social conversation afforded through easy access to posts and RSS feeds. Anne believes that her students began to value how they can use blogging as conversations to assist each other in their work. Their blogging

> created a sense of community where students were free to exchange ideas and anxieties, protest and receive feedback without fear of reprisal or a lower grade. The students were engaged with posting to their blogs because they enjoyed sharing their ideas in ways that went beyond simply fulfilling a writing assignment. They shared tentative responses to their reading. They sought out advice from each other on how to write their papers. They provided encouragement to each other.

Also, as noted in chapter 1, it is important to encourage students to perceive blogging as a social conversation in their own personalized "third spaces"—the public arena associated with phase 2 writing (Glogowski, 2006). Students can design their blog template, layout, color, and font in a manner that marks it as their own space. They can also easily embed images or video clips into their posts to convey their messages or illustrate their ideas. In some cases, they may focus primarily on the use of images evident in what are known as photologs such as Fololog.com (@ = Photologs).

In creating an attractive appearance for their blogs, students can then appeal to other members of their blogosphere community. In reflecting on blogging in Elizabeth Boeser's class, Josh Hiben noted that:

> It's awesome because of the community of it. You have your blog and it's
> different from any work sheet that you fill out and hand back to the teacher.
> You can look at your 20 other classmates and learn from them and their
> humor. It's more connected. Instead of the teacher-student thing, it's like a
> teacher-student and then you see whatever else one puts in.

Central to blogging as social conversation with peers is the ability to cite and link to other posts by using others' posts acquired through RSS feeds to formulate one's own ideas or positions. As David Parry (2006) notes, "One only has to look at the most successful blogs to understand the extent to which the ability to cite and link to sources is crucial for garnering an audience. By learning to use RSS, students can cull from a large number of resources to provide this citationality" (p. 2). Rebecca Blood (2002) notes that bloggers rely heavily on others' blogs to construct their knowledge. They *scour* other blogs on their particular topics and/or check on feeds to their blog. They then *filter* what they find to extract the most relevant, valid information. They then *post* their findings by linking to others' posts.

This process of scouring, filtering, and linking reflects how blogs are constructed within the context of the classroom or larger blogosphere in which posts and comments are linked together as a vast network of cross-referenced texts related to specific topics. These topics are organized according to tags or keywords that are listed at the bottom of posts; students can then search for posts related to specific tags or keywords.

Blogs are also linked through the use of RSS feeds. By linking to their peers' posts, as well as posts from outside the classroom, students are learning to formulate their ideas within the nexus of a range of competing positions that are linked together, as if they are at a large, noisy party in which they have access to all the conversations going on simultaneously in the room. Bud Hunt (2006) argues that rather than simply put their writing onto blogs, by linking to other posts, students are using blogs as a tool for drawing on and interacting with others within the context of a blogging community. From reading and responding to each other's posts, students learn to formulate their positions and develop convincing evidence to support those positions.

For example, students can use blogs to participate in online book clubs. Sharon McDermott of Northfield Community School, Northfield, Minnesota, created a book club blog (http://www.ncs-nj.org/blogs/bookclub) to foster responses to books that enhanced their classroom discussions. Students at Urbana High School, Urbana, Illinois, share their online responses on a blog (http://uhsbookclub.blogspot.com) as part of their book club meetings in the school library.

Students can also readily connect with worldwide audiences. In the previously mentioned *The World Is Flat* blog project (Davis, 2006), students in Georgia and

Bangladesh shared their work using the blog the Georgia-NJ Connection (http://weblogs.hcrhs.k12.nj.us/georgia) to work collaboratively on researching topics. And in studying the book *The Secret Life of Bees*, students at Hunterdon High School in New Jersey shared their responses to the book with the book's author, Sue Monk Kidd (http://weblogs.hcrhs.k12.nj.us/beesbook).

Given the centrality of participating in a social conversation, blogging requires the ability to synthesize key ideas from, and comment on, others' blogs. Ryan Bretag (2007) suggests building instruction in reading of others' blogs by adding different kinds of blogs to Google Reader, then noting and discussing new posts that appear. When students continually read one another's blogs, they perceive it as a public, social conversation with peers and larger audiences who provide alternative perspectives that push them to expand their thinking. Based on his idea of writing within "third spaces," Konrad Glogowski (2007) describes five stages associated with creating blog entries about a topic:

- *Discover.* At the discover stage, students begin to focus on a topic that interests them by visiting sites to identify topics that they want to know more about.

- *Define.* At the define stage, students begin to post entries in which they begin to share ideas about their topic.

- *Immerse.* Students immerse themselves as researchers in their topic by using RSS feeds to link to and create a network of resources and experts through their posts.

- *Build.* Students use their posts to document what they are learning about their topic and to interact with others about their topic.

- *Contribute.* At this final stage, students contribute their knowledge about their topic by creating their own resources for others—a video, podcast, artifact, or creative writing—a production that reflects what they learned about their topic.

Students like the fact that they can receive comments from other students in the class (Davis, 2007). In her use of blogs, Jean Burgess (2006) found that the students who were most socially active in terms of social engagement in the classroom were also the students who were most likely to post comments or create blog links. To ensure that students receive comments from their peers in his classes, Richard has students serve as "blog partners" who are required to provide comments to each other.

Students often prefer blogging to writing traditional papers because they can express themselves in a more natural, conversational voice associated with communicating with their peers. One of Elizabeth's students, Josh Hiben, values the informality of language use in his blogs:

> It was like a journal, I could write whatever I wanted, and it wasn't so strict, but you could still communicate that idea, you can use the language of our friends. The informality is important. When you are writing a paper, you have to get into the perspective of someone who's academic and educational and you have to write it in that sort of syntax in terms of what the teacher expects. But as opposed to a blog, you can get at the core ideas that are in your head and lay them out as you see fit in your own words as opposed to a paper, where there's more finality to it.

Because blogs are public, students also adopt a public voice. dana boyd (2006a) uses the metaphor of the soapbox speaker in a community square to describe the process of adopting a public voice. She quotes one blogger, Jennifer, who noted the following:

> You're basically standing on a soapbox and reading something out loud, only with a blog it feels like there's a big community square and everyone's got a soapbox and they're about the same height and everyone's reading at the same time. So it's a matter of people going and listening to one and oh, I don't like what you're saying, and blogging with someone else and listening to what they're saying until you happen to find someone who is saying something interesting or you happen to know where your friend is on his soapbox saying something. (p. 3)

boyd notes that Jennifer perceives herself as "speaking, performing her thoughts to a conceptualized audience" (p. 3).

Students shift to a more informal language style because they are now writing to peer and Web audiences. Kathleen West (2008) noted that her students were expressing their responses to literature as part of conversing with peers:

> I found that students come to see through their blogs that their individual responses to class texts matter and are worthy of an audience of peers. As such, they're written in language that is meant to appeal to that audience, peppered with sarcasm, pop-culture references, and abbreviations that invite age-mates in. I found that blogs are a safe virtual space to bring students' "outside" identities and literacies into the classroom.

In an analysis of some of her other students' blogging (West, 2008), she argues that this shift in language style reflects a hybrid of school and popular culture discourses that deviates from traditional language use in the English classroom:

> Because almost all basic rules of English usage are abandoned on these websites, students resist the current push for standardization. On a situational

level, too, power dynamics have changed as a result of the weblog project. When the students work on their blog, there is no teacher standing at the front of the class. Instead, I'm seated at a computer, writing my own blog and commenting on others...they also disrupted AP notions of language embedded in the curricula of their school by incorporating out-of-school literacies into their work. (p. 597)

Fictional Blogs

In adopting these hybrid styles in their blogs, students are experimenting with shifts in voice and style. They could reflect on how their use of voice in their blogs serves to define their persona as writers across different contexts. (For an activity on analyzing voice in literature and in student blogs, see @ = Chris Polley's activity on voice.)

Students can also create fictional blogs in which they adopt characters' voices in constructing an ongoing narrative across different posts. Angela Thomas (2006) describes different types of fictional blogs: a series of posts in narrative sequence, blogs that employ a lot of hyperlinks and blog features to create a narrative, use of blogs that tell a partial story linked to FanFiction sites, role-playing blogs, character diary blogs, or blogs used for publishing literary texts or for commercial purposes. Consistent with the idea of the serial novel, one popular type of fictional blog consists of diary accounts of one or more protagonists containing extensive links to other posts or sites. When readers provide comments, the writer then uses material from these comments in later episodes (@ = Fictional blogs).

After engaging in the Fighting Sioux online role-play debate in chapter 1, students in Elizabeth's college writing class then used a blog (http://schooledthewriteway.blogspot.com) to create the roles of fictional high school students coping with the issues facing adolescents portrayed in Laurie Halse Anderson's (2006) *Speak* and Stephen Chbosky's (1999) *The Perks of Being a Wallflower.* The students used their roles to write letters to Charlie, the main character in *The Perks of Being a Wallflower*, providing Charlie with advice on how to cope with the difficulties of being a social outsider in his own high school.

To help them create a role within a fictional high school setting, Elizabeth first had students create descriptions of towns or cities for their fictional high schools, and then a description and image of a school mascot that represented the local culture of their town or city to post on the blog. To create their descriptions for places such as Rivendell, New Zealand; Phoenix, Arizona; Chicago, Illinois; Myrtle Beach, South Carolina; Camden, Maine; and Denver, Colorado, students conducted searches using keywords about towns and cities on Google, Flickr, or

Google Images, leading them to create multimodal descriptions of different schools with images and text. For example, one student, Katie Nelson, used the image of a Dole pineapple to create a "Dole High School," noting that "it would appeal to the kids in our class."

The students voted on what they perceived to be the best site in terms of providing the most thorough overall information and images, selecting Kyle Rushnacko's Maui High School, Honolulu, Hawaii:

> Aloha Everyone! If you're looking for that special place to bring your kid to school, you don't have to look any further. Hawaii has given you and your child a place to feel comfortable when it comes to getting a proper and fun education. Smack dab in the middle of the city of Honolulu is Maui High School. Hawaii is known for its natural beauty, its history, and its overall friendliness. What better name for a school? Maui High School, as it was appropriately named, is well recognized for its new beauty, its accomplishments in history, and its genuine friendliness, generosity, and companionship. It is among the top schools in the district of Honolulu and has won numerous awards for its academic skill and leadership.

> Maui was named after the demigod Mâui, who, in Hawaiian mythology, was said to have pulled Hawaii up from the bottom of the ocean. Legends tell of how he went fishing with his brothers and accidentally caught his hook on the ocean floor, thus raising the islands of Hawaii to earth's surface. Maui's evident impact on Hawaii is portrayed through the High School. Maui High has had and continues to have a great impact on the students of Honolulu. [Learning] substantial life skills and the highest possible level of academics, students graduating from Maui High School have had one of the highest success rates in the entire state of Hawaii.

> Looking far back into the history of The Aloha State, the beginning of Hawaii began with the Polynesians. The Polynesian people make up 16% of the population and [are] the top populating group of Honolulu and the rest of Hawaii. A majority of Polynesians, if not all, believe that Tiki was the first living man. It is also believed, according to Polynesian mythology, that Tiki is a sculpture carved in the shape of a god that houses a spirit. We at Maui High School believe in sportsmanship and high levels of school spirit. In the way of the Tikis, we can bring the ancient spirits into the doors of our school and show Honolulu's rivals what we're really made of!

The students then created their own characters and posted an image of their character along with biographical characteristics of their characters, following directions Elizabeth put on a wiki: (http://highschoolcharacters.pbwiki.com).

Selecting a Blog Platform

The first step in using blogs in your classroom involves selecting a blog platform from the many available options—for example, Blogger, Edublog, Vox, LiveJournal, TypePad, WordPress, Movable Type, Manila, SquareSpace, Radio Userland, DiaryLand, or Xanga (@ = Blogging platforms, @ = Books on blogging).

One of the more popular free blogs is Blogger (Gardner & Birley, 2008). To set up a Blogger blog, students go through the following steps:

1. Create an account. To create a blog using Blogger, students go to http:// www.blogger.com and set up a Google account, which they can use with other Google tools. To create an account, they need to enter a user name for signing into their account, a password, a display name that appears on their blog, and an e-mail address (this is not shared with third parties without students' permission). It is important that in entering the name to be used, students do not reveal their last names; they can also create a pseudonym so that they cannot be identified by online readers. Students should not use any last names on their posts or in their comments.

2. Create a blog name and address. Students need to decide on both a name for their blog as well as words to insert in the blogspot URL for their blog: http://XXX.blogspot.com. They need to select a relatively unusual name because common names may have already been claimed. They need to make sure that they use an easy-to-remember name for their URLs because once their URL is set, they will not be able to change it.

Students will be given a choice of different template options with different layout, font, and color options for their blog. They choose a template by clicking on their preferred template; they can also preview different templates.

Once students select a template, Blogger then creates their blog. To activate their blog, they must create their first post entry. To do so, they need to enter a post title and a posting. Students can personalize their blog by going into "Settings" and adding information about themselves; again, however, they should not use their last names. Students can also create a "blogroll"—a list of other blogs they are reading.

Alternative Blogging Sites

Blogger is only one of many different blog-hosting platforms (@ = Blogging platforms). In deciding on which site is most appropriate for the classroom or school, the teachers may want to experiment with different blogs, given their needs related to ease-of-use for younger students, support, and safety features. In addition to popular platforms noted above, the following are some of the other platforms that are being used in schools:

- WordPress (http://wordpress.org) is a popular platform that needs to be installed on a school server and therefore enhances security; it contains a lot of powerful features.

- Edublogs (http://edublogs.org) is a free platform built on the WordPress platform but does not need be installed on a school server; it is designed particularly for use in schools given the privacy features and extensive training support available for teachers and students.

- Angelfire (http://www.angelfire.lycos.com) has an easy-to-use editing tool, Lycos-Qumana, for inserting links, tags, and images into blogs.

- Typepad (http://www.typepad.com) is a commercial platform with a lot of features that make it easy to use.

- Platforms such as Blosxom (www.blosxom.com), blojsom (http:// wiki.blojsom.com/wiki/display/blojsom3/About+blojsom), and Textpattern (http://textpattern.com), as well as course management systems such as Moodle (http://moodle.org) and Drupal (http:// drupal.org), contain blogs; these platforms, like WordPress, require installation on a school server (Hendron, 2008). One advantage of housing these platforms on a school server is that they provide for more control and protection, particularly if they can block out spam.

- Blogs designed specifically for schools, such as Class Blogmeister, Gaggle Blogs, Learnerblogs, Kidzblog, or 21Publish: Classroom blogs. Class Blogmeister, created by David Warlick, requires teacher monitoring of student postings. Elgg (http://elgg.net) and Industrious Kid's Imbee.com are designed particularly for elementary and middle school students because they provide a lot of security, interactive features, and secure storage space (@ = Creating blogs).

Using Twitter and Tumblr for Microblogging

Another optional platform is Twitter (http://www.twitter.com), mentioned in chapter 3 as a cross between synchronous IMing and chat room and asynchronous blog and chat room exchanges. Students can use Twitter to share short messages or "tweets" of 140 characters or less (@ = Twitter). Unlike synchronous chat, this can be used to post messages at any time and place. Unlike blog posts, they are much shorter—a form of microblogging that works for mobile postings using cell phones.

Because some students may be initially intimidated by creating blog posts, Twitter may be a less intimidating, more conversational option to blogging. Given the conversational nature of sharing messages, students are often more likely to receive a reply than is the case with a blog.

In the classroom, given the public nature of Twitter (which may mean that it is blocked), teachers could have students set up their Twitter as private and then list students in the class as followers. It could then be used to exchange information and ideas about topics or books; teachers can also use it to send out announcements or messages to students. As with any site, teachers and students should avoid sharing private information.

Students can use Twitter to collaboratively construct stories (Carvin, 2007). For example, one teacher, George Mayo, created Manyvoices (http://manyvoices.wikispaces.com) for students to each contribute "tweets" to a collaborative story. Students can use Youth Twitter, a tool mentioned in chapter 1 in which, consistent with phase 3 in which teachers can still participate, students are initiating conversations outside completing school assignments.

Students can use a microblogging tool, Tumblr (http://www.tumblr.com), by just clicking on the "Share on Tumblr" icon on their browser tool bar for posting to private groups—for example, just students in a class.

Using Blogging Tools

Students can use a number of blog tools to enhance their blogging experience.

Offline Connections to Blogs Using Blog Editors

Blogging requires a broadband connection to the Web, something that students may not have at home. They may not always be connected to their blogs in their classrooms. For situations where students are not connected, they can compose their posts offline using a blog editor that sits on their computer and that will then connect to their blog when they are connected.

There are three types of blog editors: Word/Google Docs, Web browser extensions/add-ons, and dedicated blog editor applications.

Students can use Word 2007 to create their post by clicking on "New" on the Office button in the upper left-hand corner, then "New Blog Post," then "Create," then "Register Now" to select their blog platform—for example, Blogger—and then their blog URL, username, and password. They then compose their post and click "Publish" to publish their post on their blog.

In writing in Google Docs, once they want to export their post, they click on the "Publish" tab on the top right-hand side, enter information about their blog platform, log in information, click OK, and select "Post to Your Blog."

Students can add extensions or add-ons to their browser to link to their blogs. Blog platforms include icons that can be added to browser tool bars—for example "Typepad Quickpost." If they want to quote sections of a post or an article, they highlight that material and click on the icon to link to their blog, and then the material is added to their blog. Or they can use add-ons or extensions for Firefox such as Scribefire (http://www.scribefire.com) or Dashblog (http://addons.mozilla.org/en.us/firefox/addon/7215) to post from Firefox.

Students can use applications housed on their computers such as w.bloggor (Windows), ecto (Windows and Mac), Qumana (Windows and Mac), Windows Live Writer (Windows), Flock (Windows), MarsEdit (Mac), BlogJet (Windows), or Zoundry (Windows) to create posts offline and then export to their blogs.

Students can use e-mail to send in posts to a Posterous blog (http://posterous.com).

RSS Feeds

As noted in chapter 2, students can subscribe to others' blogs using RSS feed aggregators such as Bloglines or Google Reader (@ = Using feeds with blogs). When students use a feed aggregator to subscribe to a blog, they receive notice each time new posts are added to that blog. Rather than reading separate blogs, students can go to their aggregator and peruse the different post titles to read those posts that interest them or that are relevant to topics they are addressing in their posts.

To have students create feeds, students can use their blogging site to create a feed URL—a URL that differs from their blog URL. Students can use Feedburner (http://www.feedburner.com) to create blog feeds. With their Blogger sites, students can create a feed by clicking on "Settings" and then clicking on "Site Feed." At that point, they need to determine whether they want to provide only the first paragraphs of their posts by selecting "Short" or the entire posts by selecting "Full."

When students view their blog, they will now see "Feed (Atom)" added to their blog. When they click on the feed, if they have an account to Bloglines, Google Reader, or any other feed service, they will be asked to "Subscribe this feed to" and select those services on which they want to house their feed.

Students can turn to other users who they assume have expertise or interest in certain topics and access these other users' feeds for their own use. For example, if a student recognizes that a blogger has extensive knowledge of scuba diving, then that student would want to access the kinds of feeds this expert blogger is drawing on. Because bloggers can now easily add a link to their Bloglines or Google Reader feeds as "my feeds" to their blogs, students can go to that link and access these feeds. They can then add them to their own feeds, expanding their own feed lists.

When students create their own feed lists, they can readily share those lists with other students.

Tagging Blog Posts

Even when students have access to other feeds, they can be overwhelmed by long lists of posts. To further help them narrow down their search and review of posts, they can utilize tagging systems, such as Delicious, Diigo, or Furl (http://www.furl.net), described in chapter 2 to find and subscribe to relevant blog (@ = Tagging sites). Students can also promote their own blog by tagging their posts with certain keywords so that their peers or other audiences can find their posts. In doing so, they need to employ relatively specific words, but not be too specific because these words have to reference a number of different posts.

On some blogs, students may find lists of keywords or "tag clouds" in side bars, with the more frequently referenced tags in larger or bolder font than less referenced tags. Much as chapter titles in a book, these lists or tag clouds provide readers with some understanding of the topics dealt with in a blog. Users can then click on keywords to search for posts addressing certain topics.

Students can also use social bookmarking tools to make their own feeds and tags public. For example, for students using Google Reader, when they find a post they wish to share with others, they can click on the "share" icon, and that post then becomes part of a public page available to others. If students are using Blogger, they can easily add their public Google Reader page icon to their blog. They need to open up "Settings" in Google Reader and find the "put a clip on your site" option. By clicking on the button, the Google Reader shared items are then placed on their blog.

Comments

Students connect by making and receiving comments on one another's posts—often the more comments they receive, the higher the level of engagement in blogging. One advantage of using blog partners is to ensure that students receive at least some comments. Knowing that they can anticipate some response to their post may then help them formulate their post in a certain manner.

"Comment starters" can be used to prompt student comments (Davis, 2007), such as "This made me think about . . .," "I wonder why . . .," "Your writing made me form an opinion about . . .," "This post is relevant because . . .," "Your writing made me think that we should . . .," "I wish I understood why . . .," "This is important because . . .," "Another thing to consider is . . .," "I can relate to this . . .," "This makes me think of . . .," "I discovered . . .," "I don't understand . . .," "I was reminded that . . .," or "I found myself wondering . . .," Students also need to invite comments from their peers as well as react to comments as a means of encouraging further conversation by asking questions such as "Do you agree?"

Learning to make effective comments as well as creating their own posts in response to others' posts requires that students go beyond simply restating what their peers are *saying* to interpreting what their peers are *doing* in writing their posts—their purposes, agendas, and strategies. Joseph Harris (2006) argues that in reading others' posts, students are "coming to terms" with others' posts by posing the following questions about their peers' aims, methods, and materials:

> Aims: What is a writer trying to achieve? What position does he or she want to argue? What issues or problems does he or she explore?

> Methods: How does a writer relate examples to ideas? How does he or she connect one claim to the next or build a sense of continuity and flow?

> Materials: Where does the writer go for examples and evidence? What texts are cited and discussed? What experiences or events are described? (p. 19)

Classroom Versus Individual Blogs

In setting up blogs, teachers face the choice of using individual blogs or one single classroom blog. Choosing between individual blogs and a single classroom blog often comes down to determining the purposes for using blogs in the classroom.

Using Classroom Blogs

One advantage of using a classroom blog is that all posts submitted to the blog can monitored so that only teacher-approved posts end up being published. Another advantage is that because they are exposed to their peers' posts, students are more likely to read and provide comments on others' posts than is the case when each student has an individual blog (@ = Classroom blogs).

One example of a classroom blog from a middle school is the Room 613 Student Blogs (http://hetherington.learnerblogs.org/) developed by Mike Hetherington for his sixth-grade social studies class at Horace W. Porter School, Columbia, Connecticut for the 2005/2006 school year (Figure 6-1).

Hetherington created this classroom blog with WordPress in which he is the site administrator, allowing him to approve any postings. To create student subscribers, he went back to Learnerblogs.org (now Edublogs.org) and created a blog for each student with the first name, or first name and last-name initial, as a user name and created e-mail addresses for each student. He then received passwords from Learnerblogs and in the "Add User to Community" box on the class blog entered student user names and set the option as "subscriber" for each student entered. He then provided each student with a user name and password on index cards, along with the URL for the Room 613 Student Blog (see: http://mhetherington.net/blogs/?p=8).

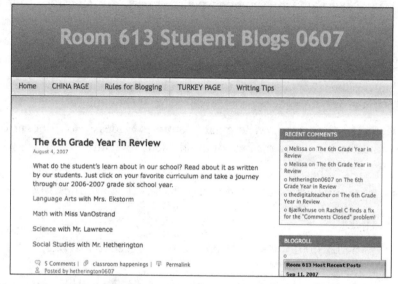

Figure 6-1. Sample Class Blog

Each student's name appears on the blog's side bar. Students click on their names to add their own writing. Hetherington has his students assume the role of scribes who summarize what their class is studying or learning on particular days, which that enhances students' agency as contributing members of the class.

One drawback to creating a single classroom blog is that as the administrator, Hetherington needed to go the "manage" page to find student posts and determine if they can be published or if they require editing, which that can be time-consuming. To address this issue, for his classroom blog for 2006–2007 (http://hetherington0607.learnerblogs.org), Hetherington employed Google Reader to capture feeds from his students' posts that are then posted on the centralized Google Reader aggregator. He also suggests setting up categories in which students can store their posts; these could be student names, topics, subjects, or assignments. For example, in the blog shown in Figure 6-1, the post created by Hetherington at the end of the school year was filed into the category "6th grade year in review."

Classroom blogs are particularly useful in teaching an online course because they serve to centralize students' writing in one place, which is the case with online forums. Students are then continually exposed to others' writing, fostering extensive commenting on that writing, which is particularly useful for online writing course instruction. (For an example of a classroom blog used in an online composition course taught by Krista Kennedy at the University of Minnesota, see http://blog.lib.umn.edu/kenne329/3401s07.)

Using Individual Blogs

One drawback to using a classroom blog is that it may be perceived as simply a site for completing teacher-initiated assignments consistent with phase 2 writing rather than to encouraging self-initiated posts consistent with phase 3 writing. One advantage of using individual blogs is that students may experience a greater degree of ownership of their blog, leading to more self-initiated writing, although self-initiated writing can obviously also occur on a classroom blog. Students can create their own template, profile, blog roll, and subscription links that add to their sense of ownership.

To ensure that students are reading and commenting on individual blogs, students can serve as "blog partners" who have RSS feeds to each other's blogs. To centralize access to all student blogs, teachers can use RSS feeds to subscribe to each student's blog linked to their own or a classroom blog; links can also be posted on a class wiki. Or teachers can use tools such as Suprglu (http://suprglu.com/) or FeedShake (http://www.feedshake.com) to combine feeds in one central site. If the entire class is working on separate blog reports related to a particular project, students can use Suprglu—which employs a newspaper-type layout—to create a final class report.

The major disadvantage to individual blogs is that they need to be monitored to ensure that they are password protected and that students are not disclosing private information in their profiles or posts or being attacked by spammers.

Another disadvantage of individual blogs is that students may encounter difficulties setting up their blogs, requiring additional assistance; this suggests the need to select a blog platform that is relatively easy to use.

To choose between classroom versus individual blogs, we recommend making that choice based on the different purposes for using blogs. For the purpose of encouraging students to value and interact with their peers as audiences and modeling blogging practices consistent with phase 2 and 3, a classroom blog has advantages over an individual blog. However, individual blogs may serve to encourage students to engage in self-initiated writing consistent with phase 4 development.

Educators Blogs

One of the primary challenges that teachers face is that they often work in isolated contexts with little contact with others who teach similar subjects. Because a lot of teachers have created their own blogs, they can access these blogs for teaching ideas by setting up RSS feeds to those blogs that are closest to their subject matter interests and grade level (@ = Educators' blogs). For example, Will Richardson's Weblogg-ed (http://www.weblogg-ed.com) and Stephen Downes's (http://www.downes.ca/news/OLDaily.htm) are popular blogs about use of Web 2.0 tools; middle school teachers share their experiences teaching middle school (http://www.middleweb.com/mw/aaDiaries.html); Susan Sedro (http://ssedro.blogspot.com) blogs about the use of Web 2.0 tools in elementary school. Teachers at Arapahoe High School in Littleton, Colorado, use their blog (http://thefischbowl.blogspot.com) to share reflections on blogging and learning. Teachers in Australia use the Digital Chalkie blog (http://www.digitalchalkie.com) to provide support and information to each other.

Teachers can also use blogs or Twitter to pose questions about their teaching to receive advice and information from others. Teacher bloggers are grateful to receive comments to their postings that contain questions and will generally respond to those questions. They can then create some online conversations with others about issues they face in the classroom. Miguel Guhlin (2006) describes his own process of creating such conversations:

> I began simply with one or two education-related blogs such as "Bud the Teacher" (http://budtheteacher.typepad.com/) and "Moving at the Speed of Creativity" (http://www.speedofcreativity.org/) and then added blogs as I went. But adding blog feeds to my RSS Aggregator is not what digital conversations are about. It's not enough to read; it's also important to write. To accomplish that, I started leaving comments relevant to the blog entries posted on others' blogs. As I posted each comment, I included a link back to my own blog "Around the Corner" (http://www.edsupport.cc/mguhlin/blog/).
>
> On my blog, I would expand on the conversation in a way that I only hinted at in the comment. In this way, I invited other bloggers to visit my blog and, in turn, leave comments on my site. And the nature of the comments left on my site has been very helpful, primarily because they give me information and advice that I wouldn't have had if I had depended on my "traditional" PLN [personal learning network], comprised [sic] of the people with whom I interact every day at work and in my personal life. Thus, in a way that Email lists could never accomplish—because not everyone can be subscribed to every Email list on which I work—blogs enable me to learn from strangers.

Guhlin can therefore continually receive feeds from a wide range of educator blogs that are then, in turn, linked to his blog. All this serves to create the kinds of social networks that provide professional development support for teachers.

David Warlick (2007), a leading authority on classroom blogging, notes that teachers can use their blogs to inform parents and district administrators about what students are learning in their classrooms, assignments, project descriptions, and examples of student achievement. At the same time, teachers also need to be cautious about sharing any criticisms of a school, engaging in business or commercial activities, or disclosing personal information about students, all of which suggests the need for schools to establish ground rules and professional development for both teachers and students.

Challenges in Using Blogs in the Classroom

Devoting Time for Blogging

Blog posting on a regular basis can be time-consuming for students (Watrall & Ellison, 2006). It takes students time to become comfortable and accustomed to blogging on a regular basis. Students can become frustrated when their blogs are not read; they may also have difficulty locating interesting content on postings.

As previously noted, students may perceive writing on blogs as just one more homework assignment. In studying his students' blogging, Steven Krause (2006) noted wide variation in the extent to which his students posted messages, as well as the quality of the posts. He found "very little writing that could be described as reflective, dynamic, collaborative, or interactive" (p. 2). He realized that he could not assume that students will be engaged to "just write" in the blogs, given the novelty of blogs. He attributed the low quality of the writing and lack of engagement to his not posting his own posts. Once he starting posting, student engagement picked up.

By sharing their posts with students, teachers are modeling blogging practices for students. In a national study of teachers' blogging as both a means of communicating with students, parents, and the community and a form of instructional practice, Jeffrey Felix (2007) found that teacher blogging increased peer interaction among students, teacher interaction with the students, and sharing of ideas, and fostered more positive student attitudes toward learning. For example, those teachers who reported posting daily to their blogs indicated that they post writing assignments 60% of the time on their blogs. Teachers also reported that students were motivated by their modeling to communicate with peers within and outside their classrooms. In using her blog to model ways of describing her eighth-grade students' experience of going on a kayak trip, Kathleen Gilroy (2005) notes how she also connected with audiences beyond just her students:

> Blogging has really helped me to connect with my audience and especially myself. It helped me connect with my audience by showing me how to really express myself when I'm talking about my personal feelings and also

how to give proper instructions. It was like presenting to the audience directly. I had to have everything on point but still try to make everything sound good and fun. I really tried to put myself in their shoes. I wanted people to learn a lot from my instructional blogs. This opportunity felt great and was amazing. Having perhaps hundreds or thousands of people reading and actually caring about what we did and how much we accomplished is overwhelming. (p. 3)

This suggests the value of teachers sharing their blog posts along with reflections on blogging strategies. Devoting more class time to blogging also provides teachers more time to model ways of linking blog posts using feeds to make connections between blogs and for students to write comments on other posts. As Barbara Ganley (2006) notes in describing her use of blogging:

Teaching with blogs the way I do—which means not applying them piecemeal but integrating them fully in all their messy, flexible, fluid promise—means you have to let go of control of the classroom, give up the stage and create opportunities for learning magic to occur. The trick is to weave the learning and the tool so seamlessly together that the blog is the class and the class finds the blog indispensable.

Rather than having students writing *for* a teacher, consistent with the shift to phase 2, teachers devote classroom to writing *with* students so that students value the teacher as one more member of the social conversation. For further resources on using blogs, see the Blogs for Learning site (http://blogsforlearning.msu.edu, @ = Using blogs in the classroom).

Safety and Privacy

Another issue has to do with safety and privacy, as well as the use of offensive or inappropriate content on blogs. Given potential legal challenges related to these issues, administrators and parents are rightfully concerned about these issues. Administrators may therefore adopt an overly cautious stance and not allow the use of blogs, and block access to them. Given reports of child predators who frequent social networking sites, administrators and parents are also concerned about the need to protect students from adults who are accessing their blogs.

Based on her research on MySpace, danah boyd (2006b) notes the following:

Statistically speaking, kids are more at risk at a church picnic or a boy scout [sic] outing than they are when they go on MySpace. Less than .01% of all youth abductions nationwide are stranger abductions and as far as we know, no stranger abduction has occurred because of social network services. The goal of a predator is to get a child to consent to sexual activities.

> Predators contact teens (online and offline) to start a conversation. Just as most teens know to say no to strange men who approach them on the street, most know to ignore strange men who approach them online.

All of this means that it is important to set up procedures that do not allow unknown people to contact students. This would include having students do the following:

- Use only first names and not disclose personal information in personal profiles on their blogs—for example, their addresses, e-mail, or phone numbers.

- Use only blogs that are secure and password-protected, so that the only people who can make comments are the teacher and their peers in a class; one advantage to a classroom blog is that teachers have more control over access than when students have individual blogs, particularly for limiting spam.

- Be aware of issues of privacy and disclosure of personal information on the Web, as well as issues of access to their blog.

- Avoid language, personal attacks, and flaming that would cause harm to other students or compromise their privacy.

To encourage students to adhere to these practices, schools adopt "acceptable use policies" that students sign, indicating their agreement with these procedures. For use in his school, Bud Hunt (2006) has drafted an acceptable use policy:

1. Students using blogs are expected to treat blog spaces as classroom spaces. Speech that is inappropriate for class is not appropriate for your blog. While we encourage you to engage in debate and conversation with other bloggers, we also expect that you will conduct yourself in a manner reflective of a representative of this school.

2. Students who violate the agreements here shall forfeit their right to school Internet access and will face other sanctions deemed appropriate by the administration.

3. Student blogs are to be a forum for student expression. However, they are first and foremost a tool for learning, and as such will sometimes be constrained by the various requirements and rules of classroom teachers. Students are welcome to post on any school-appropriate subject at any time, outside their classroom requirements.

Teachers also need to send letters home to parents informing them about how and why blogs are being used in the classroom, a rationale for using them in teaching writing, the protections created related to privacy and access, and a request that they grant permission for their child to participate in using blogs in the classroom. Hunt sends home a letter to his students' parents describing his use of blogs in his classes and requesting permission (@ = Parent communication).

Because blogs are public spaces, students may have difficulty knowing where to draw the line in terms of sharing private, confidential information or criticisms of peers, teachers, administrators, public officials, or parents. They need to realize that sharing private, confidential information or criticisms of others to an unknown public can have serious consequences—in some cases, even legal charges of libel. Although the courts have recently protected journalists' use of blogs to voice criticisms under the First amendment, students are not journalists and thus still need to be cautious about what they share when they do not know who will be reading their blog (@ = Blog safety).

Because students will be including material and links from the Web on their blogs, administrators and parents are concerned about students' accessing and importing inappropriate or "adult" material on their blogs. Schools are required by the Child Internet Protection Act to filter out such content as well as formulate a policy regarding their students' protection from such material. However, such filtering often does not block certain content and blocks other material that may be beneficial. Students then do not have access to material for legitimate academic purposes. If they are doing an assignment on certain topics related to sexuality, violence, terrorism, gambling, and so on, they may find that access to sites on these topics has been blocked, leading them to use "circumventor" sites to skirt blocking or filters.

All of this suggests the need for schools to develop proactive rather than punitive policies regarding online access and to share these policies with students and parents. Schools may be rightfully concerned about the costs of potential litigation if they have to address problems with blog use. However, in attempting to ban blog use, particularly if that use occurs outside school property or as part of a school assignment, they could face legal challenges related to free-speech rights.

Teachers may also want to keep attuned to research on these issues to inform their practices based on scholarly information (@ = Research on blogging).

Use of Copyrighted Materials

As we noted in our discussion of copyright in the last chapter, students need to be aware of their use of copyrighted material or images on their blogs related to fair use in schools. At the same time, in creating blogs, they may want to give permission for others to use their material through the use of what is known as the Creative Commons tag or logo (Lessig, 2002). By adding this tag or logo to a blog, students grant different degrees of permissions so that others can build on this blog material.

Summary

In this chapter, we discuss the use of blogs to foster student online academic writing, which draws on practices involved in public and personal uses of blogs but which also focuses more on *academic* uses of blogs to foster learning. Like dialogue journal writing, writing with blogs provides students with opportunities for social interactivity with their peers and audiences from around the world through use of hyperlinks or RSS feeds to blogs. Although the potential for writing to these audiences serves to motivate students to write, teachers need to assume an active role in fostering the use of blogs through their own contributions and prompts. Teachers also need to take a number of proactive step to ensure the safe, secure uses of blogs in their classrooms.

Chapter
Seven

Using Digital Audio
and Video Productions

Paul Allison (2006) is a high school teacher who heads up the Teachers Teaching Teachers podcast on the EdTechTalk network (http://www.edtechtalk.com) for teachers using Web 2.0 tools to teach writing and who also uses podcasts extensively in his teaching. He recounts his experience with Derek, an African American student who was a leader on his high school basketball team. The team lost its first game to a close rival. Derek, who had not done a lot of writing, decided to create a podcast describing his disappointment over losing the game and what his teammates needed to do to improve their play for the rest of the season. He chose to do a podcast rather than write a blog post because he was more comfortable speaking than writing his thoughts thorugh a podcast.

After he posted his podcast on his blog, some members of the rival team who happened to be reading his blog provided him with comments, noting that they were impressed with his own and his team's play and how they created a strategy to win the game. Allison argues that receiving these comments enhanced Derek's appreciation of the value of sharing his writing with others, serving to motivate his engagement with writing in the classroom. He notes that Derek's personal reflections and analysis of the game represent more engaged forms of writing than had he simply written a school newspaper sports report, particularly because he was using a podcast to give voice to his feelings about losing the basketball game.

The Value of Digital Audio and Video Productions

In this chapter, we discuss the use of digital audio and video productions using podcasts, audio and video conferencing, Ed.VoiceThread, and vlogging tools. Using these digital audio and video production tools helps to bolster students' confidence in their ability to communicate. Students such as Derek are often more confident about their oral speaking than their writing skills. By using a podcast, Derek received positive comments from his peers, which served to bolster his confidence in his communication skills and gave him a confidence that may then assist him with his writing.

Allison's (2006) example of Derek's use of a podcast suggests the value of building on students' oral communication skills through use of digital audio and video production tools, consistent with two of the National Council of Teachers of English and International Reading Association standards (http://www.ncte.org/about/over/standards):

- Students adjust their use of spoken, written, and visual language (e.g., conventions, style, and vocabulary) to communicate effectively with a variety of audiences and for different purposes.

- Students use spoken, written, and visual language to accomplish their own purposes (e.g., for learning, enjoyment, persuasion, and the exchange of information).

These literacy practices have been described as "sonic literacies" (Comstock & Hocks, 2006), related to the ability to create and employ audio and video texts as part of writing instruction (@ = Teaching "sonic literacy").

In creating podcasts, students are doing a lot of writing. They may often write a script or notes to read aloud on their podcast. In performing their script or notes, they may then recognize the need to revise or edit their writing to enhance the sound of it. Attending to the sound of their writing encourages students to experiment with adopting different voices that engage audiences through the use of shorter sentences with "punch," pauses or silences, and a sense of rhythm.

Because digital audio and video productions are digital, they have a number of advantages over live audio performances. The primary advantage is that they can be saved as files for creating RSS feeds for distribution to audiences beyond the initial performance event. Knowing that their performances can be readily accessed by audiences beyond the classroom means that students have some incentive to engage their audiences.

Podcasting

A primary audio communication tool is podcasting designed to create MP3 audio files that can be posted onto a server, a podcast aggregator such as iTunes, or a blog that students readily access for listening to on their iPods and other devices (Farkas, 2006; Fontichiaro, 2008; Hendron, 2008; King & Gura, 2007; Morris, Tomasi, & Terra, 2008). Because students can listen to podcasts at any time and place, they have become a popular means of acquiring and sharing information.

Podcasts have also changed the ways in which coursework can be delivered. Teachers create "coursecasting" lectures so that students can listen to lectures on their iPods—for example, lectures from courses at University of California, Berkeley (http://webcast.berkeley.edu) or Duke University (http://dukecast.oit.duke.edu). Students create podcasts to share their writing or performances of texts with peers and teachers. They can also use autocasting software such as Talkr to convert their blog posts into audio for sharing with others.

Podcasts have changed media communication. Hundreds of podcast production programs have sprung up on a wide range of topics, including education and technology, providing access to a whole other knowledge base for students to access. Radio and television programs have RSS feeds for podcasts of their programs, so that, as with TiVo and television viewing, audiences can access programs to listen to according to their own schedules.

Teachers can access professional development podcasts at iTunes University (which has a K–12 section), EdTechTalk, (http://www.edtechtalk.com), the Education Podcast Network (http://epnweb.org), Digital Campus (http://digitalcampus.tv), Podomatic (http://www.podomatic.com), Podcastalley (http://podcastalley.com), Podcastpickle (http://podcastpickle.com), and Wesley Fryer's Moving at the Speed of Creativity (http://www.speedofcreativity.org) (@ = Educator and classroom podcasts).

Using Podcasts in the Classroom

Students could listen to podcasts, and evaluate their effectiveness based on the following features:

- Use of clearly defined titles or use of what are called ID3 tags to display titles that are consistent with the content of a podcast

- Effective voice enunciation, sound production, and editing as well as use of music or sound effects to create the sense of a show

- Effective use of well-organized time to focus on the topic or subject in some depth without excessive extraneous talk that consumes extra time

- Use of voice and language that conveys interest in a topic or subject
- Consistent productions of podcasts on a regular basis so that a podcast builds an audience who can expect a series of shows
- Interactions with audiences through inclusion of interviews with audience members, soliciting audience e-mails, calls, and comments, providing show notes on a website, and/or creating a blog to receive comments

Once students are familiar with the nature of podcasts, they can use them for a variety of activities (Sprankle, 2006) (@ = Creating podcasts and podcast reviews). Just as blogs can be used for written role-plays, podcasts can be a useful tool for involving students in debates or role-play, because students can record and then reflect on their recordings. In her ninth-grade social studies class at South View Middle School in Edina, Minnesota, Gina Nelson created a role-play on the Constitutional Convention of 1787 (http://constitutionconversations.pbwiki.com). She asked her students to adopt the roles of five different delegates to the convention: George Washington, James Madison, Benjamin Franklin, Gouvernuer Morris, and Alexander Hamilton, and, working as a group, create a podcast based on these participants' conversations.

To prepare students for writing scripts for their podcasts, students acquired and shared information about their delegates on a wiki. Students also created a character map on which they identified each delegate's beliefs and traits concerning each issue. Students then had to write a script in which they created a scene for their delegates' meeting, a description of each delegate, and each delegate's perspectives on four issues: the New Jersey–Virginia plans, the Three-Fifths Compromise, the electoral college, and the possible addition of a Bill of Rights.

Students recorded and edited their podcasts using Toolfactory (http://www.toolfactory.com). Drawing on a rubric devised by Caroline McCullen (Figure 7-1), Gina then evaluated their podcasts in terms of the development of information about each issue and delegates' perspectives, the number of issues addressed, evidence of cooperative group work, and the quality of their oral presentation in terms of voice clarity and projection.

Students can create "soundseeing" audio tours of places or sites they visit on vacations for sharing with others. For example, they can create "podguides" (http://podguides.net/index.html), in which they can link up to numbers representing specific places on a map and their commentary about those places, such as the 10 most interesting works of art in a museum exhibit. These audio tools can then be made available on cell phones for others to use.

Given current interest in spoken-word poetry performances (Jocson, 2005), students can create podcasts using oral interpretation techniques for performing their own or others poems, short stories, autobiographical writing, children's literature, or folktales (@ = Podcasting unit on folktales). In a literature class,

	Beginner 1 point	All Right 2 Points	Cool 3 points	Awesome! 4 points
Content	Includes little essential information and one or two facts.	Includes some essential information with few citations and few facts.	Includes essential information. Includes enough elaboration to give readers an understanding of the topic.	Covers topic completely and in depth. Includes complete and thorough information. Encourages listeners to know more.
Introduction	No introduction or information on the delegates.	Needs to add an introduction. Needs to add who is speaking,when and where the conversation is happening.	Gives background of delegates. Needs to add what the conversation is about. Needs to tell when the conversation is happening.	Gives backgrounds of delegates. Tells the audience what toexpect in the conversation. Mentions the date and scene.
Requirements	Only one issue is addressed.	Only two issues are presented.	Only three issues are presented.	All four issues are presented in-depth.
Cooperative Group Work	Cannot work with others in most situations. Cannot share decisions or responsibilities.	Works with others but has difficulty sharing decisions and responsibilities.	Works well with others. Takes part in most decisions and contributes fair share to group.	Works well with others. Assumes a clear role and related responsibilities. Motivates others to do their best.
Oral Presentation Skills	Great difficulty communicating ideas. Poor voice projection. Little preparation or incomplete work.	Some difficulty communicating ideas, due to voice projection, lack of preparation, or incomplete work.	Communicates ideas with proper voice projection. Adequate preparation and delivery.	Communicates ideas with enthusiasm, proper voice projection, appropriate language, and clear delivery.

Figure 7-1. Rubric for Evaluation of Podcasts

students were asked to record a 5-minute reading of a passage from literature being read for a class discussion followed by a 5-minute reflection on the reasons for their choice of the passage, analysis of the passage's language and themes, and how it related to the larger text (http://acad.swarthmore.edu/weblog/e52b) (Evans, 2006).

Students can record their reading of stories by passing a digital recorder around a circle, with each student reading a section or paragraph. Their readings can then be edited on GarageBand or Audacity and shared with the students to help them understand the story. Students can add material—images, music, links—

to portray their interpretations of the story. For example, junior high students at West Junior High School, Hopkins, Minnesota, listened to stories about the town of Lake Wobegon on Garrison Keillor's *Prairie Home Companion*. Because they had created their own fictional town populated by characters, they created a radio play podcast based on stories about their characters in this fictional town, using Garageband to add sound effects to their production.

Students could perform a reader's theater production (http://podtheatre.pbwiki.com/Background) based on existing scripts in the public domain (http://www.teachingheart.net/readerstheater.htm), by creating a 10-minute play (http://www.10-minute-plays.com/index.html), or by creating their own scripts based on issues they face in their lives.

From listening to news podcasts such as CNN Student News (http://www.cnn.com/education), students can create their own classroom or school news podcasts as a radio broadcast similar to the Radio WillowWeb broadcast (http://www.mpsomaha.org/willow/radio) produced by students at the Willowdale Elementary School in Omaha, Nebraska. In doing so, they write scripts for minidramas that include the use of sound effects or conduct interviews with people about their perceptions of news events. To obtain ideas for shows, they can listen to BlogTalkRadio (http://www.blogtalkradio.com), which hosts student-produced shows.

Students can use podcasts to communicate with different parts of the world. Students participating in the global Rock Our World project (http://www.rockourworld.org), share podcasts and videos across seven continents. In the International Teen Life project (http://teenlife.pbwiki.com), students from four different countries engage in exchanges using Skype calls to discuss issues they face in their own countries and how they relate to those issues. In foreign language classes, students exchange podcasts with other students all over the world using eLanguages (http://www.elanguages.org) as part of learning to communicate using different languages.

Using Podcasts as a Teaching Tool

Teachers use podcasts to provide students with lectures, summaries of or reflections on readings and discussions, or study guides that students can listen to on their own—for example, podcasts on issues in writing (Krause, 2006). Students like the fact that they can listen to the podcasts for reviewing readings and notes when they are studying at home.

The use of podcasts as a teaching tool is reflected in the efforts of Bob Sprankle, a teacher at Wells Elementary School in Wells, Maine, a primary school. (His Bit By Bit podcast [http://bobsprankle.com/bitbybit_wordpress] features discussion of the use of Web 2.0 tools). For many years, Bob created a podcast, Bob Sprankle's Room 208 (http://bobsprankle.com/blog/), featuring his third- and fourth-grade students. This podcast received such attention that it was syndicated on iTunes. Students created weekly podcasts based on their own topics, as well as reports on school events or field trips. The students learned to work collaboratively to create their podcasts on Mac computers that recorded into GarageBand for editing. As Sprankle (Apple Education, 2006) noted:

> Instead of me teaching the kids discrete skills in isolation—such as research, writing, and making presentations—in the process of making podcasts they've started teaching each other these skills…In their small groups I'll hear them say, "That's not right; you have to change this." Then when they come together as a whole group, they'll do it again. The instruction is just so genuine. (p. 1)

Sprankle noted that having to create a polished performance influenced their attention to editing:

> They'll call someone on a grammatical error that I would have let slide, thinking it was too sophisticated…They may not know how to name it, but they know it's incorrect. Creating the podcasts has completely changed their writing and language skills. (p. 1)

Sprankle posted the podcasts with RSS feeds on his blog, and parents subscribed to these podcasts on iTunes so that they could listen to their students' work, school concerts, or a field trip report.

Then, in 2006–2007, Sprankle became the school's tech coordinator and promoted the use of podcasts to foster a sense of community for students, teachers, and parents. As he worked with students at different grade levels, he created podcasts that provided weekly reports about students' uses of technology tools, including interviews with teachers about classroom activities and students' descriptions of their experiences.

Creating Podcasts

In creating podcasts, students should first determine the purpose and audience. They should also select a specific topic for a production, given the fact that audiences who may want to listen to their podcast are doing so based on their selection of that specific topic as listed on a podcast directory (Farkas, 2006).

Because some students may feel awkward sustaining a monologue podcast, they could join with one or more other students to create a conversational podcast.

Many podcasts consist of two or three people sharing their ideas in a conversation, including phone interviews with guests using Skype.

To organize their podcasts, students could create a script, outline, or set of notes that highlights the key points and information they want to convey, which serves to organize and focus their podcast. Having a well-organized script helps to limit the podcast length. Because long podcasts consume storage space on a server, it is important to keep their podcasts relatively short by avoiding a lot of unnecessary extraneous chatter.

Producing podcasts essentially involves recording into a computer using a USB or internal microphone, editing the program, and then exporting the file for distribution as an MP3 file, usually attached to a blog so that audiences can subscribe to the blog's feed. There are numerous online tutorials listed on the wiki site (@ = Creating Podcasts and Podcast Resources)—for example, the PoducateMe guide (http://www.poducateme.com/guide). Inexpensive equipment such as microphones, recorders, mixing boards, and headphones can be purchased at discount online sites or stores (@ = Podcasting equipment and software). For reviews and advice on use of these tools, see @ = Reviews of podcasting tools.

In selecting tools for producing podcasts, it's important to recognize that students do not need to have high-end, expensive equipment to create podcasts. In most cases, current computers include their own internal microphone. If not, students need a USB microphone that plugs into a computer. Students can use either condenser USB microphones that provide high-quality audio or dynamic USB microphones that are less expensive. If they use a high-quality condenser microphone, they should also employ a windscreen or pop filter that filters out hissing or popping sounds made by *p*'s. For recording online phone calls, they should use a headset microphone to eliminate noise (@ = Recording equipment and use of Skype).

Students can record onto iPods using the Belkin Voice Recorder or Griffin iTalk recorders or other digital recording devices such as the iRiver T recorders (http://www.iriveramerica.com) to record audio. However, these recorders may have limited memory capacity, so they may not be useful for longer sustained recordings. Students can also record on Webcams such as the iSight camera, which contains a directional microphone that sends an audio signal to QuickTime Player.

To record their podcasts, students first need to connect their USB microphone to their computer or to a mixing board and audio interface. They may want to use a mixing board and audio interface if they have several different students recording using different microphones. Students also need to have headphones to listen to the actual podcast recording rather than listening to the recording through computer speakers that create feedback. If they try to monitor their recording without headphones, they will experience some feedback noise. Students can get relatively inexpensive headphones or a combination microphone and headphone set such as the Logitech USB Headset 250 (http://www.logitech.com).

Students record directly into their computer using free programs such as Audacity, Cakewalk Home Studio 2 for Windows, WavePad, Audio Hijack Pro, Mix Cast Live, or Apple Garageband 3 or 4, programs that can also be used to edit. For example, Apple Garageband 3 or 4 includes a Speech Enhancer feature that can be used to reduce what can often be annoying background noises. They can also use sites such as PodcastPeople (http://podcastpeople.com) for creating and storing podcasts for a relatively low monthly subscription fee.

Recording and Editing Podcasts

Students need to record and edit their podcasts using software such as GarageBand (Mac only: with iLife), the open-source Audacity (http://audacity.sourceforge.net), or software such as WireTap Studio, Audio Cleaning Lab 10, Audio Hijack Pro, Cakewalk Home Studio 2, or Propaganda (@ = Podcasting editing software).

Before recording, students should check their computer preferences to make sure their microphones are selected and that the mute buttons are off. In recording and editing in Audacity, students create different audio tracks to adjust the sound level in each track. Students can then remove errors or silences, as well as add sound effects, or insert interview answers if they are using a double-ended technique, and/or add music.

To use Audacity, they first need to set up their preferences in "Edit Preferences." They select "Audio I/O" (Input/Output)—with output as their sound card and input as their microphone option. Under the "Sound Quality" tab, they can then set the sound quality—the higher the rate, the larger their file. The 44100 Hz/16 bit will generate good quality.

Under "File Export," Mac users should select "16 bit AIFF," and Windows users could select "WAV 16 bit" for use in exporting their files.

Then, under "File," they select "Save Project" and give their file a name. Then, under "Project," they select "New Audio Track," and a gray-colored track will appear. They then click on the red record button to start to record a test of their voice—to hear how they sound on their headphones on a playback. They can then record—and their voice appears as a blue waveform.

They can edit out silences or noises, as well as add music to another track. They choose the Selection tool and then move their cursor over the blue waveform to highlight the section that they want to edit. Then, under the Edit menu, they select "Cut" to delete the section (or "Delete" in Mac or "Backspace" in Windows) or "Copy" to move the section elsewhere using "Paste." (They should not select "Trim"—that will cut everything else but their selected material).

Once they are done, they then select "File" to export their file as an MP3 file. To do so, they need to install a separate, free encoder, LAME (http://audacity.sourceforge.net/help/faq?s=install&i=lame-mp3). When they click on "Export as MP3," they will be asked to link to the "lame_enc.dll file" on their computer.

They can also create ID3 tags that provide listeners with a display of the podcaster's name, an image, podcast and episode title, date and/or genre, and copyright information on an MP3 player.

In using GarageBand 3 or 4, students choose "Track" and then the "New Track" option and then select the option "Real Instrument," because they are recording using their voice. They then select the "Male Voice" or "Female Voice" tracks and test out their microphone recording level by noting the amount of green that appears in the right section of the Voice panel. The Podcast Track is for adding images; the Jingles and Radio tracks are for adding music or sounds; the No Effects is available if they don't want to use the male or female voice options—but it generally works better to select the male or female voice options. They then click "Record" to record their podcast and click on "Record" again to stop recording (they can also click the shift bar).

To edit, students select the track with the waveform at the top that then creates the Track Editor on the bottom for editing that track. To edit a section of the track, they select an area they want to edit using the mouse—that section appears in dark blue. They can then select "Edit" and "Cut" to remove that section, resulting in a gray gap. To close the gap, they use their mouse to slide the right side to close up the gap.

As with Audacity, students can add in loops available on Garageband—sound effects, jingles, or music—as well as raise or lower the voice sound, and add in visual images that cue audiences about a podcast's different segments or chapters.

Students may also import online music or sound effects to include in their podcasts, but they must pay royalties for copyrighted music and sound effects. For free music, students can go to Freeplaymusic (http://www.freeplaymusic.com), or for free sound effects they can go to PartnersinRhyme (http://www.partnersinrhyme.com/pir/PIRsfx.shtml). They may also use free Creative Commons (http://creativecommons.org) licensed music that requires that they cite attributions to the musicians. To review legal considerations related to the use of copyrighted material on their podcasts, students can go to the Creative Commons Podcasting Guide (http://wiki.creativecommons.org/Podcasting_Legal_Guide).

Students then export their files. Because GarageBand doesn't export MP3 files, they need to select "Send Song to iTunes" in GarageBand. Then they find their file in iTunes and, under "Advanced," select "Convert Selection to iPod." To add ID3 tags, they select "File," "Get Info," and then fill in information for the name, artist, year, album, track number, composer, comments, and genre (select podcast).

Uploading and Distributing Podcasts

Once students have completed their MP3 files, they upload their files to a school server, using FTP (file transfer protocol), to iWeb (Macs) or free sites for storing podcasts such as Ourmedia.

However, if they want to distribute their podcasts using blogs or on iTunes, they still need to use RSS 2.0 feeds. The key step in terms of distribution of the podcast is to create a 2.0 RSS feed using Feedburner (http://Feedburner.com), FeedForAll (http://www.feedforall.com), or Podomatic (http://podomatic.com). In Feedburner, they go to "Settings" and select "Formatting." Then, they find the "Show Link Field" and click on "Yes."

To add a feed to a Blogger blog, they first add their MP3 file to their blog by going to Posting-Create, adding a title and show notes, then adding a link to the file and publish—creating a URL link. They then go to "Setting-Site Feed" to obtain a feed address—which is in Atom. To convert their Atom Feed to an RSS 2.0 feed, they go to Feedburner, and paste in the Atom feed URL to create an RSS feed for inclusion in iTunes (for further information about podcast promotion see Van Orden, 2006 and Morriset al., 2008) (@ = Publishing and promoting podcasts).

Audio and Video Conferencing

Podcasts often consist of guest interviews recorded using VOIP (Voice over Internet Protocol), audio or video conferencing tools such as Skype (http://www.Skype.com), Gizmo (http://www.gizmoproject.com), or iChat (Mac only). These tools can be used to engage students in synchronous interviews with experts, authors, parents, and students in other classrooms. These interviews may or may not be recorded for use in podcasts—students may simply engage in a live, synchronous chat that may not be recorded.

To engage in phone interviews, students can use a Radio Shack Recorder Control linked to a digital recorder. Or they can use their computers as recorders, using Phone Valet (http://www.parliant.com) or CallCorder for PC (http://www.callcorder.com). However, the most common approach to audio conferencing is through use of Skye, Gizmo, or iChat. Skype (http://www.skype.com) is a free telephone software for communication between Skype users (Fryer, 2006). (If students are calling someone who is not a Skype user, they need to employ the fee-based SkypeOut that charges 2 cents a minute.) They can use Gizmo (http//www.gizmoproject.com) or iChat, which involves a lot of the same features as Skype. Skype and Gizmo can be used record the conversation to produce digital files for creation of a podcast; for recording interviews with iChat, students need to switch to GarageBand to record the interview (Hendron, 2008). There are also tools such as GabCast (http://www.gabcast.com), which can be used to record calls and, for a fee, store them on a server. Another option is to employ commercial program such as Call Recorder for Skype (Mac), WireTap Pro (Mac), Hotrecorder (PC), KishKish (PC), PowerGramo (PC) (@ = Recording techniques and use of Skype).

However, for use in podcasting, they will need to record their calls. For recording Skype calls, students can use AudioHijack Pro (http://www.rogueamoega.com)(Macs), WireTap Studio (http:// www.ambrosiasw.com/utilities/wiretap) (Macs), Hotrecorder (www.hotrecorder.com)(PC) or CallBurner (http://www.callburner.com)(PC) (for a useful screencast: http://conversationsnetwork.org/forum). In Gizmo, a caller or guest can simply select a record button to create a WAV file to edit and create a podcast (Hendron, 2008).

Students can create video conferences using tools such as iChat (Mac), NetMeeting (Windows XP), Windows Meeting Space (Windows Vista), Adobe Breeze Meeting (http://www.adobe.com/resources/breeze/meeting), Orbitalk (http://www.orbitalk.com), Voxwire (http://www.voxwire.com), or VoiceCafe (http://www.voicecafe.org).

Using Cell Phones in the Classrooms

Given the ubiquitous, mobile nature of cell phones and iPhones, rather than ban them in the classroom, teachers can exploit their use to engage students in a range of different digital writing activities (Kolb, 2008) (@ = Using cell phones in the classroom):

- Recording messages using Gabcast (http://www.gabcast.com), Gcast (http://www.gcast.com), Hipcast (http://www.audioblog.com), or Yodio (https://beta.yodio.com) to post on blogs or podcasts (Kolb, 2008; Krause, 2006). Students can use Jott (http://www.jott.com) to send an e-mail message to cell phones, as well as to Twitter, FaceBook, Blogger, Livejournal, and other third-party applications. Cell phones are particularly useful for recording specific field notes when students are traveling or on field trips.

- Searching for information on Google using Google Mobile (http://www.google.com/mobile/search/index.html) or sharing of information as part of a social network on Cellphedia (http://www.cellphedia.com).

- Gathering information on students' opinions or attitudes using Poll Everywhere (http://www.polleverywhere.com) and then projecting the results as bar graphs.
- Using the cameras in cell phones to take pictures of information or notes on white- or blackboards or images for use in blogging. Students can also send cell-phone photos directly to Flickr via their e-mail (http://flickr.com/account/uploadbyemail).

Using Ed.VoiceThread

Another popular tool for fostering audio communication is Ed.VoiceThread (http://ed.voicethread.com) (@ = Using Ed.VoiceThread). Ed.VoiceThread can be used by students to add verbal or text commentary to a slideshow of images for posting on the Web. In contrast to the more public VoiceThread.com, Ed.VoiceThread was created in early 2008 for use only by K–12 students, educators, and administrators. (Because the free accounts on VoiceThread are often blocked by school districts, there is a $10 verification fee for educators or a monthly schoolwide fee of $100.) One advantage of using Ed.VoiceThread is that because students can have their individual accounts, students can then retain their own Ed.VoiceThread accounts for their entire school career, making it an ideal tool for use in long-term e-portfolio reflection on their writing.

In a class of 15 eighth-grade struggling readers and writers, students took photos of different parts of their school: the lunchroom, media center, gym, classrooms, and so on. Working in groups, they then wrote descriptive commentary on storyboard maps describing specific aspects of their images. They recorded their comments onto Ed.VoiceThread, in some cases choosing to add only text comments. Knowing that their productions would be viewed by audiences served to motivate students to generate descriptive writing about their images.

Creating Vlogs

Another option for students to communicate in a multimodal manner is the use of vlogs—blogs with video content (Bryant, 2006; Dedman & Paul, 2006; Verdi & Hodson, 2006). To create a vlog post, students can post their video clips on YouTube, create a URL link, and then insert that link in their blog. Rather than simply producing a blog post as a print text, students create a video to convey their message. Their entire post could be just a video or would use a video to supplement their written post (@ = Vlog tools).

Students can create video podcasts or vodcasts that are similar to vlogs by combining audio voice-over and video (@ = Video podcasts). Students may create photologs in which they share their photos along with commentaries; for examples, see Fotolog (http://www.fotolog.com), Photoblogs (http://www.photoblogs.org), or TextAmerica (http://www.textamerica.com). They can also submit photos or videos directly to their blogs using cell phones—what is described as *moblogging*. In moblogging, they are sending a picture or video to an e-mail account that then posts it to their blog (to create moblogs for Blogger, see http://www.blogger.com/mobile-start.g).

Given the increased use of video viewing on iPods, iPhones, and MP3 players, vlogs have increased in popularity. Vlogs can be used to provide audiences with visual demonstrations of how to do certain things. Richard created some tutorials on vlogging (http://digitalwriting.pbwiki.com/Vlog+production+tutorials); see also a tutorial by Steve Garfield, John Barth, Jason Crow and Four-Eyed Monsters (http://projectnml.org/examplars/06vlog).

Vlogs provide an interactive means for sharing videos. Rather than simply creating videos to park on YouTube, through the use of RSS feeds to their vlogs, students can share their videos with others in the class as well as larger audiences. Audiences can then comment on vlog posts, providing producers with a sense of audience reaction to their work.

Students can best learn about vlogs by viewing vlogs found on vlog directories such as Mefeedia (http://mefeedia.com), FireAnt (http://fireant.tv), iTunes (http://www.apple.com/itunes), or VlogDir (http://www.vlogdir.com) (@ = Vlog tools). In viewing these vlogs, students could analyze their quality and rhetorical effectiveness in terms of how they engage audiences through use of video shooting techniques, sound, lightening, and editing. They could also analyze how vlogs convey producers' strong interest or passion about a certain phenomenon through their delivery, nonverbal cues, and knowledge. They could note how producers keep vlogs relatively short (no more than 10 minutes) through use of editing techniques.

Producing Vlogs

In producing vlogs, students need to consider their purposes and audiences for use of video. Video lends itself particularly well to talking-head interviews—with a family member as part of an oral history project, an interview with people concerned about a certain issue, or a student producer providing a visual walking tour of a certain place or site—images that themselves serve to dramatize people's verbal perceptions in ways that are superior to simply quoting these people.

To organize their vlogs, students should create a script that highlights the different parts of their vlog, along with any voice-over narrative they will be using. They can then use their script to create a rough storyboard that sketches out the different shots and locations, as well the length of shots and use of any music or sound effects. If they are inserting video clips, they can go to sites, such as YouTube.com, Voeh, BlipTV, or metacafe.com, that allow users to share non-copyrighted video clips.

If they are going to be using a lot of different shots in different places rather than just shooting themselves or someone else talking, they should create a storyboard with stick people to determine the kinds of shots or angles they want to employ: close-ups versus mid-shots (waist up) versus long or establishing shots of a setting, as well as the use of cutaway shots showing people's reactions to actions. They also need to provide ample lighting when shooting indoors, and when shooting outdoors, to avoid shooting into the sun. They should use a tripod to keep the camera steady.

Students need to know that because they are compressing their video typically to a 320 x 240 screen size for online sharing, they do not necessarily need to employ an expensive, high-end digital camera for filming.

In shooting their vlogs using a digital video or still camera, they need practice in shooting themselves as they are walking or shooting interviews by holding out the camera in a comfortable position. They also need to keep the camera in close enough to themselves or other speakers to ensure high sound quality.

If students are simply creating a talking-head vlog of themselves, they can use a computer with an internal Webcam or a plug-in Webcam or camcorder. If they are using a Mac, they can open up iMovie and record right into iMovie for further editing. On iMovie, they move the button from edit to record (the video camera icon) and push down on the space bar. When they have completed recording a certain segment, they push down the space bar again, and the clip of that segment appears in the iMovie clip box. Similarly, on a PC, they can use Windows Movie Maker. When they start up Windows Movie Maker, they first need to turn on the Webcam on the top of the screen so they see themselves on the screen. They can then record their video and edit it by dragging clips into the strip along the bottom of the screen.

Students can use YouTube to record videos on a Webcam using the YouTube Quick Capture. They need to go to "Upload videos" and provide information about their video. They then select "Use Quick Capture" and then click "Record." Their video will then be stored on YouTube so that they can then copy the embed code to their blog.

Although students can store their videos on their computers, because these computers may have limited space or they may be using mobile laptop computers in a school, they will need to store them on DVDs, 2 GB USB flash drives, portable external hard drives, or a school server.

Once students shoot their video, they then import that video to their computers for editing with iMovie, Windows Movie Maker, or any number of other editing tools. Students can also combine iMovie with iChat AV and iSight in which they conduct online videoconferences to then include in their productions. The introduction of Web-based editing tools such as Jumpcut, Eyespot, Grouper, VideoEgg, and Motionbox means that students can do all their editing on online sites.

Once students have imported their clips into a galley on iMovie or Windows Movie Maker, they then move them into the clip viewer or timeline along the bottom to edit these clips. They can then cut unnecessary material, and add titles, transitions, and royalty-free music (http://www.royaltyfreemusic.com). They need to save and compress their file to create a Quick Time file using iMovie or by creating .wmv files using Windows Media.

In using a blog, students need to store their video on a video host such as their school server, the Internet Archive (http://archive.org), Ourmedia (http://ourmedia.org), MeFeedia (http://mefeedia.com), Blip.tv (http://blip.tv), dailymotion (http://www.dailymotion.com), or Uth TV (http://www.uthtv.com). If their video is less than 10 minutes or 100 MB, they can store their video on YouTube. They then can then add a link to their blog to create RSS feeds to syndicate their vlog.

Student Engagement With Vlogging

Creating vlog posts can be engaging for those students who prefer to convey their ideas in a more multimodal format. Trish Devine, a student in Elizabeth Boeser's college writing class, responded on her own initiative to the novel, *Montana* (Watson, 1993) by creating vlog posts in which she recorded her analysis of the novel. Although her initial posts were simply talking-head commentaries, as she created more posts, she began to add pictures and sound clips using iMovie. In an interview with Richard about her vlogging, she noted that creating vlog posts enhanced her own sense of voice and self-expression:

> It was a more creative way to express myself because you can do a lot more with adding pictures and sounds; it allowed me to put in parts of myself into it by picking the pictures and sound clips. I put in a lot of music that I like as background music or pictures that you personally like so that you can show parts of what you are, like your personality.

She also varied her outfits in ways that reflected the topics of her posts. For example, in her first post (Figure 7-2), she is wearing a cowboy hat when talking about the characters.

Figure 7-2. Cowboy Hat

She attributes much of her motivation in doing vlogging to her sense of her teacher, Elizabeth, as an audience who would appreciate her use of video (Elizabeth also teaches a video production class) and her creativity: "Sometimes I liked to incorporate the different outfits so that it would be more visually appealing for Boeser to watch . . . she's friendly to her students, so it was like making a blog for a friend, so it wasn't nerve-racking."

Elizabeth used blog comments to support Trish's multimodal experimentation. In responding to her initial vlog post, she notes:

> I am flattered by not only the picture but also the hat. I enjoyed listening to your thoughts, especially about the homemade skis. I also like that you add in pictures of the guns. That little gun is soooooo little. I'd like to see how you add in your pictures. Your technology rocks. Maybe that's why you are Techno Trish.

After her initial post, Trish started to add images and music. For example, in her second post, in describing the fact that the sheriff in the novel was also a farmer, she included a picture of a farm. And in describing the father and grandfather, she posed with a mustache and added background music (Figure 7-3):

Elizabeth then responded:

> I love your mustache! What a great disguise. I can hardly tell it is you. How do you choose your musical selections? I like the costumes and pictures. More than that, I like how you tie it into the text.

In discussing the theme of racism in the novel, she embedded her drawing of racism (Figure 7-4), with the Beatles's song "All You

Figure 7-3. Mustache Pose

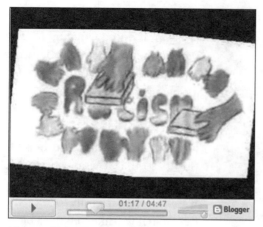

Figure 7-4. Racism in the Novel

Need is Love" playing in the background.

In a final e-portfolio reflection, Trish described her vlogging experience:

> I didn't have any vlogging experience before this class. I thought it was a really awesome way of blogging. It's a very intimate situation because it's just me in front of a camera talking about my feelings. There's no text to hide behind. It helped me to overcome some of my shyness especially when the class watched them. I was happy that people enjoyed watching them. It was a real confidence booster.

Trish also noted how her vlogs appeal to her peer audience:

> When you make a video, you're more proud of it than something's written because it's different so that people acknowledge that—people will say that they really enjoyed certain parts of it. They are a lot of work and time-consuming, but they are something I look back on and I'm glad I did them.

Using Digital Audio and Video Production Tools With Students With Learning Disabilities

Another important use of digital audio and video production tools has to do with working with students with learning disabilities who need certain accommodations as required by law to assist them with their writing (Graham, Harris, Fink, & MacArthur, 2003). Schools are legally obligated to provide support for these students so that they can complete homework assignments and teachers do not have cause to exempt students from doing their homework—an illegal denial of student access to instruction (Beckman, 2003). Schools must also provide support staff who know how to employ assistive technology, foster collaboration between teachers and speech therapy staff, train teachers in assistive technology use, provide physical space that is not noisy for use of the hardware, and award academic credit for students learning to employ these tools (Follansbee, 2003).

One of the primary challenges in working with learning-disabled (LD) students, as well as other students who struggle with writing, is the disparity between their proficiency in oral versus written text production (Follansbee, 2003).

Although these students may be relatively proficient in speaking their thoughts, they may experience difficulties in translating their speech into writing (Graham et al., 2003). If they have difficulty in handwriting, their hand movement may not be able to keep up with their thinking. If they have difficulty spelling words, they may struggle in writing words, leading to frustration and a lack of motivation to write. Teachers therefore employ digital audio or video production tools to help LD students address their difficulties in the following: (Troia, 2006, p. 329)

- Generating or organizing ideas, given their lack of organizational structures
- Planning for writing and shifting those plans
- Revising texts, given their inability to adopt audience perspectives or recognize errors
- Coping with handwriting or spelling
- Being motivated to write, given their frustrations in producing writing

Given these challenges, Trioia (2006) argues that writing instruction for LD students needs to do the following:

- Recognize individual differences in students' particular strengths and difficulties
- Create meaningful writing tasks with real purposes and audiences
- Provide students with explicit instruction in writing processes and strategies
- Focus on students' spelling and handwriting

Digital text-to-speech and speech-to-text tools can help these students in moving between oral and written discourse. In the past decade, various organizations have created a range of software tools to assist students with learning disabilities in their literacy learning (@=Learning disabilities software).

Text-to-Speech (TTS) Tools

Text-to-Speech (TTS) tools transform print texts into audio for visually impaired students or students who learn better from listening to than from reading a text. LD students are more likely to identify errors in their writing when they hear their writing than when they just read their text (Graham et al., 2003). For students who have difficulty writing, when they create texts using TTS tools such as Texthelp Read&Write (http://www.texthelp.com), Readthewords (http://readthewords.com), Apple Voices (on OS 10.5), or Write: OutLoud (http://www.donjohnston.com/products/write_outloud/index.html), they can then hear that text read to them. They can also use tools such as TextAloud (http://

www.nextup.com) or HearWho (http://www.hearwho.com) to create MP3 files for podcasting and CAST's eReader (http://www.cast.org) to insert links or clips or take notes as they read. Students can also select from a range of different voice types—melodic versus monotone—allowing them to then experiment with relationships between their writing and creation of different kinds of voices (Montgomery & Marks, 2006) (@ = Text-to-speech software).

Students can create audio versions of their blog posts using what is known as autocasting software using Talkr (http://www.talkr.com), Bluegrind (http://www.bluegrind.com), Switch (http://www.nch.com.au/switch/), NaturalReader (http://www.naturalreaders.com), TextAloud (http://www.nextup.com/TextAloud), or Spoken Text (http://www.spokentext.net). They can listen to their posts to hear instances of language use they could revise. To listen to their own writing, they could also use Clicker 5 or Writing With Symbols 2000. When students select pictures, words, letters, or phrases from the screen, they hear the word, or the word that goes with the Clicker Writer word processor; they can hear what they have written with the Clicker Writer.

LD students can also use TTS word-processing programs such as IntelliTalk 3 (http://www.intellitools.com), Kurzweil 3000 (http://www.kurzweiledu.com), or WriteAway 2000 (http://www.specialneedscomputers.ca/c-wa.htm) to listen to their writing to detect editing issues (Barbetta & Spears-Bunton, 2007). Students with dyslexia can use programs such as WriteAssist or DyslexiWrite that provide them with oral suggestions for words as they are typing these words.

LD students also benefit from word prediction software such as Co:Writer 4000 (http://www.donjohnston.com), Aurora (http://www.qurora-systems.com), or Word Q (http://www.wordq.com), which predict subsequent words based on word frequency and context (Barbetta & Spears-Bunton, 2007). Based on the initial letters typed, this software predicts the word a student is intending to type as well as sounding out the words (MacArthur, 2006). It provides students with word-choice options of correctly spelled words so that they are not slowed down by word selection or frustrations with correct spelling (Montgomery & Marks, 2006).

Deaf or hard-of-hearing students can employ iCommunicator (http://www.myicommunicator.com), which translates their speech into text and text into speech, and provides video sign-language communication so that students can view a person signing text on the screen.

Speech-to-Text, Voice-Recognition, and Dictation Tools

LD students, as well as students with low literacy skills or high writing apprehension, benefit from speech-to-text dictation tools. Voice-recognition or dictation tools assist students who have difficulty with editing and spelling issues by helping them focus on what they are trying to communicate. Students can use Dragon NaturallySpeaking (http://www.nuance.com/naturallyspeaking) (PC), IBM ViaVoice (http://www.scansoft.com/viavoice) (PC and Mac), iListen (http://www.MacSpeech.com)(Mac), QPointer Voice (http://www.enablemart.com), and CoolSoft Voice Recognition (http://www.coolsoftllc.com/main.asp). It is also the case that Windows XP and Windows Vista include Windows Speech Recognition (http://www.microsoft.com/enable/products/windowsvista/speech.aspx) (@ = Speech-to-text dictating software).

Dragon Naturally Speaking Preferred or Pro versions are particularly effective for use with LD students, for they contain features such as verbal feedback to the student as well as synthesized reading back for what appears on the screen so that as with text-to-speech software, students can hear the text they have produced (Follansbee, 2003). This means that as students hear verbal feedback or the words they have created, they can then correct those words.

When using the Dragon Naturally Speaking Pro dictation software, LD students can use the KeyStone ScreenSpeaker (http://www.keyspell.net/catalog/product_info.php?products_id=30); in the initial training of this software, students listen to their own words as they are read back to them (Beckman, 2003). As words that they dictated appear on the screen, they will be read back to the student will note misspellings. Students can use the Kurzweil 3000 (http://www.kurzweiledu.com) or the Don Johnston Draft: Builder (http://www.donjohnston.com/downloads/templates/) to dictate according to well-defined organizational templates that serve to structure students' thinking (Beckman, 2003).

Although speech-to-text software is particularly helpful for LD students in terms of improving their writing quality (MacArthur, 2006), there are a number of challenges involved in using voice-recognition software; this software may work effectively only for certain students. Students need to be fluent, articulate slowly, not have speech impediments, dictate punctuation, recognize that dictated speech in writing still needs revision, and be willing to devote time for training (Follansbee, 2003; Hecker & Engstrom, 2005). Although newer versions of this software are more consistent with natural speech than older versions that required students to pause between words, the software may still lack accuracy, producing incomprehensible text.

Translation Software

All this assumes that students are fluent in English. However, there is an increasing number of students in schools who are orally fluent in their native language but who need assistance in acquiring both oral and written English. These students often have difficulty when trying to read Web-based texts or websites that are only in English. To build their confidence in their language fluency, it is also useful to provide these students, as well as their parents, with documents written in Spanish or other languages. The free IBM TradúceloAhora! (Translate Now!) software (http://www.traduceloahora.org/en/home.html) translates e-mails and Web pages into Spanish (Murrey, 2007). There are also numerous other programs that can translate English into other languages, as well as translate students' writing into their native language into English (@ = Translation software).

Summary

The various digital audio and video production tools described in this chapter can serve to enhance writing instruction by providing students with a means for performing their writing to audiences and attending to the sound of their words, leading to further revision and editing. By creating podcasts or vlogs, students can share their productions with audiences on the Web. Audio digital software can assist LD students in dictating their writing as well as providing verbal recordings of their texts.

Chapter
Eight

Designing and Editing
Digital Writing

When users go online, they expect to find texts with images and icons that are engaging and easy to navigate and read. For example, the e-zine *Teen Voices*, written by and for adolescent females (Figure 8-1), provides a forum for this group to address issues that concern them.

Figure 8-1. Teen Voices Online

161

The opening page employs bright colors, images, icons, and language to welcome adolescent females to the *Teen Voices* site. The major titles: "Go Home," "Get Published," "SUBSCRIBE," "Make Some Noise!," "Infosites," and "Back Issues," highlight the different sections of the page. The page is organized by two major horizontal columns, each in its own color. The purple column on the left focuses on descriptions of *Teen Voices* itself, with a parallel structure of verbs—"Welcome" and "Visit," are designed to attract audiences into the *Teen Voices* community. The central right column includes an image of the magazine with a description of future stories and events on the right side. A reader's eyes first goes to the "Welcome" column and then moves to the right side to read about the magazine contents.

The language, with repeated uses of you, and "Read along—and then head outside" serve to create a bond between text and audience. The summary "Welcome to Teen Voices Online" describes the focus of the current issue on the 2008 Summer Olympics and topics related to females' participation in athletics, as well as "poetry and fiction that takes you right onto the field," invitations to engage the reader.

The design of the *Teen Voices* page involves the use of visual rhetoric to engage audiences. Analyzing visual rhetoric involves focusing on effective design of sites using images, links, video, icons, audio, and text. As the Digirhet group (2006) notes:

> Writing today means weaving text, images, sound, and video—working within and across multiple media, often for delivery within and across digital spaces. And, perhaps now more so than ever before, writing requires a deep attention to context, audience, and meaning-making across the multiple tools and media available to us as writers. (p. 241)

In this chapter, we discuss the importance of teaching students principles of visual digital design—how to select, combine, format, and edit text, images, videos and sound in ways "in which the author creates an *ethos* that requires, encourages, or even discourages different kinds of interactivity for that audience" (Hocks, 2003, p. 632) (@ = Visual rhetoric).

Given the multimodal nature of digital texts, it is important to focus on aspects of design throughout students' creation of such texts. As previously noted, in initially creating their blogs, students need to focus on making design choices in terms of templates, color, font, and layout consistent with the look they want to project. J. Anthony Blair (2004) notes that visual arguments can imply reasons for changing or accepting attitudes, intentions, or behaviors. He cites the example of a television political ad used in the Lyndon Johnson—Barry Goldwater presidential contest, which portrayed a little girl picking flowers followed by a countdown to the explosion of an H-bomb with President Johnson's words in the background, "'These are the stakes, to make a world in which all God's children can live, or go into the darkness. Either we must love each other or we must die'" (p. 50). The ad concludes by urging people to vote for Johnson.

Blair notes that the visual display in this ad implied that Goldwater, known for proposing the use of H-bombs in wars, might use the H-bomb, resulting in the death of the little girl, and that to prevent Goldwater from becoming president and using the H-bomb, voters needed to vote for Johnson. This reasoning was not conveyed solely through the verbal content of the ad; it was primarily conveyed through the emotional impact of its images.

Similarly, documentary filmmakers employ visual images to build visual arguments for their positions. In his documentary *Sicko*, Michael Moore (2007) makes the case that the health care system in America is dysfunctional in contrast to the health care system in other countries. To argue this position, he uses the visual image of taking a group of people who can't afford treatment or expensive drugs on a small boat as they travel from Miami to Cuba, where they can purchase drugs at a fraction of the cost charged in the United States.

Many students already manipulate visual information when they use digital media, such as adding pictures to Facebook pages, creating cartoons, or editing existing images using programs like Photoshop. However, they may not be skilled at the effective use of visual information to create arguments or design multimodal texts. It is therefore important that they learn how to think about the use and design of visual images combined with text and audio to engage in visual rhetoric.

Analyzing Digital Design

One first step in helping students attend to digital design is to have them consider how the use of different formats or designs communicates different meanings to audiences. To focus her students' attention on design features, Anne Wysocki (2004b) has her students complete some writing in crayon instead of on a keyboard, which they find to be challenging. Students discuss the differences in what they wrote, how they wrote it, and how they thought their audiences would respond to their writing. They recognize that the writing with crayons projects a certain persona that differs from that of texts written with word processing.

Students then analyze design features of specific examples of blogs, websites, wikis, digital poetry and storytelling, zines, and other digital texts in terms of how easily and quickly they can comprehend the material and navigate to other pages or links. Students pair up and self-consciously describe think-aloud responses to *how* they are comprehending or processing information on a Web page in response to the following questions:

- What do I notice first on the page? What do I notice next?
- What specific images, icons, font size, color, and sections draw my attention to what things are on the page?
- How quickly and easily can I find things on this page?
- How engaged am I in reading this page?
- If I want more information, what do I do next? If I want to go to another page, do I know what to click on and where I will be going?

Once students are aware of how design features influence their experience, they can then reflect on how design options convey different meaning. Students go to the Blogger set-up site, where they find a wide range of different blog templates to choose from (Figure 8-2).

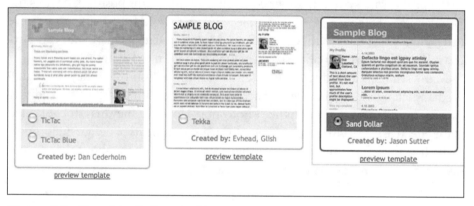

Figure 8-2. Template Options in Blogger

Then, working in pairs, they select those templates and color options that they believe will best serve their purposes and best represent the persona or ethos they wish to project on their blog. They discuss how different images, language, layout, and color on the blog templates have different appeals to their audiences by addressing the following questions:

- What are the specific images and words in this template?
- What is the relative size of the images and words?
- What kinds of information are located where on a page? Are they easy or difficult to find?
- How are these images and words arranged or aligned on the page in the template?
- What is the relationship of images and words in the template?
- What icons, buttons, or words are used to help you navigate the template?

In identifying these different design features of a text, students consider how these features are being used rhetorically to communicate to different audiences and why they might select certain features over others. To engage in this analysis, student can address these questions:

- Who is the audience for this blog?
- What is the message or idea being communicated to this audience in this blog?
- How are the images and words being used to convey this message or idea?
- How do the size, arrangement, and alignment of images convey this message or idea?

Students review actual blogs, as well as other sites, sharing their reactions to how the design features and layout convey the intended messages or content (@ = Blog/wiki/website design). Students reflect on use of the above features in creating websites using Google Page Maker (http://pages.google.com/-/about.html).

Students study examples of "mashups," which combine different websites to create new websites—for example, combining Google Maps with a restaurant guide to provide users with maps for restaurant locations (@ = Mashup examples). Combining different sites requires some attention to how the design features of one site mesh with the design features of another site.

Assessing the Readability of Digital Texts

Another key factor influencing digital design has to do with the ease of comprehension of a digital text or its readability—how easy a text is to comprehend, given readers' search for relevant information on site (Kress, 2003).

Readability is often defined in terms of the level of difficulty of words or sentences, the number of syllables or sentence length, or the number of words in a sentence. Students can use Word to obtain a readability score for their Word documents or employ online readability tools (@ = Readability formulas). However, it is important to note that determining readability simply in terms of words and sentence difficulty does not capture a number of other factors that contribute to an audience's ease of understanding of digital texts. Reading and navigating texts on a screen differs from reading print texts. For example, online users need a lot more white space on a screen to orient their attention than is the case with print texts. It is therefore important to consider a number of other principles of readability contributing to audience comprehension unique to processing digital texts.

One of the differences in how audiences process online versus print texts has to do with their purposes for reading online texts. When audiences go online, they are often looking for certain information—the latest news reports about a political campaign, movie ratings, sports scores, book purchases, medical advice, and so on. In contrast to reading print texts, in which readers' eyes move from left to right and process information in a linear manner, when reading online texts, readers' eyes focus initially on whatever information is most relevant to their purpose or needs (Kress, 2003). If they are shopping for inexpensive cameras, they may first focus on the camera prices.

By recognizing that their readers are seeking information most relevant to their needs, students can design texts that help readers quickly and efficiently locate relevant information or ideas. Too much text information, information located in too many different font sizes, a confusing use of background color or font color, or a misuse of banners or columns can limit easily locating relevant information.

Students might analyze the ways in which images and words are aligned with each other on a page. If there is too much information or it is difficult to determine the function of certain parts of a page or site, then they have more difficulty processing that information. Students can analyze alignment by creating a grid in which information is organized into columns or vertical sections. In this grid, the top vertical sections assume more importance than those images or words on the bottom section.

Students can also determine how readability influences a site's overall appeal. For example, as a writing teacher, Candace Doerr (2007), who works for the Minnesota Writing Project, frequents local National Writing Project sites. In reflecting on the readability of sites, she found that many of these sites included too much information on their front page so that she had difficulty readily locating relevant information. In contrast, she found the layout of the Red Cedar

Writing Project (Figure 8-3) associated with Michigan State University, engaging and easy to navigate:

Figure 8-3. The Red Cedar Writing Project Website

> What jumps out at me about this website is its placement of the teacher front and center. The image almost functions as a hook into the site, by leading you to the story about the teaching consultant who is working on the podcast. This placement of image and content speaks volumes about what the Red Cedar project is: teachers teaching teachers.
>
> As for organization of content, there are two main navigation bars. The top bar placed just above the photo seems to be geared toward those outside the writing project, including information on the summer institute to recruit new teachers. The bottom bar, placed just below the photo, seems to be geared to those teacher consultants already in the writing project, with icons linked to pages related to news, events, and related networks.
>
> This organizational formatting continues with similar black tool bars and headings continuing into the following pages, with headings at the top of each page to remind you where you are.

Doerr (2007) is defining the relationship between use of design features and her engagement with this site.

Another difference between print and digital texts is that in contrast to reading print texts, readers of digital texts quickly scan pages without reading every word. Eye-tracking research on how readers read news sites found that they initially scan for headlines, summaries, and captions; when they read the articles, they read only 75% of the articles (Torkelson, Petersen, & Torkelson, 2002). Given this scan-and-skip reading process, student need to consider how to highlight items as well as how to slow down their readers so that they actually attend to certain key bits of information. For example, providing readers with lists of items rather than sentences or paragraphs functions to summarize important information for quick scanning while also slowing down the reader who is attempting to skip over information.

In light of scan-and-skip processing, students also need to put key information in the beginning of their text. In the traditional essay, students learn to start with an introductory paragraph that provides background context for a topic or thesis articulated later in the essay. In contrast, in writing in their blog or wiki, writers employ an "inverted pyramid" organizational structure by initially stating their overall topic summary in the beginning of their text.

Students can use titles or headings to provide readers with an overall organizational schema for understanding the logical relationships among different sections of a text, which is particularly important in creating a wiki. It is also important that the titles or subheads be retained in the same place on different pages so that audiences know where to look to determine a page's content. On our wiki resource site, the side bar with chapter titles is constant on all the pages.

Students need to limit the amount of information they provide on a page (for example, in PowerPoint), so that they do not overwhelm the reader with too much information to process at any one time. They are then using the white space itself to help readers focus their attention on significant information.

Students need to recognize that the amount of information available is related to how much information in available on a screen—something that differs from reading print texts. In reading screens, readers want to see the front page captured within their initial screen space to avoid scrolling down to find needed information.

Students can analyze and use different fonts or typefaces to convey different meanings associated with the type of font selected—for example, using a larger font size for titles of more significant stories and a smaller font size for less significant stories (@ = Text editing). Wysocki (2004a) distinguishes between the "decorative" use of font (as employed in a stand-alone header, title, or advertising slogan) versus the use of font for "extended reading" as part of the regular text (p. 127). She finds that certain fonts are used as decorative typeface: script, gothic, postmodern, or fonts associated with certain arts movements. For use in extended texts, she identifies a range of different categories of font: Roman, Modern, Slab serif, and Sans serif—differences associated with different levels of formality.

Another readability principle has to do with guiding readers' expectations for navigating across different pages, something previously discussed in terms of navigating hyperlinks. Because readers want to quickly navigate pages, they need a clear idea of where links will take them so that they do not become lost in an endless maze of pages. Readers also need a clear understanding of the content of a link so that they know whether to click on that link to acquire certain information. To guide reader expectations, students need to clearly identify their hotlinks using specific words or phrases summarizing the content of the linked material.

Analyzing Image-Text Relationships

Another important aspect of digital design is the use of visual images—either still or video—to illustrate certain concepts or ideas (@ = Visual design). Students can study the meaning of images by using digital editing software such as the free Photoshop Express (http://www.photoshop.com/express) to vary images and reflect on differences in the meaning of these images. By making an image or a font darker or larger, moving objects around in a frame, or cropping an image, students can anticipate differences in potential audience responses to alternative versions of images.

Students can also analyze the representations of concepts or ideas through images or clips by going to Google Images, Flickr, Yahoo Images, or YouTube and entering certain topics or tags associated with the concepts or ideas they are addressing in their writing. They can then review the different images or clips that appear and discuss how those images or clips effectively capture or convey the meaning of a certain concept or idea. For example, on Flickr, a search for Creative Commons images using the concept *environment* brings up a photo by Isaac Mao, *Environment in China* (Figure 8-4).

Figure 8-4. Isaac Mao's *Environment in China*

Mao's image effectively captures the relationship between air pollution caused by smoke from factories in the background and people's health by showing the woman wearing a protective-mask.

Students can analyze the use of images on book, magazine, e-zine, or yearbook covers to determine their effectiveness in capturing the content of these texts. For example, 17-year-old Jean Beauchamp created a Creative Commons yearbook cover for a 2007 yearbook (Figure 8-5) that shows students looking at a sky-plane creation of the number 2007.

Students can analyze how images are employed in these covers to capture readers' attention and convey the storyline or subject matter in a manner that interests the reader. Beauchamp's cover conveys the idea of students looking at their graduation year, 2007, as well as their future through the image of the blue sky.

Figure 8-5. Jean Beauchamp's Potential Yearbook Cover

Applying Digital Design to Creating Texts

By analyzing texts for their digital design and visual rhetoric, students can then create a range of different types of texts themselves.

Digital Scrapbooks or Posters

Students can create digital scrapbooks, photo albums, or posters including images and texts as a record of their school year, a project, a class field trip, and so on (Nerius, 2007). Students can use iPhoto or Shutterfly Studio (free download from Shutterfly), Clipmarks, Plum, or Tabblo to collect, annotate, comment on, organize, or remix blog posts, images, Web pages, and RSS feeds which can then be shared as a collection with others students and/or turned into a PowerPoint or Ed.VoiceThread presentation (@ = Digital scrapbooks).

Students can use digital scrapbooks to portray their response to a reading. Judy Annan (2006) created an activity in which students identified certain topics and themes based on their reading of the online version of *The Adventures of Huckleberry Finn* (http://www.telerama.com/~joseph/finn/finntitl.html). Students first view an example of a digital scrapbook in the form of a PowerPoint presentation about Mark Twain, "Mark Twain: An American Icon" (http://www.readwritethink.org/lesson_images/lesson787/MTScrapbook.ppt).They then review sites related to the topics and themes portrayed in the novel, find images that reflect their interpretations of these topics and themes, save these images in folders, and copy and paste the images into PowerPoint, as well as saving the URLs on the Landmark Project's Citation Machine (http://citationmachine.net). As they are saving these images, students are also keeping notes for writing about the images. They then reflect on their work, based on the criteria that they need to collect at least 10 scraps of information imported to their PowerPoint. Students share their presentations with their class, and they are evaluated with a rubric that includes criteria for content, design, variety of material, citing of source information, mechanics, understanding of the topic, topic focus, and quality of the final presentation. Students can also create online digital posters using the Web Poster Wizard (http://wizard.4teachers.org) or Gliffy (http://gliffy.com). In doing so, they need to focus their message and rely on visual appeals.

Classroom Newspapers or Newsletters

In support of their digital writing, students can analyze and produce online classroom newspapers or newsletters. In a program sponsored by the American Society of Newspaper Editors, 470 schools now publish online editions available at Myhighschooljournalism.org (Eschoolnews, 2006); see also the Write Site (http://www.writesite.org), designed for middle school students. Students can analyze the use of layout in their school newspaper in terms of how stories are blocked out on pages as well as the effective use of font size, titles, columns, white space, and use of images, or they can consider how these features are used successfully in well-designed online newspapers such as the award-winning Paly High School, Palo Alto, California, newspaper, *Paly Voice* (http://voice.paly.net).

Students can create their own digital classroom newspapers or newsletters to share their writing with parents, peers, or administrators using blogs, wikis, Drupal, Moodle, Google Page Creator, Bricolage, Typo3, or commercial programs such as Apple's iWork Pages 2, to select different layout options for designing classroom newspapers or newsletters (@ = Classroom Newspapers/Newsletters).

In his journalism class at Edina High School in Edina, Minnesota, Jim Hatten has his students analyze the school newspaper and create their own classroom newspaper:

> For 2 years I have used digital literacies in my Introduction to Journalism classes with much success. I created a class website using Google Page Creator. Students are trained from the first day in the semester that class connections should be made through this vehicle (http://edinajournalism.googlepages.com). The first assignment of the semester is to create a blog for the classroom using Blogger.com or WordPress.com, both free blogging services. As a part of this assignment, students learn to comment on the teacher blog to tell me the User Requirements Language (URL) of their blog. I take those URLs and create a new webpage on the class website for all students to find each other's blog pages. Students post story ideas, answers to assignments, and news stories on their blogs. In addition, we use wikis for group work and also for glossaries of terms and techniques in journalism. Discussion boards allow for more writing practice, moving classroom discussion to the digital arena. Sometimes for homework, I assign students to read two blogs and comment on them. Eventually, I use the blogs for critical analysis of one another's work, the works of professional newspapers, and our own high school newspaper. I find that these online tools increase productivity and quality of student work.
>
> In addition to these general classroom Web tools is an online newspaper I created for my Intro to Journalism class (http://edinajournalism.googlepages.com/gazette), which was linked to the class website. I wanted to create an online newspaper for this class because the class had no direct link with the school newspaper, and I wanted my students to have the real experience of being published. Creating an online newspaper allows them the opportunity to have both an audience of their classroom peers and a real-world audience that extends far beyond the classroom walls (including to their parents).
>
> It is my hope that my Introduction to Journalism class's newspaper will become as widely read as the school newspaper, if not more so. The stories that students wrote were electronically submitted to me, and a student editor and I copied and pasted them onto a new Google Page, which was hyperlinked to the class newspaper page. I feel students "owned" their articles more than classes without a means of publication did, because they knew their work would be on the website for all to see. Students also discussed in class which student should have the lead story on the website and why. Discussions revolved around news judgment, writing abilities, and audience analysis. Through discussing which story would appear in which

part of the online newspaper and which stories would be more promi-nently featured, the class applied nearly every aspect of the course goals in a collaborative culminating activity.

Another particularly effective activity was a blog assignment the students created impromptu the day the school newspaper came out (the newsprint version done by the newspaper publication class—a class of students separate from my Introduction to Journalism students). My students requested to critique the other newspaper and have me lead a discussion on the topic. Instead, I assigned the class a blogging assignment in which they could critique a full page or two of the school newspaper. In addition, I asked that each student read two other blogs and comment on other critiques. I also commented on each critique, giving each of my students' electronic feedback that was visible to anyone who wished to see it. Two of the students in my class were also staff members of the school newspaper. Because staff members of the "real" newspaper read our class blogs, the critiques gained a new level of importance. The blogs allowed the students a space where they felt they could honestly and genuinely critique the work of their peers and explore the major foundations of journalism, which were either being upheld or disregarded.

Online newspapers create an inexpensive mass medium for students to experience a real-world application of the skills and efforts they develop in class. Because the audience is open-ended and public, students tend to self-edit better, challenge themselves in their own writing, and think critically when given another student's work to read. It is easier for me as a teacher to manage student homework and monitor missing assignments. Students value their work more and take ownership of their own abilities and downfalls as writers. For each of these reasons (and so many more), digital literacy resources are infinitely valuable to my journalism classes.

Comic Books and Graphic Novels

Another form of digital writing that combines images with text is the digital comic book or graphic novel (McCloud, 2006; Withrow & Barber, 2005) (@ = Comics/graphic novels). Many students are reading graphic and manga novels in print and online (http://www.manga.com), and teachers are assigning sophisticated graphic novels such as *Maus: A Survivor's Tale* (Spiegelman, 1993), *American Born Chinese* (Yang, 2007), and *Persepolis: The Story of a Childhood* (Satrapi, 2004).

To prepare for creating comic books or graphic novels, students can analyze how comic book artists vary their images to position the reader in relationship to the unfolding story. Artists employ changes in focus—moving closer to an object or person (close-up shot) versus farther back (long-shot), to position readers as looking down on an object or person or up at a person. Students can also analyze how writers vary their perspectives and angles within blocks, use blocks to develop a storyline, and employ dialogue in bubbles to portray characters' relationships and conflicts.

They can then use software such as Comic Life (http://plasq.com/comiclife), My Comic Book Creator (http://www.mycomicbookcreator.com), Make Beliefs Comix (http://www.makebeliefscomix.com), or Toondoon (http://www.toondoo.com/Home.do) to access templates, images, balloons, and other features for creating comics. Students then select different template options and import their own digital photos or clip-art images from the program. They can then add dialogue bubbles to create a storyline. For example, using photos of different works of art taken on a field trip to a local art museum, students can create a comic book in which they import the images of the artworks and then add dialogue bubbles describing their reactions to the art.

Students can also create comic book adaptations of the many noncopyrighted literary texts available online, using comics software to create blocks for scenes in stories and avatars for characters. They can then copy and paste characters' dialogue into dialogue bubbles. In doing so, they can create what Kathleen Yancey (2004) describes as "pop-up" writing, an idea based on music videos that include visual pop-up bubbles that contain interpretations, background contexts, or critiques of the music video. In teaching the novel *The Octopus* by Frank Norris, Yancey has groups of students choose at least two of eight contexts related to the novel: epic, romance, gothic, western, railroad history, California history, naturalism, and Norris. They then create pop-up links to these contexts for group presentations as posters, PowerPoints, or websites. She then has students write individual essays in which they interpret stories in the novel through the use of related images, allusions, references, and other texts.

E-Zines

In online e-zines, students use parody, satire, and spoofs to voice their social or political perspectives on issues that concern them, particularly issues of gender or race inequities or the environment (@ = Electronic zines). Because they can publish these e-zines on the Web using a blog, wiki, or website format, they can attract a potential audience with little or no expense. Since they are writing for their peers, they know that they need to engage their peers through a multimodal format. One study of three adolescent girls who published their own e-zine, *Burnt Beauty*, found that they employed intertextual links to other magazines, newspapers, and the Web, both in terms of clips and critical reviews (Guzzetti & Gamboa, 2004). This e-zine featured a discussion of feminism and reviews of TV programs, films, and music, as well as popular culture portrayals of females—for example, a critique of Barbie dolls.

Creating an e-zine as a classroom activity or assignment means that students may be limited in the extent to which they can criticize the school or community, given potential censorship by school administrators. On the other hand, if students want to choose to create an e-zine, they should be supported in making that choice. Tobi Jacobi (2007) argues that using e-zines in the classroom to challenge status quo notions of culture leads to learning. Based on a project in which students in a Colorado high school created zines, she values

> the chaos it inspires, and "zine" terminology has come to symbolize the kind of exploration, collaboration, and debate I want to encourage in students. They need to be mired in conversations about wordplay, document design, and context just as I need to have my expectations about Standard English and genre challenged. Such issues inevitably deepen our classroom conversations and our collective understanding of what it means to be writers whose words circulate in the public sphere. (p. 47)

Rather than grading the e-zines, Jacobi developed a set of guidelines for creating zines that emphasized the value of collaborative, construction of zines, experimentation with alternative forms of writing, distribution of zines outside school, and the creation of a "space for dialogue on the ethical issues surrounding the co-optation of zines into the classroom" (p. 48).

Interactive PowerPoint Presentations

Although PowerPoint, Keynote, or Kid Pix Deluxe 3 presentations are frequently employed in classrooms (@ = Presentation tools), these presentations can be one of the least interactive, dialogic forms of digital writing. Presenters often simply read off of their slides without engaging audiences in an interactive manner (Tufte, 2006). Making these presentations more interactive requires a shift in design and content to reduce the amount of information on slides by using short, bulleted lists of topics—fewer than seven bullets, with each item under seven words (Harrington & Rekdal, 2007).

To display online material, students can also use the hyperlink feature to link slides to websites. For example, in creating a PowerPoint for studying the characteristics of the different states of the United States, students could begin with a slide of a map of the United States with links to each state (Siegle, 2006). Then, working together as a class, students create links to further information about each state.

Students can import clip art, photos, and video clips to their slides by going to sites such as Empressr (http://www.empressr.com) or Toufee (http://toufee.com).

When importing clip art and photos, they need to adjust the size or crop the image so that the image fits within a slide along with any captions or other language. Because digital photos often take up large amounts of memory, slowing down loading time, the images need to be optimized by using the "Compress Pictures" option under "Format."

Students can also add audio or video clips to their presentation by embedding an audio or video file into the presentation or by linking to a file in the computer's hard drive, ideally stored with other files for that presentation in the same folder. In adding audio to a slide, students select "Sounds" under "Insert" and then choose whether they are using sound from a gallery, file, or CD, or recording their own sound. They then select whether they want the sound played automatically when they reach a slide or when they click on a speaker icon on a slide. When importing a video file, students select "Movie Insert" and then, as with audio, determine if the video is played when they reach a slide or when they click on the video icon. They can also have the video fill up the full screen by selecting "Play Full Screen" (@ = Digital video).

Students can add any of 59 transitions to move between slides using fades, dissolves, wipes, or other transitions. In creating transitions, students should employ the same, consistent type of transition by selecting "Slide Sorter" and then a global transition.

In presenting their PowerPoints, students need to learn how to do more than simply read their slides by using the slides as summary highlights of their more expanded oral presentation. They also need to avoid rushing through their slides to allow time for audiences to reflect on the information and even pose questions. They can include questions on their slides or blank slides on a handout for peers to engage in free-writing or images and video clips to prompt discussion. To help them move through their presentation, they can employ Presenter View (in PowerPoint 2007), which provides thumbnail lists of the different slides under an active slide as well as notes, time elapsed, slide number, and forward and backward buttons.

Students can publish their presentation on the Web by going to "Save As" and selecting "Single File Web Page"—saving it as a "Mime HTML" file—or selecting "Web Page" to create a folder for uploading to a server. They then select options in "Publish as Web Page" to modify their presentation to make it appropriate for the web.

Students can create online presentations using Slideshare (http://www.slideshare.net), Spresent (http://www.spresent.com), Google Presenter (within Google Docs), or Zoho Show (http://show.zoho.com). One advantage of putting presentations on the Web is that as students are viewing the presentation, they can pause the presentation and type their comments in their blog or in a chat room.

Creating Interactive PowerPoint Presentations About a Novel

In working with her 10th-grade students in a communications class, Heather Johnson of North High School in North St. Paul, Minnesota, used an online PowerPoint presentation to foster students' blog responses to the novel *The Secret Life of Bees* (Kidd, 2004):

> The required communications course that I teach is a comprehensive course that covers public speaking, interpersonal skills, nonverbal skills, conflict resolution, and listening skills. That trimester, I decided to create a blog for my students as a forum for this course where they can go and share examples of how to and how not to communicate. I kept the specifications quite broad to start, telling them to keep it related to communications. The blog has thus become a forum not only for the examples but also for the students to share ideas for upcoming speech topics, and inquiries on how to write the outline.
>
> For a required blogging assignment I gave to my English 10 students, I set up a time for us all to go the computer lab, and students participated individually in an interactive PowerPoint presentation that I found online, created by Mr. Harrington, Mrs. Scott, and Mrs. Thompson, Normal Community West High School, Normal, Illinois, at http://www.unit5.org/ncwhsimc/ Hotlists/Secret_Life_of_Bees.ppt
>
> Students accessed the presentation (and the follow-up blog) on my teacher page at http://northhighschool.webaloo.com/msjohnson.aspx.
>
> This PowerPoint is an interactive tool that explores various aspects of Sue Monk Kidd's novel, *The Secret Life of Bees*. The three teachers created a fantastic PowerPoint, five pages in length, providing many fascinating links leading to aspects of the book that will help students understand the novel on a deeper level. For example, the PowerPoint links to an interactive beehive; the animated movielike beehive details bee behavior, feeding habits, mating, and fun facts.
>
> The students absolutely loved this interactive component of the PowerPoint. Additionally, the novel opens at a crucial time in American history: 1964. Understanding the timeline and having a historical context is critical when reading this particular novel, and the PowerPoint led students to various timelines and calendars exploring the history of this era.
>
> Creating a PowerPoint with active links is something that I would like to do with the novels I teach in the future. The students seemed to truly have a valuable experience, which they reported in their class blog. Once they were done with the PowerPoint, they were required to post a response

on their blog, discussing what they learned from the PowerPoint, what they liked, and any overall reactions to what they learned. I required the responses to be at least three to four sentences in length.

As the following excerpts from their blog posts about the novel suggests, the PowerPoint helped students interpret the novel:

AJ Swanson:

> The PowerPoint helped to explain more about the time period and what the main character is going through. I thought it was interesting learning about the actual life of bees in the interactive hive.

Michelle Pokorny:

> The presentation has a great timeline that shows various events that have taken place before and after the Civil Rights Act was passed. For example, on May 4, 1961, students called "freedom riders" volunteered to test the laws which prohibited segregation.

Students at times did not even seem to notice that they were learning; they were so excited to blog and explore online on their own. I have rarely seen such a level of excitement for a novel, and I plan to continue activities such as these in the future. Digital writing has opened up new opportunities in my classroom, and I look forward to expanding on this new form of writing in my English and communications classes. It was a "virtual" field trip of sorts, and the follow-up blogging piece added a productive way to share student ideas and responses.

Alternatives to PowerPoints and Keynote

Rather than use PowerPoint or Keynote for presentations, teachers or students can employ a wiki coupled with a digital note-taking tool so that teachers and/or students can collaboratively add material during or after a presentation (Morgan, 2006a). One example of using a wiki as a presentation tool is BlogShop Lite, developed by Brian Lamb (2006). Audience members add material to this wiki and are then notified of revisions through subscribing to feeds.

At the University of Washington, Richard Anderson (2006) developed the Classroom Presenter tool (http://www.cs.washington.edu/education/dl/presenter), which employs a Tablet PC so that a teacher can write notes on slides during a presentation that are then projected to a screen in the classroom. For example, if a teacher is showing a slide with a graph of figures, the teacher may use digital ink to circle or underline certain data in the graph or to write down student comments about the graph. Students can add their own notes to the slides and instructor notes; the teacher can then display those notes to the class as a means of furthering class discussions.

Rather than adopt the role of passive consumers, students perceive themselves as contributors to a presentation.

Online Tools for Editing for Grammar and Spelling

Another important set of digital tools for editing are grammar and spell-checkers, for example, those in Word or AbiWord. These tools are particularly valuable for students who are prone to make a lot of errors. One study found that middle school students who were having spelling difficulties were much more likely to correct spelling errors when they used a spell-checker than when they did not (MacArthur, Graham, Haynes, & De La Paz, 1996) (@ = Grammar and spelling checkers).

Students need to recognize some of the limitations of grammar and spelling checkers (MacArthur, 2006). Although grammar or style checkers may flag errors, they may be based on erroneous assumptions about language use. One study (Kies, 2006) indicated that grammar checkers often incorrectly identified errors, particularly the use of subject-verb agreement and passive voice. For example, use of passive constructions may be noted as problematic when in fact it is appropriate. Writers may use the passive when they want to deflect attention from the agent as actor, as in "Company employees were fired by the CEO," as opposed to "The CEO fired company employees." Grammar checkers may also identify problems of usage as grammar errors. Students therefore need to understand differences between grammar as a matter of syntax and usage as a matter of acceptable language, particularly in the context of dialect differences.

Students have difficulty correcting grammar because they lack the vocabulary to explore alternative syntactical structures or to avoid use of word repetition. To find appropriate vocabulary, students can employ online thesauruses such as *Roget's Thesaurus* (http://www.bartleby.com/thesauri), Thesaurus.com (http://thesaurus.reference.com) or WikiSaurus (http://en.wiktionary.org/wiki/WikiSaurus) for generating synonyms for replacing repetitive words (Montgomery & Marks, 2006). To get help addressing grammar errors, students can go to various online sites available at university online writing centers (@ = Online editing resource sites).

There are also problems with spell-checkers. They may simply not identify misspellings or may identify proper nouns as misspelled, as well as words that have not been put into a spelling dictionary. If the spell-checker provides a list of optional spellings, students may not be able to select the correct option (Montgomery, Karlan, & Coutinho, 2001). Montgomery and Marks (2006) suggests using an "InSPECT" approach for coping with spelling errors: "In the document, Start the spell checker, Pick correct alternatives, Correct additional errors, Type in your corrections" (p. 35). They also suggest using games or work sheets that provide alternative spellings, as well as having students work together in editing conferences to correct one another's errors. Students could also sound out difficult syllables such as *ence* versus *ance* in *independence* or associate problem words with certain topics (Dobie, 2007). For example, to note that *cemetery* has *e's* in it, a student could associate that word with *eerie*.

Citing Material

Students need to recognize when to give credit for the use of an original work, including recognizing the differences between direct quotes and paraphrasing a writer's text, which requires that they cite references (@ = Citations-reference styles). Students need to know that they must document any reference to or paraphrase of a writer's article, chapter, book, or website, regardless of whether they quote that writer. Students also need to know how to employ the different types of reference styles: the MLA (Gibaldi, 2003) and *The Chicago Manual of Style* (University of Chicago Press, 2003), which are typically used in literature or the arts, and the American Psychological Association (APA) (2001) style, typically used in the social sciences. When citing online sources, students should realize the value of citing sources—that they are also providing readers with a service by including a current, correct URL with the reference. Students should therefore include the authors, the title, the date they retrieved the document, and the URL. For example, for excerpts from the fifth edition of the APA Publication Manual, the author of the site would be noted as the http://APA Style.org; the date is the copyright date on the website, 2003; the name of the site is Electronic references; the date of retrieval is October 16, 2006; and the URL is http://www.apastyle.org/elecref.html; resulting in the following reference: APA Style.org. (2003). Electronic references. Retrieved October 16, 2006 from http://www.apastyle.org/elecref.html

Using Reference Software

Students can also use reference or citation management software to create and organize their references (@ = Reference tools). One advantage of this software is that they can create their own reference database or library for use in writing different papers. Thus, whenever they need to add references to their papers, they can go to their databases for these references rather than having to hunt them down. This software also formats both their citations as they are writing their papers and then adds references according to a selected citation style.

The two dominant commercial citation management software programs are EndNote and RefWorks. EndNote and RefWorks can be used to create bibliographic databases that students can continually draw on for different papers. RefWorks, which is found only on the Web, is typically sold as site licenses to schools and universities and is less expensive than EndNote. Another similar service, CiteULike (http://www.citeulike.org) as well as Scribe 2.5, Wikindx, or JabRef, can be used to organize notes according to citations, automatically link a citation in the text to a reference list, format references in MLA or APA style, and create reference lists. For CiteULike, because citations are stored on their server, students can access it from any computer and share their library with others.

Because students in K–12 classrooms may be using only a limited number of references, they could then turn to free citation software programs such as StudentABC's Citation Creation Machine, Citation Builder, CiteULike, Connotea, or David Warlick's Citation Machine. For example, to use Citation Machine, the program most suited to K–12, students can select their choice of style format, type in the source, and create citations in a relatively straightforward manner. Another useful free tool is Zotero (http://www.zotero.org) that students can use to not only store references for searches, but to also tag references as they would in using delicious.com. K–12 students can also use tools within Noodletools such as the free NoodleBib Express or NoodleBib MLA Starter (for students in Grades 1–5).

Summary

Learning to employ digital design involves creating digital texts that are engaging and easy to read, based on principles of readability and digital layout. By analyzing their own engagement and comprehension of texts, students recognize how specific aspects of layout, white space, font, and images, as well as grammar and spelling, can enhance engagement and comprehension. They can also apply design principles to create interactive PowerPoint presentations to engage their audiences. Finally, students need to know how to effectively employ grammar and spelling checkers and citation software.

Chapter
Nine

Using Digital Tools for Formative and Summative Evaluation of Writing

Students are most likely to improve in their writing when they receive helpful feedback while they are writing that will lead to revision, as well as feedback on their final products. Many teachers are discovering the benefits of using digital tools to provide timely feedback during and after students' writing. Anne Beaton, a high school English teacher at Armstrong High School in Robbinsdale, Minnesota, has this to say about her decision to use digital tools in word-processing programs to provide feedback on her students' papers:

> I needed to find a way to better utilize their face-to-face time in the classroom. In addition, reading papers and writing feedback by hand had become taxing and frustrating—I never felt as though I was able to fully communicate my thinking to the writer. I found myself leaning on catchphrases like, "nice" or "??" or "unclear" rather than taking the time to fully explain myself in the margin. Time spent commenting was replaced by rubrics that served as a quick easy way to distribute comments to the masses. I could simply place an "X" in the box and let the student decipher why their effort fell there.
>
> But X's do not teach. I was determined to find a better way to reach my students and then I stumbled across the "track changes" and "comment" tools offered in Microsoft Word. I had used them with my own writing, but had not considered their effect with my students. Jumping directly into a

text to rewrite a sentence or attach a comment to their work was intriguing. I was curious about how my ability to offer direction and feedback to students might be augmented with the help of these tools. How refreshing to truly *show* a student a variety of word choices instead of jotting "w/c" or reconstructing a sentence to *show* a grammatically correct version or place the period *inside* the quotation marks. I realized that with the help of electronic feedback, I could provide visual examples that served as mini lessons tailored to each student.

In previous chapters, we examined how digital tools can be used for a variety of writing activities. In this chapter we examine how digital tools can be used to provide two kinds of online feedback: feedback to help students revise during composing (formative) and feedback to help teachers evaluate completed texts (summative). By formative feedback, we mean feedback that occurs before an assignment is due, while a student is writing and revising drafts. Formative feedback could take the form of teacher comments on student drafts, teacher-student conferences, student peer review, or tutoring. By summative feedback, we mean feedback that assesses and evaluates a final product and assigns a grade. Summative feedback is provided by a teacher and involves a set of evaluation criteria, or a rubric, or some other method of evaluation.

Although online feedback can be engaging, it is not something that comes easily or intuitively. On the contrary, using digital tools to provide online feedback takes some getting used to. One reason is that online feedback can seem less personal than handwritten or face-to-face feedback; teachers and students alike may feel less of a connection to other writers. Another reason is that online feedback can interrupt texts, disrupting the sense of author and reader roles as well as the idea of stable text. Interruptions also occur as readers are empowered to edit, draw, provide substantial commentary, rewrite, and even record voice comments over text.

Drawing on the discussion of online discussion tools in chapter 3, we also want to distinguish between synchronous versus asynchronous feedback. Synchronous, real-time feedback occurs in chat sites, whereas asynchronous feedback does not.

It is also important to recognize that giving feedback to the kinds of digital writing discussed in this book requires criteria relevant to the uses of digital communication associated with the uses of multimodality, hypertextuality, and interactivity. These criteria differ from those applied to evaluating print texts. For example, an effective student blog involves uses of images and video, links to other blogs and sites, and strategies for engaging audiences, considerations that are less relevant for evaluating students' print essays.

Formative Feedback Strategies

Although past research about formative feedback is mixed in terms of fostering self-assessing and revision (Beach & Friedrich, 2006), digital tools such as conference-style synchronous chats, small-group student chats, online peer review, and annotated sample papers can be used to provide effective formative feedback.

Providing Formative Reader-Based Feedback

In providing this formative feedback, it is important to focus on a few central aspects that need the most work, rather than overwhelming students with too many issues. It is also helpful to give descriptive, reader-based feedback (Elbow, 1973) regarding specific aspects of a draft that engage, confuse, please, puzzle, or require more information, rather than judgmental feedback (Beach & Friedrich, 2006). Describing how one as a reader is processing specific parts of a text provides a student with a sense of how the reader is experiencing a text. In responding to a description of high school students' gambling problems in a blog post, a reader-based response may be: "When I read your opinion about problems with high school students' gambling, I was expecting some specific examples of these problems." In this feedback, the teacher is describing *how* he or she is responding *as a reader* based on genre expectations that in identifying a problem, one typically provides reasons for that problem.

In responding to students' blog posts, teachers can provide this feedback in blog comments that describe their experience reading the text that led to some suggested revisions. For example, in David Nunez's class, North Vista Education Center, Robbinsdale, Minnesota, Brittney wrote the following story as a blog post:

> "I have cancer." That's all Thomas heard as he stared at his mother, as the words came out, he just couldn't believe it. How could this be happening, what about Tito and Tati? Racing thoughts started going through his mind... "I need you to take care of Tito & Tati, the doctors said I'm getting weaker, and more sick, I'm going to have to quit my job." After a slight pause her voice rose. "Thomas! Do you hear me?" He replied "Yea..." not sure of what all he had heard, but the one thing that he was still racing through his mind. Not saying a word he got up and walked away, confused, hurt and unsure of what the situation really is. He drops down on the couch not realizing he's falling asleep, until the moment he wakes up.
>
> He wakes up and it's late, everyone is asleep. The heat was on a little high, so he thought he'd take a walk to cool off, to think things through some. He couldn't stop thinking about his mother. It was hard enough coming up

already but without her it would be harder. Ever since his father died it was tough, then Tito and Tati were born—it just made it harder. A single mother raising 3 kids, but now it would be him, Thomas just didn't know what to do. He never had to take care of kids, he went to school and worked to save up for college. His mom took care of all of them always. He never had to worry about anything, although he still did, he knew it had always been hard for his mom to raise all of them. She always made it, though, even when it got really tough.

The next morning Thomas woke up and was still stuck on the same thing, he hadn't talked to his mom since she told him. He thought maybe now would be a better time to talk to her, seeing as the situation kind of sunk in a little. He wasn't sure what to say or if he should just touch base a little; he wasn't sure if the topic would hurt his mother to discuss her medical problem. He knew that he could do what she was asking, taking care of Tati and Tito, but that would mean giving up a lot. "Hey mom," Thomas started out the conversation. "You were outa here before I could even finish last night," she stated. "I'm sorry, I was just in shock I mean I never had this happen before, we can't lose you, we need you still, Mom, you're the only parent we got." Now Thomas was a little emotional, trying to hold back a few tears, his Mother could see them in his eyes, though. "Thomas, I'm sorry, but life comes with unexpected things, and I guess we just have to work with it, I didn't ask to get cancer, I don't want to leave you guys anytime soon, but things happen. I just hope I last longer then they say I will, I don't want to hurt you guys, but you need to be strong, for Tati and Tito." Just then Tito and Tati came bursting in the house from outside, dripping snow everywhere. "Mommy!! Tito pushed me in the snow!!" Tito giggles as Tati starts crying and telling their Mom. "Tito, why'd you push your sister in the snow?" Tito starts laughing some more, ignoring his Mom. "Tito!! Go to your room!" she yells at him.

In providing feedback to Brittney's story on a blog through a comment, David focused on issues of character development:

You've written a very nice start to a story here, Brittney. I love how difficult a topic you've taken on and how well you are handling it. The main character seems really shocked to me.

I think you should start thinking about where the story is going and how it will end, though. You don't need to tell the story all the way to the point where the mother dies if you don't want to, that might be very long. Rather, think about change.

> The main character in a story usually changes. That change, good or bad, is what makes us feel like it is a complete story. How will your character change?
>
> My advice is that Thomas accepts his mother's death and realizes that he wants to take care of Tito and Tati. Maybe after spending some time with them. We haven't met the two kids yet, and that might be nice. You don't have to do this, but it would give a sense of change in the main character.

In reflecting on his feedback, David noted that:

> I chose to address what I thought was the biggest issue in this student's writing rather than attacking smaller issues such as spelling and grammar. We can address those points later. But, for this first post of hers, I gave her some positive feedback and then wrote about how I felt that the main character of her story needs to change over the course of the story. This is a classic writing workshop critique, and a major issue that needs to be addressed in any story.
>
> I think it's important to keep online feedback positive and constructive—especially with something as personal as creative writing. Students can easily misconstrue written text because it carries so much less tone than verbal comments.

Conference-Style Synchronous Chats

A key aspect of providing feedback is to create conversations about a student's writing that allow teachers or peers to scaffold students' self-assessing so that they learn to identify issues and revisions to address those issues on their own. Synchronous chats are well suited for conference-style chats using real-time IMing or online chat room interactions on sites such as iChat, Adobe Acrobat Connect, Moodle, Desire2Learn, Nicenet.org, or Tappedin.org (@ = Synchronous conference chat). Synchronous chats tend to be used in ways similar to face-to-face writing conferences, such as brainstorming ideas for topics and revisions, discussing progress on writing, and providing interpersonal support for writers.

Chats can work well for a series of teacher-student conferences that allow teacher and student to not only brainstorm ideas on the fly but also to document those ideas for future reference. In an account of a student-teacher conference, Eric Crump (1998) describes online chat in terms of a "hybrid" language—somewhere between talk and writing. He suggests that chats are great for brainstorming ideas, that they are engaging to students, and that they create positive energy about writing and revision. Another advantage of chat environments is that they help form social ties, because they tend to be less formal. When they occur between teacher and student, teachers can get to know their student's writing and the student even better.

Similarly, teachers can set up "virtual office hours" in which more than one student could "stop by" and ask questions about an assignment. Many students have experience with IM environments; opening the door of teacher-student communication in this way can be a powerful source of formative feedback on student assignments, as well as serving as a means of modeling peer-group feedback (@ = peer-group/instructor feedback).

Conference-style chats also occur in tutor-student online environments, such as online writing centers (@ = Online writing labs). For example, at the University of Minnesota Center for writing (http://writing.umn.edu/sws/index.htm#sessions), students submit their drafts online to the tutoring site, and then, after 30 minutes (which gives time for the tutor to prepare feedback), they engage in a synchronous chat with the tutor. Both tutor and student can view the draft on the computer window and the student can then make revisions.

Eventually sites such as this one will include a Webcam shot of the tutor's and student's talking heads. For example, Wimba Pronto (http://www.wimba.com) combines IMing with audio or video sharing for audio or video conferencing along with the students' writing displayed on the screen.

In one study, Beth Hewett (2006) describes how synchronous conferencing in an online tutoring center involved whiteboard interactions. Her analyses of synchronous "talk" demonstrated that two-thirds of the synchronous dialogue reflected discussion about ideas for revision, generated either by student or tutor. In addition, half of the dialogue reflected interpersonal interactions, suggesting that chats are a good forum for making interpersonal connections in a conference setting.

One structured chat activity is a brainstorming chat, in which chat participants offer suggestions for paper topics and other ideas for what they might write. This kind of chat could take place in a computer lab classroom and take only about 15 minutes of class time. Students work in groups of three or four working in different chat rooms. Students then respond to three structured prompts: (a) for the first 5 minutes, students chat about topic ideas they might have for a paper assignment; (b) for the second 5 minutes, students chat about examples, sources, or evidence they might use; (c) for the third 5 minutes, students brainstorm further about any ideas or questions they have about the assignment. At the conclusion of this chat, students report on what they discussed to their peers.

Schools can also set up an online writing center staffed by trained student tutors or even volunteer adults. If these centers can be staffed both during and after school, students could then obtain feedback when they are most likely to need that feedback. One model for online peer feedback sites is SWoRD (Scaffolded Writing and Reviewing in the Discipline) developed at the University of Pittsburgh (http://www.lrdc.pitt.edu/schunn/SWoRD/index.html) (Cho & Schunn,

2007). On this site, students submit their drafts to SWoRD, which assigns them to peers, who give feedback and grade the drafts. Students revise their drafts, which are then returned to the same peers for further review. Because students rate the helpfulness of their peers' feedback, the peers are graded according to these helpfulness ratings.

Why use online conferencing when you can provide feedback in what could be more intimate face-to-face conferences? One major advantage of online conferences is that students are not limited to scheduling conferences during class time—students can hold conferences at any time—for example, when they are working on their writing in the evening. Another advantage of an online written chat conference is that students have a record of the feedback they received so that in later revising their text, they can go back and review suggestions for revisions. For example, by conducting chat conferences on Tappedin.org, students can receive an e-mail transcript of their chat. They then have a record of their self-assessing and revisions in different conferences to refer to in revising their writing or to include in their portfolios as evidence of change in their ability to self-assess and revise.

Asynchronous Formative Feedback

In addition to synchronous chat feedback, teachers or peers can also employ asynchronous tools to provide formative feedback—e-mail, IMing, blog comments, or digital recording to give feedback during the drafting process. For digital recording, teachers or peers can use a digital recorder and e-mail a voice file to students or they can create an MP3 file for students. Or this audio can be used to create a written text file to be sent to students' e-mails or blogs using Jott (http://jott.com). For brief comments, teachers or peers can use a cell phone to call in their feedback to a Jott phone number that creates a text message that is sent to the student's e-mail or blog.

As with chat feedback, one advantage of these tools is that students can receive assistance relatively quickly. As April Stasko, an English teacher at Hayfield High School, Hayfield, Minnesota, notes:

> Students like e-mailing and writing knowing that they will get fast feedback. Also, e-mail and blogging conversations can be much more private than a discussion in the classroom. So, since more students like this, I spend more time online responding to students. Also, many of my students use their parents' account to e-mail stuff, so I am very aware that parents will read my comments, which makes the audience quite different (and again takes more time).

Teachers or peers can also provide asynchronous feedback using a threaded bulletin board forum such as Moodle, Drupal, Ning, Joomla, or Nicenet.org (see chapter 3). Students post their writing and receive immediate comments from peers on the bulletin board (Hayes, 2006). One value of using a bulletin board rather than personal e-mails is that a teacher can control student access and comments, which then discourages students from making overly judgmental or derogatory comments. Also, rather than the more ephemeral chat interactions, the students' comments can be saved for later use.

Sandy Hayes of Becker Middle School, Becker, Minnesota, describes how she uses bulletin board technology for large-class peer review at the middle school level.

> The most successful activity I've found to engage students in more thoughtful and productive responses than typical peer conferences or read-arounds is the use of an online bulletin board. Although I do not promote it initially as a revision activity, it yields higher quality work in ongoing assignments, because students internalize perceptions of quality, encounter an array of possibilities they could try, gain a sense of writing for an audience, and show improved attitude and motivation toward writing. For middle school students, the activity works best for units in writing poetry or short prose pieces, in which a single comment or two is adequate. With older students and longer pieces of writing, I would initially provide a list of reflective prompts to guide substantive responses and to discourage focusing on editing issues.
>
> Process
>
> - Students post a piece of their writing to the class bulletin board or blog. To include students who may not have Internet access, we use class time for posting and responding. This gives a rather unusual context to the usually asynchronous nature of the medium since the posting of the piece and the comments may be as synchronous as online chat and since a student may be responding to the classmate sitting at the next computer.
>
> - So why don't the students just talk to each other? Everyone posts a response to everyone's writing and everyone can read every comment. As a classroom discussion, this would be a cacophony. In the computer lab, students are so focused that flurries of keystrokes are the only sound.
>
> - Encourage positive and specific comments. Students don't need to write a comprehensive response to a peer's paper. If each student writes just one comment on every classmate's piece, the writer gets

a wealth of feedback. Even the "me, too" responses are valuable, for they reinforce an aspect of the writing that was especially effective.

- The process works best if the bulletin board or blog can thread a student's work and allows replies to replies so there is a chronological organization to the work, comments, revisions, and comments on revisions. (I use http://www.nicenet.org. It's free, with no advertising, and teachers can limit access and edit content.)

- If students post their writing as portfolios, classmates see not only the quality but also the quantity of the writing of their peers. This can be a reality check for those students who have an unrealistic perception of the depth of their body of work.

- Tolerate IM talk. This is a naturally engaging environment for today's text-messaging generation. The sprinkling of LOLs and smilies in their responses adds to the spirit of community.

- Critical mass is critical. For an even larger body of work, create a site where students can post a short piece of writing so students can read writing from other classes. Or pair up with another teacher and cross-pollinate classroom bulletin boards.

- Participate. I strive to post a specific, positive comment or a clarifying question on at least one piece of writing for every student. My comments, as well as comments of more adept peers, serve as a model for expanding students' response vocabulary as they are picked up and modified by others. When I wrote to Jenny about a line from her poem that gave me goosebumps, and I later read Jeremy's comment to Hilary about a line that sent shivers down his spine, I know we've gone beyond *"Good job. I liked it."*

Online peer review can also be done using simple e-mail with attachments (word-processed documents). Students can view one another's documents and provide electronic comments embedded directly in the text. Anne Beaton describes her approach to using online peer review in her Advanced Placement English 11 course:

When introducing the use of electronic feedback into my classroom, I started on a small scale; I tested it with my own reading of student papers. I stumbled across the "track changes" and "comment" tools offered in Microsoft Word. I had used them with my own writing but had not considered their effect with my students. Jumping directly into a text to rewrite a sentence or attach a comment to their work was intriguing. Reading my students' papers on my computer was an entirely different experience than paging through paper copies. I noticed that I am no longer restricted to the margins. I have access to the text and can highlight, underline, change, and comment. In this particular writing class, we focus on the *way* in which a piece is written, and electronic feedback has given me a chance to comment on very particular aspects of my students' writing in a clear, efficient manner. I have used the highlight function, for example, to expose to a student her "telling" rather than "showing" for the opening paragraph of her essay:

> I walk into the classroom where the meeting is being held. The coaches tell us all the demands and expectations of being on this team. I bring home the registration papers and my parents give their consent and write a check. Sunday night I make sure my bag is packed; I have a water bottle and shoes. I'm ready.

> Here's the comment I inserted: Throughout the first paragraph you are noticing very intimate details of what it is like to be in this situation, but you never invite the reader in. Notice how much you are telling. Think of the Wolff opening. Why is it that we can feel the tension without him saying? Steal from his work and apply it to your opening.

I can use the "track changes" tool to step into a paragraph and manipulate the text to show a student a better way to communicate her ideas:

> I was three months old, and my dad laid me down in my crib and said, "Dani, we're moving." Apparently my reaction was "a small giggle and a dirty diaper."

> *Comment: I'm not sure that you need to quote this, but perhaps mentions who said it?* What I can say is that, at three months old, I was extremely upset; I did not want to leave the cheese-loving state of Wisconsin and make my way down to Mississippi.

I can comment throughout my students' papers to help them to link ideas about their writing from previous papers in addition to stepping back and providing feedback about entire paragraphs. At the end of each paper, I can quickly write a personal note to each student in which I often cut and paste from the original document (or from a different source) to help teach my point. In addition, students have appreciated handouts that I am able to easily create by cutting and pasting student examples to a single document to stress common errors or "what works." So often, the teacher is the only person to read *everything*—and reap the benefits; the handouts and overheads have helped my students to learn from one another's successes and failures and have helped me to address the needs of a particular group of students. The added ability to communicate with my students in multiple ways is invaluable.

Having demonstrated to my students what electronic feedback looks like on their own papers, I spent some time directly instructing my students in a "how to" session in the computer lab (complete with handouts). We have since established a system of trading papers electronically with our small groups *the night before* the draft is due in class. I give my students a list of elements on which to focus for the given essay, and they spend time individually working their way through the rough drafts of two group members: highlighting portions of the essay, offering changes, and jotting comments. The following day in class, my students arrive with copies of each partner's paper, including the reader's added electronic changes and comments. Because they have already read all the drafts and thought through possible critical responses, their preparedness drives the peer-review sessions to greater depths. My students' attention to and care in revising their classmates' writing (and, subsequently their own) has invited a new level of focus to peer-review sessions that we did not have with the previous method.

Three common forms of electronic feedback include intertextual commentary, footnote commentary, and endnote commentary. Intertextual commentary involves line-by-line comments, suggestions, even corrections (such as grammatical or mechanical edits) to text (Monroe, 1998). Most word-processing programs allow for some kind of electronic intertextual commenting tools; as Anne mentioned, Microsoft Word has a "track changes" function (found under "Tools"), which, when enabled, allows a writer to delete text, add, or change text using underlining and strikethrough visuals that preserve the original text.

Besides these editing tools, writers can use simple text editing techniques such as writing text in a different color or font to distinguish teacher, tutor, or reviewer comments from the author's text (Monroe, 1998), as employed in the following sample paper with comments made using simple font and boldface changes:

My writing process is very hard to predict. It varies from paper to paper, I often don't do the same thing twice. But many times I start my paper by sitting down to watch my favorite TV program. **How does this help you write your paper?** It seems that I can't start writing until the very last moment, sometimes at 10 pm the night before the paper is due. When I am finally forced to start writing a paper, then the words start coming. I usually sit down for a half hour and write until I can't write anymore. **What happens then? Are you done?**

Students could also provide comments using some kind of footnote feature in which a reviewer marks the text in some way, like a footnote, and writes a comment using a split screen. These comments work well to provide suggestions and explanations about specific passages in the text, much like handwritten comments in the margins. Typically these comments are seen as less invasive and provide ample space for longer comments. Naturally, the footnote feature of any word-processing program can be used to create these comments. However, a better alternative is a "comment" function, common to many word-processing programs (in Microsoft Word it is found under the "Insert" tool bar).

A "comment" function allows reviewers to highlight a word and insert a comment. The comment function opens a split screen, much like a footnote would, where the comment can be typed. As illustrated in Figure 9-1, the comment function can be seen more easily than footnotes; when the computer mouse rolls over the highlighted word, the comment appears much like a "sticky note" on screen.

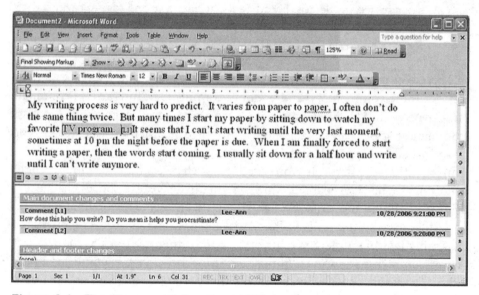

Figure 9-1. The "Comments" Function in Word

Of course, if footnotes or comments are inserted using electronic word-processing tools, it is important to have e-mail access so that the documents can be delivered electronically. Attaching the word-processed documents to an email message or a bulletin board accomplishes this task easily. April Stasko notes that her students not only value their peers' online editing feedback, even if it's anonymous, but also benefit from learning to edit others' writing:

> They like getting into their classmates papers with a different font and making comments. Students don't know who did the purple font versus the green font, so the anonymity is safe. When I have students edit online, they have certain guided questions (restate the thesis) that they answer on paper

that the author can see and I eventually get and score. Then they also comment in the paper. Most students walk away from this with a better picture of where they are. They have read several classmates' papers and can see if they are on the right track or completely missing the boat. When they see several papers, it can give them the guidance or reassurance they need to get to work on theirs. I think they get more out of the reading of others' papers than they do the actual comments on the written paper. I do feel that most use the comments in their paper in the other color font to improve their paper. Overall I really enjoy this activity and see improvements in writing as a result.

Students can also use annotation or tagging tools such as Diigo or Trailfire (a Firefox extension) to highlight and write notes or annotations about peers' online texts and post their notes for group members to see (for a screencast demonstration of using Diigo for highlighting and annotating students' online texts, see Diigo: A Social Bookmarking Research Tool [http://www.screencast-o-matic.com/watch/cij0ev4l]).

Students can also provide peers with endnotes that summarize overall reactions to the text and make general suggestions for revision. Some websites are actually designed to accommodate endnote commentary on drafts; sites such as FanFiction (http://www.fanfiction.net), The Next Big Writer (http://www.thenextbigwriter.com), or Writing.Com, in which people post writing and others can write reviews or rate the writing (@ = Online review or rating sites). The benefit of endnote commentary is to provide a general sense of reader response and overall thoughts about revising a document—suggestions usually involving global concerns such as organization, thesis development, or content.

In preparing for online peer review, it is helpful to organize the peer review based on a series of steps and deadlines for students to follow. Monroe (1998) suggests using intertextual comments throughout a document, followed by an endnote that summarizes overall impressions and suggestions. The intertextual comments could be made using word-processing tools, and the endnote could be typed as an e-mail message. When used consistently, this protocol creates an expectation for the online experience, which is very helpful to students unfamiliar with online environments.

Research about peer review does not suggest that peer review results in better papers; on the contrary, students sometimes do not offer constructive criticism and may not know how to comment, resorting to the "sounds good to me" comment (Beach & Friedrich, 2006). However, research also suggests that peer review is valued because it supports process-based writing, encourages students to think about their audience, and provides students with practice talking about writing (Spear, 1993).

All this suggests the need to train peers to provide effective feedback by model-ing reader-based feedback. For example, David Nunez focuses on the need to train his students to provide constructive criticism:

> The way that I am training my students to perform online feedback is that we spent some time talking about constructive criticism. We looked at a simple poem that I wrote badly and we went around the room and came up with ways to write criticism. Next, they are required to post three times on others' blogs, but I moderate all the comments initially. I haven't had to deny publication for any of my students' comments. Then, as a class, we are going to look at the first comments and try to figure out which ones were good and why they were good.
>
> I require that they have three good comments, and they will keep post-ing until they have given three interesting constructive comments to their peers. (On a feedback sheet I will let them know how many they have that count and why they are good comments.)

In response to Brittney's story, her peers provided both positive comments and suggestions:

> Viola: When I read the part about when he stood, and was still thinking, I want to know what he was thinking about. Great plot. I love (or hate?) the way the characters are sad and upset.
>
> Melissa: i like the story, but it's kind of sad. he was thinking about what he's gotta do after his mom died but she already did???..... well it [sic] good, i think you should give more detail.
>
> Lia: I think that your story is really good but I think that it would be better if you can tell more about the mother and son's relation-ship. I think that is all, but it is really good—I just want to read more about it. Like how did the mother get cancer and did the mother die. I don't know, maybe just something like that would help me out [to understand] what is going on.

Research is beginning to show that online peer-review feedback can influence revisions in two interesting ways (Hewett, 2000; Breuch, 2004). First, some stud-ies have reported that online peer-review feedback tends to be more directive or assertive than face-to-face comments and that such comments result in increased revision. That is, revisions may happen more often when reviewers have pro-vided concrete and specific suggestions for revision.

A second advantage of using digital comments on texts is that they can be readily stored and shared as examples of useful comments for training peers to give peer feedback, as well as examples of students' revisions made as a result of a comment, modeling the revision process.

Creating Annotated Sample Papers

So far we have reviewed formative feedback strategies such as conference-style chats, small-group student chats, and online peer review. We'll end this section by reviewing one other formative feedback strategy: creating annotated sample papers.

New approaches to formative feedback argue that students can benefit from knowing the criteria or expectations for writing a paper before they start to work on it (Anson, 2006). Because students need to internalize standards for what counts as a successful performance in a genre, they can think about appropriate criteria for an assignment using annotated sample papers (@ = Annotated sample papers).

Creating annotated sample papers begins with creating a set of criteria or rubric that can be used to evaluate the final drafts of an assignment students are completing—criteria associated with three to five different categories based on the learning goals of the assignment. A summary, for example, might include a category about the accuracy of the content, a category about how well the summary captures the gist or main points of the original, a category about the style and structure of the summary, and so on. Each of these categories then has to be defined in writing in terms of what features are associated with a good performance within the category.

The next step in creating an annotated paper is to choose one or two responses to the assignment. It helps to save papers from previous classes (erase the students' names or create pseudonyms, and, when possible, have each class sign a form that gives permission to use their work in future classes). It is best to choose "interestingly problematic" papers—not excellent ones and not really bad ones, but ones that have complex strengths and weaknesses of different types.

Now create a verbatim copy of the first sample paper in digital form. At the end of the paper, place a rubric with its different categories and their appropriate values (for example, five categories each worth 20% of the grade). Show how many points the sample paper received in each category, with a final score for the whole paper. This allows students to acquire a feel for the entire paper with its problems and successes, its errors and effective turns of phrase; it also shows them the overall judgment of the paper based on the rubric.

For each category, create a *hyperlink* to another version of the paper, exactly like the first version. Then look for salient features in the paper that explain the judgment made for a particular category. If one category is "style," for example, choose words, phrases, and sentences that are either problematic or effective stylistically. Highlight those textual places. Use an appropriate commenting method, creating links to each highlighted piece of text. (This can be done using a split-screen approach, with comments on the right screen, adjacent to the highlighted text). Or use a pop-up approach—as students scroll over a highlighted word or text, a pop-up window appears that explains what's at stake in the high-lighted text. Or use a link approach, taking students to separate screens with explanations. At the end of the paper, offer an overall comment on the criterion from the rubric that is being discussed and why it received the points it did from that perspective.

Creating these annotations for each element or criterion in the rubric provides students with a series of "lenses" or criteria for students to look through for determining the quality of certain features employed in an assignment. Creating annotations can also be used to elicit student input on creating their own set of criteria for a given assignment. Based on an assignment, provide students with some students' previous sample writings (with names removed) for that assignment. Have students discuss differences in the quality of these samples and reasons for their judgments: what in the *text* that led them to judge differences in quality.

Then, after students complete their own writing for this assignment, have them post their writing to a class website or wiki. Students annotate the writings and, working in small groups, consolidate their annotations and create a set of criteria. Each group then shares the criteria, leading to a final composite set of class-decided criteria. These criteria become a guide for students not only as they write their papers but also for how they will be evaluated on those papers.

Summative Feedback Strategies

So far we have reviewed formative feedback strategies that can be given by teachers, tutors, or students during the composing process. Now we turn our attention to using digital tools for providing summative feedback after the writing is completed, although there is some digital writing that may never be "completed." As we mentioned at the beginning of this chapter, summative feedback is more evaluative because it carries a grade. In addition, summative commentary is less free-form in nature than formative feedback is because it often involves a set of criteria that guides the evaluation (@ = Summative evaluation).

Using a Grading Rubric

It is useful to employ a grading rubric specific to an assignment that provides students with criteria constituting summative feedback so that students know that the same criteria are being employed for all students.

Creating a rubric involves listing those features of an assignment critically important to successful completion of that assignment. As illustrated by the rubric in chapter 7 for evaluating podcasts, for each feature, develop a scale based on descriptive criteria, for example, "excellent," "good," "sufficient," or "needs improvement." Using word-processing software, create a table format listing criteria in the first column. Sites such as Rubistar (http://rubistar.4teachers.org/index.php) or Digitales (http://digitales.us/evaluating/scoring_guide.php) can be used to create and format rubrics. In using these resources, it is important to tailor criteria to specific, unique assignments, rather than using prepackaged rubrics with an overly generic set of criteria that students will not understand (Broad, 2003).

Create columns to represent the scales and save the document as a template. For evaluation of each student's paper, copy and paste the rubric into a new document and type comments in each criterion table cell. When it is finished, these comments can be sent to the student.

For example, after the students in Elizabeth Boeser's class created their roles for their high school wiki described in chapter 4 related to reading *The Perks of Being a Wallflower* (Chbosky, 1999) and *Speak* (Anderson, 2006), they then had to write a problem-solution essay in which they had to "convince the reader that adolescents in today's world struggle with serious issues and present alternative ways to deal with these issues and possible solutions for the characters' struggles: How do we provide support and/or solutions to teens who struggle with the kinds of issues presented in *The Perks of Being a Wallflower* (and/or *Speak*)?" To evaluate this paper, Elizabeth developed the criteria shown in Figure 9-2.

CATEGORY	Excellent	Proficient	Sufficient	Deficient
Paper Format, Mechanics, and Content:				
Includes name, my name, course, and date (MLA)				
Topic is defined and explained				
Introduction is complete with thesis statement and P.O.C.				
Paper contains linear, clear, insightful argument				
Solution to issue is provided and reasonable				
Conclusion incorporates summary statements and clever clincher				
All facts are cited and match the Works Cited page				
Works Cited page has at least four sources				
Essay is free from spelling, grammar, and punctuation errors				
Paper meets length requirements: four to six pages				
Keyboarded text, 12-point font, double-spaced, page numbers				
Packet, articles, rough draft, and originality report are included				
Real Life/Personal or Alternate Example:				
Example included in the paper relates directly to topic				
The relationship between example and topic is explained				

Figure 9-2. Problem-Solution Essay Grading Criteria

Another option is the use of the Calibrated Peer Review (CPR) (http://cpr.molsci.ucla.edu/), an online program that has been designed to help students learn to apply a rubric to some sample writing by comparing their evaluations with those of the teacher's evaluation. Before using the rubric, students must complete an exercise in which they apply the rubric to sample student writing that has already been evaluated by the instructor using the same rubric. CPR will calibrate the student evaluation with the teacher's evaluation to let the student know how close they are to the teacher's evaluation. When students conduct evaluations of other student writing, CPR keeps track of comments and multiple submissions of writing to see if improvement has been made.

Evaluating Blogs

The idea of rubrics can also work for evaluating other forms of digital writing, such as blogs or wikis. (For standards and criteria for evaluating digital writing, see @ = Standards related to digital writing.)

Evaluating blogs requires developing a different set of criteria that is more appropriate for the kinds of practices involved in creating and commenting on posts. In reflecting on her experience of evaluating her students' blogs, Kathleen West noted:

> We can grade blog entries in at least three different ways at different points in any blog project. Since I felt like my 8-week blog project really only allowed my freshmen to become beginning blog writers, I graded their entries on completion. That's one way to let everyone know that you're serious and that the work needs to be done. It also allows the students to get a quick base of entries under their belts and gives them a new experience to feel good about.
>
> I'm thinking that another way is to grade the entry on the quality of content based on the understood audience. If it's understood (either implicitly or explicitly) that the audience is academic, that the post is a scholarly response to a scholarly topic, grade accordingly. If it's understood that the audience is wider and less sophisticated, other language would be appropriate. So part of the blog requirements would involve a certain number of posts for each audience that the teacher is concerned with addressing. That might mean that each entry now begins with a short audience statement, but that's not such a bad thing and kids can get creative with how that statement manifests itself.
>
> The latest idea I've had about this is to grade certain entries based on the amount of conversation it generates, based on comments and other entries. So the quality of the writing isn't as important as the quality of the

idea. This helps create a culture of commenting and interacting with other bloggers.

In addition to those criteria suggested by Kathleen, other criteria or rubrics can also be related to the extent to which students do the following:

- Clearly formulate their positions or opinions
- Address topics and issues dealt with in class discussions or readings
- Provide supporting evidence for positions or opinions
- Employ links to others' posts both within and outside the classroom
- Reformulate others' material or links in one's own words
- Engage in comments to peers' posts and reactions to those comments

Evaluating Wiki Writing

Developing criteria for evaluating wiki writing involves not only using criteria similar to those involved in evaluating blogs, for example—creating links between pages—but also evaluating students' ability to work collaboratively in creating a wiki. These criteria could focus on the extent to which each student in a group clearly identified their role in the collaboration, what they would contribute, and whether they followed through on making that contribution.

Issues of Plagiarism

There is much fear among teachers and administrators that the Internet has caused an epidemic of plagiarism. Students can download entire papers and turn them in as their own. They can cut text from Internet sources and paste it into their papers without attribution in an attempt to make their work seem more sophisticated. And they can splice together entire papers from multiple sources without doing much more than creating transitions and making sure the font is the same. Under these circumstances, teachers' suspicions have grown, often to the point that they suspect some degree of plagiarism in a class of students.

Instances of plagiarism can be detected by entering a familiar, suspicious line from a student's paper into Google and see if a close match results. Entrepreneurs now offer services such as MyDropBox.com or TurnItIn.com, which will tell whether—and to what degree—students have plagiarized in their writing (@ = Plagiarism detection).

Before deciding whether to subscribe to a plagiarism-detection service (which can be done at the course level or by an entire school or university), it is important to know how these services work and why there may be more principled ways to subvert plagiarism than submit student writing to computer detection systems (Anson, 2008). For example, TurnItIn.com works by matching the text in papers submitted to its search engine against a very large database of existing work written by both students and professionals.

The technology produces what the company calls a "customized originality report" that provides an index of how much in a student's paper is copied from another source. The text of the paper is shown in a left frame; in the right frame are any sources that match the text in the left frame. For a highlighted passage, the program retrieves the original passage that appears to match the student's. In addition to looking at published sources for matches, TurnItIn's search engine scans all student essays that have been submitted before. Even if a paper submitted to TurnItIn from one class is plagiarized, any future student can never use that same paper because the system will find it.

Several aspects of technologies like TurnItIn have led many educators—and whole campuses or schools—to avoid subscribing to it or to drop their subscriptions (Anson, 2008). First, students must submit their work to the system, which then stores the papers in its database forever. Although the companies will argue that the original papers are turned into a code that in some way protects the student's copyright, this code is still a version of the students' work. Forcing them to send their work to a company that in some sense "owns" and stores it is at least ethically questionable. In one case at McGill University, a student won a suit on moral and ethical grounds that he was the owner of his work and couldn't be forced to submit it to TurnItIn. "'I was having to prove I didn't plagiarize even before my paper was looked at by my professor,'" the student argued (Alphonso, 2004, p. A1). Second, most teachers using plagiarism-detection software require at the start of a course that their students submit all their graded work to the system. Even though no one has yet committed plagiarism, it is already assumed that the entire class is potentially guilty. This can have the effect of signaling to students that they may not be trusted not to plagiarize, and that alone can work against establishing an atmosphere of respect and collaboration.

Finally, there have been a number of cases in which students have been falsely accused of plagiarism because a computerized detection system discovered some percentage of their work was not original. Chris (Anson, 2008) corresponded at length with a student who was suspended from a special honors program because a small percentage of a difficult paper she wrote was flagged as plagiarized by a plagiarism detection system. The students were not told their papers were being submitted; furthermore, they received no support at all from the teacher for writing their papers, which were assigned at the beginning of the course and collected at the end. The student had dutifully cited all her sources with parenthetical references following each instance of a quoted source, but she neglected to put quotation marks around the sentences themselves. The computer has no way to consider such cases—it does not bring the complexities of human judgment to bear on what it sees. The teacher and administrators, trusting the computer's judgment, also failed to consider the context of the so-called plagiarism, and simply rejected the student's appeals. It took filing a lawsuit to force the university to perceive the issue from more than one perspective. Computers can't "read" or understand text, and as a result there will be mistakes in the way they detect plagiarism. If a student's career can be affected by such mistakes, we ought to approach their use with considerable caution.

Much has been published about plagiarism, but there is growing educational consensus that teachers need to do their part to provide a context in which it is difficult to plagiarize and in which students are not motivated to do so—for example, by creating unique, interesting, engaging assignments instead of dull, canned assignments on which dozens or hundreds of papers have already been written. The Council of Writing Program Administrators has created a "best practices" document that advocated these and many other useful and principled strategies. They caution that the availability of computerized plagiarism detection services "should never be used to justify the avoidance of responsible teaching methods" (Council of Writing Program Administrators, 2006, p. 3).

Automated Response and Evaluation Programs

Finally, we discuss the option of using automated response and evaluation programs, otherwise known as machine-based scoring, along with a collective note of caution against using these programs (@ = Machine-based scoring).

When students submit their writing electronically to a computer program, the program reads the writing and then gives the student a humanlike, helpful response, in a sympathetic and approachable "voice," offering reactions, suggestions, examples, and other information of at least the quality a human reader would provide under the most ideal teaching circumstances—all in a fraction of a second. These programs can also grade students' writing, assigning points based on preestablished criteria.

A number of companies now offer schools and teachers opportunities to pay for "machine scoring" or "automated evaluation" of writing. Most of these services are not designed to do what the first part of our scenario described; they simply evaluate the writing and provide a score. But their marketing claims make them seem very attractive, especially to overburdened schools and teachers.

Computer Systems for Analyzing Writing

The underlying programs that allow computers to read and analyze student writing fall into two types of systems. One system is based on "mining" existing, scored papers for certain features, creating a sophisticated matrix of those features, then applying the matrix to new (unscored) cases to come up with a prediction of how humans would score them. It can do this with great consistency and reliability. But it needs to be "trained." For this reason, these programs do not work well for teachers who like to create new, unique assignments and who change their teaching from year to year. Typically, such programs are used for large-scale scoring of standardized test essays, when students are not given any information about their performance, anyway, other than a score.

Another system examines students' texts for certain features, almost all of them at the surface of a text. For example, it's relatively easy to scan a paper for words that are common and words that are less common, using a large lexicon of words with an index of their frequency of use. Papers with less common words might be scored higher because students with a more sophisticated vocabulary could be thought to be better writers. Or a computer can look for errors of syntax and word usage. The problems with such analyses are obvious: they ignore deeper aspects of writing and they can be unreliable at judging the surface features that they do look for. They assume that students who use less common words are better writers or that sentence fragments are problematic.

Programs can also use semantic analysis to look for the cohesion of words throughout a document, but they are unable to say anything about broader rhetorical concerns, such as whether a writer has successfully met the expectations of an audience, or whether a style is appropriate to the specific occasion of an assignment, such as a scenario. And they cannot detect the use of irony, humor, or other nuances of prose that we want our students to acquire. (For further critiques of specific programs, see Ericsson & Haswell, 2006.)

Given these issues, we offer a set of questions for anyone claiming to have a scoring system that will reduce or eliminate the need to evaluate students' writing:

1. Does the program rely on a corpus of existing, graded papers to grade new papers? Does this then mean that teachers need to keep using the same assignments?

2. Will students know that their writing is being read (and evaluated) by a computer? What will knowing they are writing for a nonhuman reader do to their sense of purpose and audience?

3. What happens when the system has been tested, particularly with random texts? What information does it provide? Does that information provide valid (measures important aspects of writing quality), reliable

(measurements are consistent in similar papers), and useful information for students (helps them in their writing)?

4. How does this information compare to information provided by a teacher in terms of offering a personal, helpful response?

5. If "teaching" writing is accomplished in part through feedback designed to foster self-assessment, how well does the program provide that feedback?

6. What are the ethics of paying for a service that replaces or substitutes for teacher feedback? How is this service being funded, and by whom?

7. If teaching conditions are poor—if class sizes are such that there are too many students so that teachers are overwhelmed and cannot provide adequate feedback—does paying for a service to do some of that work really change the underlying problem?

Summary

In this chapter, we have discussed strategies for using digital tools to provide formative and summative feedback. In the beginning of this chapter we claimed that using digital tools for feedback is an exercise of technological literacy, or the ability to not only use technology but to think critically about it. We hope this chapter has demonstrated the careful thought and time that goes into using digital tools for formative and summative feedback for the purpose of improving student writing.

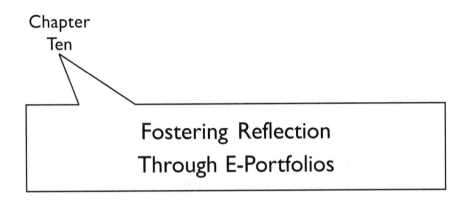

Chapter
Ten

Fostering Reflection
Through E-Portfolios

Throughout this book we have described the uses of different digital writing tools, primarily for generating discrete projects: writing on Word or Google Docs, a series of blog posts, a wiki essay, a digital storytelling production, a podcast, and so on. Throughout a course or a school career, students produce a range of these different digital writing texts in different courses and contexts. In addition to providing students with separate evaluations for each of these texts, it is also useful to evaluate their growth and development in these texts as they improve in their uses of digital literacies—for example, their ability to employ hyperlinks.

In this chapter, we discuss how e-portfolios can be used to provide this long-term evaluation of students' growth over time. Because students are producing digital texts, these texts can be readily linked to an e-portfolio for use in showcasing students' work.

Using Student E-Portfolios to Assess
Students' Digital Writing

Electronic portfolios (or "e-portfolios") are collections of digital text material organized and linked by students to foster their reflections on their development as writers over time (Dimarco, 2006; Montgomery & Wiley, 2004). They can be used for the following:

- Presenting the sum total of all the different work in a specific course
- Creating a series of documents and other materials in different modes and genres, all focusing on a specific topic, problem, or subject
- Displaying a record of all the work that went into responding to a specific assignment—for example, a blog as an invention activity or one or more rough drafts and comments on them by other class members, perhaps also with some meta-reflection by the author, and then a final draft
- Reflecting on growth with an introduction commenting on the work and introducing the viewer to it
- Displaying one's best work, perhaps to meet an assessment benchmark, apply for a job, or just document progress

Although e-portfolios are commonly created as a semester-long project in a specific course, some institutions, such as Indiana University–Purdue University, at Indianapolis; Alverno College; and Kalamazoo College, have large-scale electronic portfolio systems in which all undergraduates document their writing and other work during their academic careers (@ = School and college portfolios).

Why use e-portfolios rather than print portfolios? One key advantage of e-portfolios is that they provide extensive space for storing writing based on folders or links. This makes it far easier to access and review students' work than is the case with a paper file folder (Hewett, 2006). Because students' writing, as well as résumé, transcripts, letters of recommendation, awards, and coursework, are all online, students can grant selected access to advisors, professors, classmates, family, friends, and potential employers, and/or graduate admissions officers, who can review their work online—something that was not possible with paper portfolios. Because digital texts can be more readily linked through digital mapping or links than with paper portfolios, students can reflect on connections between their work. For example, they may organize their e-portfolio using a digital map displaying connections between the different topics and texts they addressed in a course, leading to reflection on what they learned from making those connections.

Another major advantage of e-portfolios is that students' selective work for a class or schools can be readily displayed for other students, teachers, and parents to access that work. For example, an e-portfolio was developed at Timilty Middle School, Roxbury, Massasschusetts (http://www.savetimilty.com/nuke) as part of a forum related to issues facing students in their school experience and lives. The purpose of this forum was to create a school community in which "(1) everyone writes for everyone else and not just the teacher, and (2) everyone, not just the teacher, cares about everyone's writing" (Fahey, Lawrence, & Paratore, 2007, p. 463).

The Purpose of Using E-Portfolios

It is helpful to determine the purpose of using e-portfolios: whether a portfolio will be used as a product-based portfolio or a process-based portfolio. Product-based e-portfolios focus on finished drafts of papers or other artifacts (websites, design projects) that students have worked on throughout a class. Using an e-portfolio for this purpose allows students to post their best work and save or archive it for future reference. Grades reflect the finished product posted on the e-portfolio site. Contents of a product-based portfolio might include a table of contents, final papers, design projects such as a newsletter or brochure, blog entries, websites, digital stories, and reflections on their portfolio texts.

Process-based e-portfolios are more inclusive of drafts and other formative work leading up to the finished product(s). In writing classes, for example, an e-portfolio might include first and second drafts of a paper with peer feedback. Process-based portfolios show student work as it progresses; they make the process visible. Grades reflect effort and amount of improvement throughout the process.

The Tools for Creating E-Portfolios

Gibson and Barrett (2003) contrast two types of structures for creating e-portfolios: GT, or "generic tools," versus CS, or "customized systems." Barrett (2006) perceives a GT structure associated with teacher-developed tools as more consistent with a Web 2.0 orientation in that they are focused more on bottom-up student interactivity, emergent development, creativity, constructivist learning, with open-ended feedback from peers or teachers. In contrast, CS structures employed by commercial e-portfolio products are more associated with a Web 1.0 orientation in terms of being top-down, structured, standardized, and accountability driven. For example, many of the commercial digital portfolios programs, such as Angel Learning (http://www.angellearning.com/products/eportfolio/default.html), Eportfolio (http://www.eportfolio.org), and Chalk and Wire (http://www.chalkandwire.com), employ CS server-based, customized templates based on categories for storing the texts and the use of rating scales or rubrics for assessing those texts (@ = Portfolio software). For example, Chalk and Wire uses a RubricMarker to assess specific aspects of a portfolio and then aggregate that data.

One limitation of many of these CS programs is that students often have to conform to predetermined structures that afford students little opportunity to create an e-portfolio unique to their work within their own classroom (Ellertson, 2005). One advantage of alternative open-source GT portfolio programs (http://www.osportfolio.org) is that they allow students and teachers greater flexibility in the design of an e-portfolio specific to their own classroom writing. However, given the bottom-up, idiosyncratic nature of a GT structure, for purposes of school or statewide assessments, it may be difficult to compare students in their unique classroom contexts, which, if used for writing assessment purposes, which may limit the reliability of assessment of students or programs. As a result, districts or states that want to use e-portfolios for assessment of writing quality are often forced to employ CS structures.

Using Blogs and Wikis as Portfolios

One example of a GT e-portfolio structure involves the use of blogs or wikis (Barrett, 2006; Lamb, 2006) (@ = Using blogs and wikis to create portfolios). Morgan (2006) argues that blogs and wikis allow students freedom to create their own learning spaces in which to engage in reflection consistent with their own needs. Students can readily create links between their writing, as well as use RSS feeds to share their reflections with peers and teachers. Because students may already be using blogs and wikis for their writing and revision, they could then simply add the reflective dimension to their blog or wiki writing, rather than having to transport their digital writing onto another e-portfolio site. If students are using blogs and wikis during their entire school career, they could be reflecting on their growth over years.

Blogs and wikis are also useful for creating e-portfolios that can be searched according to chronological order or topic. In using a blog as an e-portfolio in her classes, Tara Autrey (Hicks, Russo, Autrey, Gardner, Kabodian, & Edington, 2007) noted that the blog served as a means of easily organizing her students' writing:

> Now I can easily view a student's writing samples with one click of a button. Because I have laid out pieces in a linear fashion from the earliest to the most recent work, students, their parents, and I are easily able to see progress over time. The digital portfolio also allows me to instantly see whether a particular child is meeting curricular objectives. In addition, I can quickly pull up several students' work and do a collective assessment, noting common errors and successes. This helps me decide whether I have presented the required curriculum and what I need to review or introduce to students. (p. 453)

Other teachers who were using e-portfolios (Hicks et al., 2007) noted the following (p. 491):

- It is a great way to compile and display student work. I think I may use it with some of my students next year. . . . We could place the student's websites on our school's website.

- Creating the [e-portfolio] artifacts for this class has helped me gain a better idea of how I will approach my classes next year. I will also be able to help my fellow teachers set up webpages, which was recently requested by our superintendent.

- I plan on having an electronic scrapbook for each of my students, on which we will build throughout the year. I hope to move onto electronic portfolios of some type as well. I will continue to update the newsletter I created, and I will link it to the class website I will be designing during the summer.

One limitation in using blog posts or wikis for possible inclusion in e-portfolios is that students may be intimidated by the idea of having their writing evaluated, particularly if they are just starting blogging or wiki writing, and are experimenting with adopting different voices and styles (@ = Creating portfolios).

It helps, then, to have students distinguish between including all their work in an e-portfolio and selecting those texts that best illustrate the use of certain composing processes or digital literacies based on certain criteria. To store all their work, students could create a digital archive on the school server, using tools such as BackPack (http://www.backpackit.com) or School WebLocker (http://www.schoolweblockers.com), and then select those texts for inclusion in their e-portfolios.

It is important that students have a clear sense of what they are expected to include in their e-portfolios. At the Mt. Edgecomb High School, Sitka, Alaska, Todd Bergman (2006) asks students to include the following items in their portfolios:

> A personal cover page, an annotated table of contents (each item in the table of contents has a short explanation or description that explains your reason for inclusion it in the portfolio—what skills, growth, capabilities and/or accomplishments does the work represent?), a personal statement (this may be an introduction and can also be used as an application essay for colleges and scholarships or employers), a resume, transcripts, letters of reference, a minimum number of work samples (these should represent a minimal number of individual capacities or work areas—each sample should include a brief reflection on its significance), articles, newspaper clippings, certificates, photographs, or other evidence of different—nonacademic

activities (these may include sports), materials on family and culture, clubs or organizations, work experiences, community service, and hobbies. (p. 3)

One of Bergman's students, Katiana Bourdukofsky (2003), included a multicolored home page containing the title of her e-portfolio, a picture of her against a black background, and a sidebar with a table of contents. Her links take the viewer to her résumé, four academic projects, and personal material (buddies and family, community and activities). She briefly introduces each academic project and provides a context for these projects, explaining why she chose to place them in her e-portfofio. For example, at the link to her academic essay project on Shakespeare's *Hamlet,* titled "Infatuation, Loyalty, and Weakness," she explains that she included this project not only because it represents some of her best work but also because it displays her "complete understanding of the metaphor and allusion usage." On the page about her project in a course on the Pacific Rim, she includes a digital photograph of a (physical) poster she created that contains illustrated photos of Maori face painting. Another link displays her work on Alaskan native literature, and the fourth opens a project in which students studied the relationship between computer technology and the stock market (for other student portfolios, see @ = Student portfolios).

Using E-Portfolios to Foster Reflection

A primary reason for using e-portfolios is to foster student reflection about their writing. It is important to provide specific directions for students' reflections, for example, having students describe: "1) where the project was done (its context), 2) why the project was done (its purpose), and 3) what learning experiences were accomplished (learning demonstrated)" (Bergman, 2006). Teachers can also model portfolio construction by creating their own e-portfolios to reflect on their teaching (Kilbane & Milman, 2003) (@ = Teaching portfolios).

Students can reflect on reasons for differences in their writing quality due to differences in their sense of purpose and audience, interest, engagement, knowledge of the topic, expertise in using digital writing tools, and so on. For example, they may note that because they did not have a clear sense of their audience in assignment A, they had more difficulty with that assignment than with assignment B, when they had a clear sense of their audience. This may then lead them to attempt to clarify their sense of audience in their future writing assignments.

Students can also reflect on how their texts display their proficiencies in various digital literacies. For example, Elizabeth Boeser asked her college writing students to use some blog posts to reflect on their uses of digital writing in the class in response to some prompts:

- What did you learn to do well? How do you know this?

> I learned how to express my opinion. I know this because I was always scared to share my opinion because I was scared of what other people would think, but now I learned that no matter what your opinion there is always information to back up your theory and if people don't think the same way you do then you prove your opinion and come up with things to support you. (Shannon Saleck)

- What kinds of digital skills did you learn?

> I think I will start blogging more now because I realized that it helped me a lot to express my feelings about things without having to talk about it because I am so scared of confrontation. I also really enjoyed making the wiki because I never heard of a PBwiki and I thought it was so cool that I actually got to make one and have something that people can look at and it can help other people with research. (Shannon Saleck)

> I learned how to link other pages to certain wikis and also link research to certain pages and find research links, the easy way. (Breanna Ramroop)

- Copy and paste in some examples of your best work (or the work for which you are most proud) from your blog or wiki. Make a working link to that material. Explain why you think it's particularly good.

> I personally like any of the work I have done from my blog on the different blogs from *Speak*. I got to really show my true feelings about high school and really show who I really am. I really expressed myself about things that I normally would not and it makes me feel really good that I could do that.

> I think the tree that Mr. Freeman makes her draw symbolizes Melinda's growth. Trees grow a lot and I think the whole point of the trees being in the story is to show how Melinda grows though out the story. First she is she shaded, she hasn't become a seed of a tree yet. Then she begins to talk to people and become friends with a couple people. She gets stronger, and says more what is on her mind. She starts to think about boys, about being with her old friends again, she stands up for herself more and defends herself and how she feels. It is easy to grow or "draw a tree" when your [sic] small, everything you know in the world is perfect until you grow up and see what the world is really like. When you are little everything seems easy. Drawings seem easy, math seems easy, and school in general is so easy. Then you grow up, and as you do, things start to get harder. You realize that life is not so easy. Drawings get

harder, school gets harder but, the thing is, even if everything gets harder, you are growing in mind, body, and spirit." (Shannon Saleck)

I think this is one of the better blogs I have done on the group book I had read. It makes it seem that I went more into depth with this book and tried to figure out what some of the chapters or passages might have meant. I took it on a more psychological level.

As I read the last few chapters, it made me realize that most of these men are normal with a slight disability. Even though they are in a mental ward, they seem completely normal on the inside of this facility. Some of the men are just like children, because they have been cooped up like such and don't necessarily get their way when they have a group therapy session. I take it to be the Nurse Ratchet is a stern mother (sort of) and she just wants what is right for her patients. Though she does a bit more than a normal mother would, she is also killing these men little by little. (Breanna Ramroop)

- On which paper do you think you did your best writing? Do you feel this way because of how peers evaluated your work, how much effort you put into it, or the grade the teacher assigned? Explain your feelings.

  I think I did my best writing on the group book paper. I think I did my best on this because the paper we were writing about had a great topic and it was a strong paper that anyone could've written, but I just got a good feeling from finishing it and also writing. I got a good feel from it because the other group members had some of the same ideas as me and it just all worked together. (Breanna Ramroop)

- What are some things you want to work on in the future in your writing?

  The main thing that I have been deeply thinking about is using my digital skills combined with writing skills I learned in this class also combined with my passion for film and documentary to create a homelessness-awareness blog through journal entries and a short documentary series that creates awareness and a push for involvement in youth when it comes to homelessness. (Josh Hiben)

- How was peer feedback valuable to your learning?

  It helped me to hear when my peers thought something was awkward, or wordy. Sometimes my own ear doesn't catch that stuff because I wrote it. It was always nice and helpful to hear their opinion, although usually there aren't really spelling errors or anything. I wrote a better paper when there was peer feedback. (Kate Mackin)

It's different when you get comments on your work by your teacher, but when you get comments on your work by other students, you get the opinions from students your age. It's a different and helpful way to get critiqued on your work. (Kyle Rusnacko)

When it came to comments on the blogs or wikis, it really helped me see what others think and what their true opinions were on the subjects at hand. It was a mind opener. (Breanna Ramroop)

- How did teacher comments influence or change your writing?

One of the biggest things I appreciated from you being my teacher is your feedbacks and comments on all my papers. I was so happy when I got my first paper back full of comments because I was like SHE REALLY CARES. And every comment you made always made my paper that much more dominant. When it comes to college I will most likely e-mail you my papers. (Josh Hiben)

- Explain which project you worked on that you liked the best or that you found most interesting. Explain where the project was done (its context, blog, wiki, paper, PowerPoint), why the project was done (its purpose), and what learning experiences were accomplished.

I really liked the blogging for *The Perks of Being a Wallflower*. I thought writing letters was a really good idea. It helped me get more involved in the book, because as I was reading it I became more engaged. I thought to myself, "What will I write about this? What is an appropriate response?" Instead of just reading, I felt like I was involved in the book. (Kate Mackin)

I really found the wiki projects most interesting, the *Montana 1948* one because I got to learn a lot about Montana and things like that. I think it was done on the wiki because it was easier to organize things everyone could contribute to the wiki instead of just the blog because you cannot really contribute the same was as you can in the wiki. (Shannon Saleck)

I think I liked the "Schooled-the-Write-Way" wiki the most. I thought it was interesting because it took place over almost the whole term and it was nice to tie in *Speak* and *The Perks of Being a Wallflower* into it as well. I also liked how it was a step-by-step process: choosing the city, choosing the school, and then choosing the characters. I think its purpose was to pretend like we were in a different high school atmosphere than that of JHS, and deal with issues that don't necessarily take place here. I learned of different issues that people deal with and how to cope with them. It was a fun and beneficial unit to focus on. (Kyle Rusnacko)

- How did your digital writing change at all in the last two terms? Do you think you will use any of these tools in the future because of these changes?

It became more comfortable and confident for sure. I was into every response and made sure it counted. Because of this digital writing, I have become a much better writer. I will guarantee using almost all of these learning experiences next semester in my college career and in my career after college. (Josh Hiben)

My writing changed a lot over the two terms. I became a lot more outgoing in my writing instead of being scared to share my feelings. I became a lot more advanced in my writing skills. I also became more knowledgeable about many different kinds of writing styles. I think I will use a lot of these skills in the future. I plan on making a blog just to talk about things because that really helped me express my feelings instead of not talking about it. I hope to someday make another PBwiki, maybe in college, because I found it really helpful and easy to organize my thoughts and information. (Shannon Saleck)

I learned more about research and how to find things much more easily online, rather than go to the library and look through books. Some things came easier with articles online and it was much easier to cite things from the Internet and how to make a paper look professional. When I have to write things in the future, I will make sure to use all of these tools that I have learned and also to take a little time to process thoughts about writing and doing other projects. (Breanna Ramroop)

Teachers can also provide students with standards and criteria to foster self-reflection (@ = Evaluating portfolios). Rather than importing generic standards and criteria often employed in CS e-portfolios, you should employ standards and criteria specific to the digital writing unique to the class so that students have some ownership and understanding of these criteria (Broad, 2003). Students can then use these standards and criteria to identify illustrative examples demonstrating that they have achieved certain standards. For example, if one of the standards has to do with the ability to integrate images and video into their writing, then students would seek out examples that illustrate this standard to include in their e-portfolio.

Students can also use their e-portfolios to provide evidence of their ability to revise their texts, and they reflect on how those revisions served to improve their writing quality. To document revisions with wikis, they can include different versions of their writing that is housed in wikis under "history." They can then highlight changes across different versions, noting how, for example, adding more information serve to bolster the strength of their arguments.

One of the challenges of portfolios is that creating, responding to, and evaluating them can be time-consuming. Students often need time during class to work with each other on constructing their portfolios. In doing so, they can then provide face-to-face or online feedback to one another about their portfolios using the criteria you have developed. When faced with 120 students' portfolios in his high school English classes, Richard Kent (2006) employed a writing-center model in which each student was paired up with an editor who provided written feedback to the students' writing included in their portfolios. After students write a cover letter introducing their work, as well as a reflection, they also receive letters from peers, parents, Kent, and other readers responding to their portfolio work.

Using E-Portfolios for Writing Assessments

E-portfolios have been used as part of school or statewide writing assessments in lieu of standardized writing tests. Portfolios are a more valid measure of writing quality than is the case with a standardized timed exam written for unknown audiences about a topic about which a student may have little knowledge. The use of print portfolios in states such as Kentucky has been shown to have a positive influence on writing instruction in classrooms because teachers are then focusing more on composing processes than is the case in states with standardized writing tests (Hillocks, 2002).

On the other hand, using e-portfolios for external district or statewide assessments creates a very different purpose for the selection of texts and reflection on those texts than is the case with students' own uses of portfolios in their own classroom, particularly if the district or state e-portfolios employ a "CS" structure. When e-portfolios are used for school or statewide assessment, they are judged according to external assessment criteria that may not be consistent with their classroom writing experiences. Barrett (2007) argues that this use of e-portfolios for high-stakes assessment assumes that the meaning of e-portfolio texts is "constant across users, contexts, and purposes" (p. 436). In contrast, from a student's perspective, the meaning of their texts written within their unique classroom content according to standards operating in that classroom cannot necessarily be judged using externally defined standards.

On the other hand, given the value of employing e-portfolios as a more valid alternative to standardized writing tests, Barrett (2007) proposes that students create three different kinds of collections that serve different purposes: (a) a digital archive as an ongoing collection that serves their own individual needs, (b) an e-portfolio based on selected texts from the archive that captures students' use of their own voice and stories in their selected texts and reflections unique to their classroom context, and (c) an institution-centered database, or assessment management system based on specific writing tasks and scoring rubrics that can be used for school or district assessment purposes. For Barrett, the archive serves the need for "assessment for learning" while the database serves the purpose of "assessment of learning" (p. 440). Furthermore, the purpose for the archive and e-portfolio is defined by the student, organized by students based on their own selections, maintained over a long time, used to foster students' self-reflection, and is not related to high-stakes decisions. The purpose for the database is defined by the institution based on predetermined selection of texts; the development occurs at the end of a course; and the writing is scored according to an external set of rubrics related to making high-stakes decisions (Barrett, 2005). All of this reflects the importance of defining the purposes for which e-portfolios are being used.

Summary

In this chapter, we argue that e-portfolios can be used to foster student reflection on digital writing. E-portfolios allow students to include a range of different multimodal texts illustrative of their work, organize that work, and create links within that work to foster reflections on patterns in their writing. While e-portfolios can be used for district and state-wide assessments, this represents a different purpose for using e-portfolios than is the case with classroom e-portfolios. In addition to using commercial e-portfolio platforms, students can also use blogs or wikis to create e-portfolios. From documenting and reflecting on their digital writing, students learn to reflect on strengths and weaknesses in their writing, leading to growth in their writing.

Chapter Eleven

Five Ways to Grow as a Digital Writing Teacher

Engaging students in digital writing requires learning and growing in some new directions as a teacher. As a busy teacher coping with the daily demands of teaching, learning to use and integrate a whole new set of Web 2.0 digital writing tools can be daunting and difficult. Moreover, traditional professional development workshops on technology integration may not meet a teacher's unique needs or involve hands-on, follow-up support, suggesting the need for supportive professional development that serves to foster implementation, reflection, and change (Vrasidas & Glass, 2007).

In this final chapter, we suggest five ways to grow as a digital writing teacher.

1. Join Online Communities Devoted to Teaching Digital Writing

There is lot of useful information available from the growing number of online communities devoted to teaching digital writing. Teachers can access this information by using RSS feeds to subscribe to relevant blogs, wikis, and podcasts in which educators describe their use of new digital writing tools and how use of these tools influences their students' writing (@ = Educators' blogs, @ = Classroom-school-library-professional development wikis). For example, the previously mentioned weekly podcast, Teachers Teaching Teachers (http://teachersteachingteachers.org) organized by Paul Allison, involves K–12 teachers sharing their experiences using digital writing tools (@ = online professional development communities). Further information on uses of Web 2.0 technology tools is available on the EdTechTalk network of podcasts (http://www.edtechtalk.com/), including EdTechWeekly, 21st Century Learning, EdTechBrainstorm, EdTechTalk, EdTechTalk K–12, Making Connections, and Women of Web 2.0 (@ = Educator and classroom podcasts).

Teachers can download presentations from technology conferences—for example, the NECC conference (http://center.uoregon.edu/ISTE/NECC2008), the K–12 Online Conference (http://www.k12onlineconference.org), or the Learning 2.0 conference (http://learning2cn.ning.com). They can also join social networks of teachers interested in Web 2.0 technology integration—for example, School 2.0 (http://school20.ning.com) or Classroom 2.0 (http://classroom20.ning.com).

Free professional development resources are also available, including journals—*T.H.E. Journal* (http://www.thejournal.com), *Edutopia* (http://www.edutopia.org), *KAIROS* (http://kairos.technorhetoric.net), and *Computers and Composition Online* (http://www.bgsu.edu/cconline)—and professional organizations—the National Council of Teachers of English (http://www.ncte.org/collections/weblit), the National Writing Project (http://www.nwp.org/cs/public/print/resource_topic/writing_and_technology), the Apple Learning Exchange (http://edcommunity.apple.com/ali), PBS Teachers (http://www.pbs.org/teachers), Education World (http://www.educationworld.com/a_tech/index.shtml), and 4Teachers (http://www.4teachers.org).

Teams of teachers within a district could enroll in NCTE's CoLEARN Writing Intiative program (http://www.ncte.org/store/learning/116735.htm, $1,200 for 12 teachers for a year). This online in-service program provides teachers with access to full-text articles, sharing of ideas about teaching writing, online discussions with teachers from all over the country, and sessions with composition experts.

2. View and Create Online Teacher Cases

Another way to learn from online communities is to view online cases of teachers describing and reflecting on their teaching that include video clips of students' learning, examples of student work, and teacher reflection (@ = Online teacher cases). Reading cases, as well as creating cases, fosters understanding of teachers' thinking about teaching within specific classroom contexts and how teachers adopt and employ tools within their own unique, specific contexts (Anson, 2002).

The Goldman-Carnegie Quest Program (2006) site (http://gallery.carnegiefoundation.org/insideteaching/quest/collections.html) includes a "teaching gallery" of K–12 online teaching cases that contain inquiry-based, teacher reflections about teaching English language arts. For example, Pincus (2006) addresses a question about her high school students' drama class, "How can I connect students to the work of Shakespeare by infusing 'main stage' teaching with 'second stage' practices?" by showing examples of her students' drama performances.

Hutchinson (2006) examines how she can draw on her African American elementary students' oral traditions in teaching literacy. These teachers use video clips of their students' drama performance and language use to reflect on how their instruction leads to student engagement in learning. Finally, Steven Krause constructed a case study of his college "Broadcast Composition" course in which he employed audio files, podcasts, and screencasts to engage his students in audio production of their writing (http://www.bgsu.edu/cconline/krause1).

Within a school or district, teachers might create and share their own cases consisting simply of written descriptions or reflections of their teaching and/or videos of their teaching. Housing these cases within a specific school or district means that teachers already have a context for a shared understanding of their standards, curriculum, and culture.

3. Create a Personal Learning Network

One of the primary Web 2.0 digital literacies is the ability to network and build relationships online, something that students are continually doing on Facebook. In his 2007 K–12 online conference presentation, Utecht (2007) argues that while accessing online communities can provide a lot of useful information, they may not necessarily provide information relevant to a teacher's need in a "just-in-time" manner. He proposes that teachers create their own "personal learning networks" consisting of a group of teachers who interact with one another to address their needs.

To build this network, he suggests using an RSS reader such as Bloglines or Google Reader to subscribe to specific blogs, particularly their own colleagues' blogs, that address specific needs to which teachers can pose comments. He also suggests creating links to colleagues or support persons using Twitter (http://twitter.com), (@ = Twitter) IMing, or social-networking sites for sharing ideas or posing specific questions to receive immediate answers to questions.

In addition to these tools, teachers can create their social networks for a specific group using open-source software such as Ning (http://www.ning.com) (for an example, see the Education Ning: http://education.ning.com), Elgg (http://

elgg.net/), Drupal (http://drupal.org), Orkut (http://www.orkut.com), People Aggregator (http://www.broadbandmechanics.com), Virtual Learning Commons (http://sourceforge.net/projects/vlc), or iSocial (http://sourceforge.net/projects/socialnetwork) (@ = Social learning sites). In these networks, teachers can include immediate colleagues as well as other invited people whose expertise they value. Then when they try out digital writing tools, they can share successes and challenges with people for their comments and advice.

4. Conduct Teacher Action Research on Teaching Digital Writing

A fourth way to grow as a teacher involves conducting teacher action research projects about specific issues or questions related to teaching digital writing. Teacher action research involves looking systematically at the relationship between teaching and student learning (Glanz, 2003) (@ = Teacher action research). Teachers identify specific issues or questions related to their teaching—for example, whether students can use e-portfolios to reflect in a thoughtful manner about their writing. They then collect data based on observations, interviews, or analysis of students' digital writing.

Such research could serve to demonstrate the value of using digital writing tools in the classroom. For example, Ewa McGrail and Anne Davis were curious about the value of blogging in Anne's fifth-grade class, so they conducted a research project:

> Our classroom blogging research project that spanned a school year examined what happens when fifth graders blog and converse about literacies in class and beyond. A class blog was created by the blogging teacher to engage students in thinking and blogging about their learning and what it meant to them. Then student blogs were launched (http://neccposter2007.googlepages.com/linkstoclassblogsandstudentblogsattheele). Student and teacher reflections and conversations, both verbally and on blogs, were employed as a tool for deeper thinking and as a learning strategy. Students were taught the following attributes of blogging: questioning, thinking, writing, collaborating, reflecting, commenting, linking, and proofreading. To push the learning connections and stretch students to higher levels of thinking, comment starters were used. Examples included: "This made me think about…"; "This post is relevant because…"; "I don't understand…". Throughout, the class blog served as a model for composing thoughtful posts and comments. The current class blog post was shared at each session with the entire class to summarize and celebrate learning.

Dialogue in the classroom was crucial. Understanding aspects of writing in public spaces was emphasized. There was a focused effort on nurturing a community of bloggers within and beyond the classroom.

Our initial analysis began by reviewing student writing samples in a quantitative fashion (Weber, 1990). As we looked at pre- and post-grade-level scores based on counts, averages, and readability indicators by the Flesch-Kincaid formulas, we found that most students improved in grade levels, but these scores did not tell us much about the attributes of writing. Our next step was to conduct a qualitative content analysis (Creswell, 2003) by focusing on the following areas of writing: attitude, content, voice, connections and relationships, thinking, and craft.

From this analysis three larger themes emerged. First, there was a change in attitude. Students were motivated and they looked forward to reading posts and responding to comments. There was an increase in blogger confidence reflected in enthusiasm and a willingness to take risks in thinking and writing on their blogs. They were also anxious to experiment with language and were more focused in their interactions with their readers. Second, student awareness of the audience was evident as the audience became a driving force because the students cared about, related to, and interacted with them to improve their communications. They strived to make their writing interesting, engaging, and clear for their audience. They also sought feedback, support, and ideas. These student bloggers developed strong voices as relationships strengthened. Third, there were changes in the quantity and quality of writing. Sentences became longer. Students attempted to write in a more complex way. They used richer vocabulary and syntax and became more playful with blogging by using figurative language and being creative. They experimented with connected words and phrases and made an effort to explain and illustrate their ideas and thinking. This writing did not always translate into a polished product. However, they were definitely taking steps to richer, meaningful, and engaged writing. This needs to be viewed in a very positive light. If there are no attempts to take risks, there is no room for growth.

By posing questions about the value of blogging and then collecting data to address these questions, Ewa and Anne demonstrate how blogging serves to enhance students' writing ability, something that teachers can use to justify their use of digital writing tools in their classrooms.

As a social studies teacher committed to fostering a social justice, multicultural agenda, Aby (2007) was concerned about the fact that her largely white, middle class students in her fall 2007 government classes at Jefferson High School in Bloomington, Minnesota, needed to address how institutional forces related to racial differences shaped the political election process. She believed that by having students share their views about how issues of race influenced the political primary elections, they would begin to recognize the importance of the forces of racism operating in society. She also believed that by using a blog, students of different races would feel more comfortable sharing their perspectives than in face-to-face classroom discussions.

She developed a blog (http://2008presidentialrace-meredith.blogspot.com/) for use during a 10-week period that focused on the 2008 presidential primary campaigns. For her blog prompts, she encouraged students to engage in research about the issues addressed in the primaries as well as how the candidates' stances would influence racial and ethnic groups. For example, one of her prompts asked students to reflect on whether and how candidates who are African American such as Senator Obama represent the "Black vote." She also asked students to reflect on which candidates and parties were most likely to attract the Latino vote.

In addition to providing students with background readings on these issues, she also built classroom discussions around the issues addressed in the blog prompts. At the end of the grading period, she asked students to submit their best response and their best original blog post for her evaluation based on criteria of the organization of information, consideration of alternatives, disciplinary content, elaboration of ideas, evidence of research, number of posts, and writing quality.

Given her goal of fostering cooperative group work in diverse settings, she assigned students to small groups according to differences in race and sex. These groups were then responsible for creating a wiki page for their class wiki based on a review of two assigned chapters from the students' government textbook.

As a reflective teacher, Aby (2007) was curious the whether her use of the blog was helping students address issues of racial difference. She therefore conducted a research project to complete her master's program thesis requirement. She interviewed teachers and students about their perceptions of effective multicultural education; asked a colleague to observe a classroom discussion; took field notes about the degree to which her prompts served to address issues of race, her students' reactions to her activities, and their ability to work together in groups; and surveyed her students to determine their perceptions of her activities.

By comparing differences in the discussions across time, she noted improvements in the quality of the classroom discussions, differences she attributes to their blogging, which provided them with "more experiences and opinions and material to draw from. This made it easier for all of them to participate" (p. 24). She noted the following:

> The blog activity radically changed my class. It equalized participation in a way I have never been able to do in class. Quiet students did not have to

> fight to have their voices heard. In fact, my quieter students found more of a voice online. One African American girl, who is struggling academically in class, responded to two or three people every post even though she was only required to respond to one student. However, in class she is very self-conscious about speaking. Another student, an academically successful white girl who is who is terrified of speaking in class, posted lengthy write-ups. She frequently made the decision to post first, which successfully carved out a spot for her in our discussion, and set the tone for the whole class' discussion. (p. 24)

She also found that having to conduct research to complete her blog prompts helped prepare students for the discussions. She noted that:

> They successfully tied in information from other areas of study, resources they had researched independently, and posts that they read from their classmates. This is the best discussion I have ever seen high school students have about race in my eleven years of teaching. It was an academic political science discussion based on research, personal experience and observation…the blog was successful at preparing them for the activity because it used a medium they were already excited about and because it is an authentic medium for campaigns and election. The students made several connections to things they had said in their blog posts or that others had said in their blog posts.

Aby's (2007) student survey data indicated that "the blog and the candidate presentations were the activities that gave them the best understanding of the election." Although most students preferred to make their own selections of peers to work with, half of the students of color indicated that they preferred teacher-assigned groups based on race and sex because it meant that they were more likely to work in more mixed groups.

From conducting her study, Aby (2007) recognized the value of her blogging to enhance her students' collaborative learning and discussions, results she shared with other teachers in her social studies Advanced Placement professional learning community.

5. Create a Teacher E-Portfolio to Reflect on and Document Growth

Finally, as we noted in the last chapter, we recommend that teachers keep a teacher e-portfolio to not only reflect on teaching but also to document development over time, a process that can be useful for demonstrating one's effectiveness as a teacher for purposes of tenure or administrative evaluations. As noted in the last chapter, this e-portfolio could simply be a blog or wiki. One study of posts from 12 middle school teachers' blogs found that teachers use blog posts to engage in some degree of reflection about their teaching, although there was not much evidence of critical analysis of their teaching (Ray & Hocutt, 2006). It is important that teachers be willing to think critically about teaching in terms of identifying goals for improvement and then monitoring growth in achieving those goals.

Teachers can also access examples of online "course portfolios" to perceive how other teachers reflect on their courses (@ = Teaching portfolios). For example, the Peer Review of Teaching Project (PRTP) (2007), housed at the University of Nebraska, provides teachers with a repository of 240 course portfolios for review by other teachers. This project suggests the value of creating a similar repository in a school or district for sharing of teacher reflections.

Summary and an Invitation

In this chapter, we describe five things teachers can to enhance their own teaching: join online communities, view and create online teacher cases, create a personal learning network, conduct teacher action research, and create a teacher portfolio. All of these activities are designed to keep teachers informed about and reflect on methods for teaching digital writing.

We close with one more invitation to join the community of readers of this book by contributing material to the resource wiki, http://digitalwriting.pbwiki.com (password: digwriting; please do not delete material). We hope that the ideas presented in this book will serve to enhance students' engagement with writing.

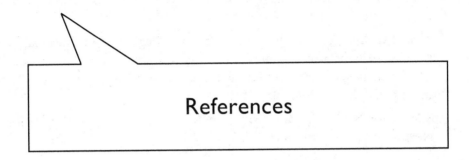

References

Aby, M. S. (2007). *Multicultural education in the suburbs: Increasing minority student inclusion in predominantly white high schools.* Master's research report, College of Saint Scholastica, Duluth, Minnesota.

Adams, J. (2006). The part played by instructional media in distance education. *Journal of Studies in Media. & Information Literacy Education, 6* (2). Retrieved September 16, 2008, from http://tinyurl.com/5dm6ag

Allison, P. (2006). Blogging is multimodal. [Podcast]. *Weblogs & Wikis & Feeds, Oh My!* Retrieved August 5, 2008, from http://tinyurl.com/2pgsjs

Alphonso, C. (2004, January 16). Student rebel beats McGill in essay fight. Globeandmail.com. A1. Retrieved August 13, 2008, from http://tinyurl.com/59b6ov

American Psychological Association. (2001). *Publication manual of the American Psychological Association* (5th ed.). Washington, DC: Author.

Anderson, L. H. (2006). *Speak.* New York: Smith.

Anderson, R. (2006). *Beyond PowerPoint: Building a new classroom presenter.* Retrieved May 2, 2007, from http://campustechnology.com/mcv/resources/solutioncenters/center/presentation/article/?msid=6&id=39827&c1p=1

Annan, J. (2006). Literary scrapbooks online: An electronic reader-response project. *ReadWriteThink*. Retrieved May 1, 2007, from http://www.readwritethink.org/lessons/lesson_view.asp?id=787

Anson, C. M. (2002). *The WAC casebook: Scenes for faculty reflection and program development.* New York: Oxford University Press.

Anson, C. M. (2006). Assessing writing in cross-curricular programs: Determining the locus of activity. *Assessing Writing, 11,* 100–112.

Anson, C. M. (2008). We never wanted to be cops: Plagiarism, institutional paranoia, and shared responsibility. In R. M. Howard & A. Robillard (Eds.)., *Pluralizing plagiarism: Identities, contexts, pedagogies* (pp. 231–246). Portsmouth, NH: Boynton/Cook.

Anson, C. M., & Beach, R. (1995). *Journals in the classroom: Writing to learn.* Norwood, MA: Christopher-Gordon.

Apple Education. (2006). Elementary school students become podcasting pros. *Profiles in success: Wells Elementary School.* Retrieved July 30, 2007, from http://www.apple.com/education/profiles/wells/

Barbetta, P. M., & Spears-Bunton, L. A. (2007). Learning to write: Technology for students with disabilities in secondary inclusive classrooms. *English Journal, 96* (4), 86–89.

Barrett, H. C. (2005). *Researching electronic portfolios and learner engagement.* Retrieved April 28, 2007, from http://electronicportfolios.org/reflect/index.html

Barrett, H. C. (2006). *Authentic assessment with electronic portfolios using common software and Web 2.0 tools.* Retrieved April 26, 2007, from http://electronicportfolios.org/web20.html

Barrett, H. C. (2007). Researching electronic portfolios and learner engagement: The REFLECT Initiative. *Journal of Adolescent and Adult Literacy, 50* (6), 436–449.

Barton, M. (2004). Embrace the wiki way. *Tikiwiki.* Retrieved October 31, 2006, from http://www.mattbarton.net/tikiwiki/tiki-read_article.php?articleId=4

Barton, M., & Cummings, R. (Eds.). (2008). *Wiki writing: Collaborative learning in the college classroom.* Ann Arbor, MI: University of Michigan Press/Digital Culture Books.

Beach, R., & Friedrich, T. (2006). Response to writing. In C. A. MacArthur, S. Graham, & J. Fitzgerald (Eds.), *Handbook of writing research* (pp. 222–234). New York: Guilford Press.

Beach, R., & Myers, J. (2001). *Inquiry-based English instruction: Engaging students in life and literature.* New York: Teachers College Press.

Beckman, J. D. (2003). *Voice recognition software for learning disabled students. Speak to write manual.* Washington, DC: U.S. Department of Education. Retrieved May 9, 2007, from http://www.edc.org/spk2wrt/manual_toc.htm

Beeghly, D. G. (2005). It's about time: Using electronic literacy discussion groups with adult learners. *Journal of Adolescent & Adult Literacy, 49* (1), 12–21.

Berger, A. (2005/2006). Playing to learning. *The Murphy Reporter.* Retrieved April 20, 2008 from http://www.sjmc.umn.edu/mreporter/winter2005/neverwinter.html

Bergman, H. (2006). *About digital portofolios.* Retrieved November 2, 2006, from http://www.mehs.educ.state.ak.us/portfolios/portfolio.html

Black, A. (2005). The use of asynchronous discussion: Creating a text of talk. *Contemporary Issues in Technology and Teacher Education, 5* (1), 5–24.

Black, R. W. (2008). *Adolescents and online fan fiction.* New York: Lang.

Blair, J. A. (2004). The rhetoric of visual arguments. In C. A. Hill & M. Helmers (Eds.)., *Defining visual rhetorics* (pp. 41–61). Mahwah, NJ: Erlbaum.

Blood, R. (2002). *The Weblog handbook: Practical advice on creating and maintaining your blog.* New York: Perseus.

Bolter, J. D., & Grusin, R. (2000). *Remediation: Understanding new media.* Cambridge, MA: MIT Press.

Boss, S., & Krauss, J. (2008). *Reinventing project-based learning: Your field guide to real-world projects in the digital age.* Washington, DC: International Society for Technology in Education.

Bourdukofsky, K. (2003). *Katania Sasha Bourdukofsky: Portfolio.* Retrieved November 2, 2006, from http://www.mehs.educ.state.ak.us/portfolios/katiab/katiab.htm

boyd, d. (2006a). A blogger's blog: Exploring the definition of a medium. *Reconstruction 6* (4). Retrieved March 3, 2007, from http://reconstruction.eserver.org/064/boyd.shtml

boyd, d. (2006b). Discussion: MySpace and Deleting Online Predators Act (DOPA); Interview with Henry Jenkins and Danah Boyd. Retrieved June 28, 2006, from http://www.danah.org/papers/MySpaceDOPA.html

Bretag, R. (2007). *Blogging: It isn't about the writing.* Retrieved January 9, 2008, from http://www.bretagdesigns.com/technologist/?p=349

Breuch, L. A. (2004). *Virtual peer review: Teaching and learning about writing in online environments.* Albany, NY: State University of New York Press.

Broad, B. (2003). *What we really value: Beyond rubrics in teaching and assessing writing.* Logan, UT: Utah State University.

Brockhaus, A., & Groom, M. (2007). *Using Wikipedia to reenvision the term paper.* Retrieved January 7, 2008, from http://connect.educause.edu/Library/Abstract/UsingWikipediatoReenvisio/45402

Brunk-Chavez, B. L., & Miller, S. J. (2007). Decentered, disconnected, and digitized: The importance of shared space. *Kairos, 11* (2). Retrieved March 5, 2007, from http://english.ttu.edu/Kairos/11.2/binder.html?topoi/brunk-miller/index.html

Bryant, S. (2006). *Videoblogging for dummies.* Indianapolis, IN: Wiley.

Budenski, J. (2007). Using visual art to assess thinking in a language arts classroom. *Minnesota English Journal, 43* (1), 186–206.

Burbules, N. C. (2007). E-lessons learned. In L. Smolin, K. Lawless, & N. C. Burbules (Eds.), *Information and communication technologies* (pp. 207–216). Malden, MA: Blackwell.

Burbules, N. C., & Callister, T. A., Jr. (2000). *Watch IT: The risks and promises of information technologies for education.* Oxford, UK: Westview Press.

Burell, C. (2008, March 4). *What is schooliness?* Retrieved http://beyond-school.org/2008/03/04/what-is-schooliness-overview-and-open-thread/

Burgess, J. (2006). Blogging to learn, learning to blog. In A. Bruns & J. Jacobs (Eds.)., *Uses of blogs* (pp. 105–114). New York: Lang.

Calishain, T. (2007). *Information trapping: Real-time research on the Web.* Berkeley, CA: New Riders Press.

Carvin, A. (2007). *Collaborative writing, 140 characters at a time.* Retrieved January 7, 2008 from, http://www.pbs.org/teachers/learning.now/2007/12/collaborative_writing_140_char_1.html

Cary Academy. (2003). *Turn of the century: New York and Vienna, 1890–1910.* Retrieved July 5, 2006, from http://project1.caryacademy.org/turnofcentury/

Center for Digital Storytelling. (2005). *Digital storytelling.* Retrieved November 2, 2006, from, http://www.storycenter.org

Center for Evaluation & Education Policy. (2005). Getting students ready for college: What student engagement data can tell us. Bloomington, IN: Center for Evaluation & Education Policy. Retrieved April 18, 2008, from http://www.indiana.edu/~ceep/hssse/pdf/college_prep_hssse05.pdf

Chbosky, S. (1999). *The perks of being a wallflower.* New York: MTV Books.

Cho, K., & Schunn, C. D. (2007). Scaffolded writing and rewriting in the discipline: A web-based reciprocal peer review system. *Computers & Education, 48* (3), 409–426.

Coiro, J. (2003). Reading comprehension on the Internet: Expanding our understanding of reading comprehension to encompass new literacies. *The Reading Teacher, 56* (6). Retrieved May 13, 2003, from http://vwwi.readingonline.org/electroniclelec_index.asp?HREF=/electronic/RT/2-03_column/index.html

Comstock, M., & Hocks, M. E. (2006). Voice in the cultural soundscape: Sonic literacy in composition studies. *Computers and Composition.* Retrieved May 7, 2007, from http://www.bgsu.edu/cconline/comstock_hocks/index.htm

Conrad, R., & Donaldson, J. A. (2004). *Engaging the online learner: Activities and resources for creative instruction.* San Francisco: Jossey-Bass.

Cope, B., & Kalantzis, M. (2005). *Putting "multiliteracies" to the test.* Retrived April 10, 2006, from http://www.alea.edu.au/multilit.htm

Council of Writing Program Administrators. (2006). *Defining and avoiding plagiarism: The WPA statement on best practices.* Retrieved September 3, 2006, from http://wpacouncil.org/node/9

Creswell, J. W. (2003). *Research design: Qualitative, quantitative, and mixed methods approaches* (2nd ed.). Thousand Oaks, CA: Sage.

Crump, E. (1998). At home in the mud: Writing centers learn to wallow. In C. Haynes & J. R. Holmevik (Eds.), *High wired: On the design, use, and theory of educational MOOs* (pp. 177–191). Ann Arbor, MI: University of Michigan Press.

Curtis, D. (2006). Building online learning communities. *i.e. magazine*, pp. 23–27. Retrieved October 28, 2006, from http://education.smarttech.com/ste/en-US/Ed+Resource/Community/I.E.+Magazine/Current+issue.htm

Cushman, E., DeVoss, D., Grabill, J., Hart-Davidson, B., & Porter, J. (2005). *Why teach digital writing?* Retrieved November 1, 2006, from the Michigan State University WIDE Research Center Collective Web site: http://www.wide.msu.edu/widepapers/why_teach_digital

Daemmrich, I. G. (2007). Novices encounter a novice literature: Introducing digital literature in a first-year college writing class. *Teaching English in Two-Year Colleges, 34* (4), 420–433.

Davis, A. (2007). *Significant comments: Improving instruction through the use of weblogs.* Retrieved March 20, 2007, from http://adavis.pbwiki.com/Significant-Comments

Davis, V. A. (2006). Wikis in education case study: Westwood Schools wiki integration. In S. Mader (Ed.), *Using wikis in education*. Retrieved April 18, 2007, from http://www.wikiineducation.com/display/ikiw/Home

Dedman, J., & Paul, J. (2006). *Videoblogging*. Indianapolis, IN: Wiley.

Digirhet.org. (2006). Teaching digital rhetoric: Community, critical engagement, and application. *Pedagogy, 6* (2), 231–259.

Dimarco, J. (2006). *Web portfolio design and applications*. Hershey, PA: Idea Group.

Dobie, A. (2007). One idea—many audiences. *E-Voice: Newsletter of the National Writing Project*. Retrieved May 12, 2007, from http://www.writingproject.org/cs/nwpp/print/nwpr/2379

Dobson, T. M. (2005). *In medias res: Usability and the digital artifact, or, reading, writing, and the digital artifact*. Paper presented at the annual meeting of the National Reading Conference, Miami, FL.

Dodge, B. (2006). *The Webquest portal*. Retrieved August 18, 2008, from http://webquest.org/index.php

Doerr, C. (2007). *Readability of the Red Cedar Writing Project Website*. Retrieved January 9, 2008, from http://blog.lib.umn.edu/doer0026/cyborgs/2007/12/mwp_website_in_need_of_a_facel_2.html

Donath, J. (1996). *MIT media Lab, identity and deception in the virtual community*. Retrieved July 1, 2006, from http://smg.media.mit.edu/people/judith/Identity/IdentityDeception.html

Elbow, P. (1973). *Writing without teachers*. New York: Oxford University Press.

Ellertson, A. (2005). Information appliances and electronic portfolios: Rearticulating the institutional author. *Kairos, 10* (1). Retrieved November 5, 2006, from, http://english.ttu.edu/kairos/10.1/binder.html?http://cissrv3.uwsp.edu/faculty/aellerts/rearticulate/home.html

Ericsson, P. F., & Haswell, R. (Eds.). (2006). *Machine scoring of student essays: Truth and consequences*. Logan, UT: Utah State University Press.

Eschoolnews. (2006). *Stop the presses: School newspapers moving online*. Retrieved November 4, 2006, from http://www.eschoolnews.com/news/pfshowStory.cfm?ArticleID=6706.

Evans, L. (2006). *Using student podcasts in literature classes*. Retrieved October 12, 2006, from http://www.academiccommons.org/ctfl/vignette/using-student-podcasts-in-literature-classes

Fahey, K., Lawrence, J., & Paratore, J. (2007). Using electronic portfolios to make learning public. *Journal of Adolescent & Adult Literacy, 50* (6), 460–471.

Farkas, B. G. (2006). *Secrets of podcasting* (2nd ed.). Berkeley, CA: PeachPit Press.

Felix, J. P. (2007). Edublogging: Instruction for the digital age learner. Retrieved January 9, 2008, from http://suptfelix.blogspot.com/2007/12/study-on-blogging-educators-is-complete.html

Fisher, C. (2007). *Studying societies at JHK*. Retrieved April 29, 2007, from, http://studyingsocietiesatjhk.pbwiki.com

Fitzgerald, F. S. (1992). *The great Gatsby*. New York: Scribner.

Follansbee, B. (2003). Speaking to write/word for word: An overview of speech recognition. *Perspectives, 29* (4), 10–13.

Fontichiaro, K. (2008). *Podcasting at school*. Portsmouth, NH: Greenwood Press.

Fryer, W. A. (2006). *Skype in the classroom: Integrating technology in the classroom*. Retrieved October 18, 2006, from, http://www.wtvi.com/TEKS/05_06_articles/skype-in-the classroom.html

Ganley, B. (2006). Pedagogical underpinnings of blogs in the classroom. *BgBlogging*. Retrieved August 25, 2006, from http://mt.middlebury.edu/middblogs/ganley/bgblogging/006557.html

Gardner, S., & Birley, S. (2008). *Blogging for dummies* (2nd ed.). Hoboken, NJ: Wiley.

Gee, J. P. (2003). *What video games have to teach us about learning and literacy*. New York: Palgrave MacMillan.

Gee, J. P. (2004). *Situated language and learning: A critique of traditional schooling*. New York: Routledge.

Gibaldi, J. (2003). *MLA handbook for writers of research papers* (6th ed.). New York: Modern Language Association.

Gibson, D., & Barrett, H. (2003). Directions in electronic portfolio development. *Contemporary Issues in Technology and Teacher Education, 2* (4), 559–576. Retrieved April 26, 2007, from, http://www.citejournal.org/vol2/iss4/general/CITEGibsonGeneral2.pdf

Gilroy, K. (2005). *Educational Weblog: How 8th graders view blogging*. Retrieved March 20, 2007, from http://www.ottergroup.com/blog/_archives/2005/6/10/927527.html

Glanz, J. (2003). *Action research: An educational leader's guide to school improvement* (2nd ed.). Norwood, MA: Christopher-Gordon.

Glogowski, K. (2006). Classrooms as third space. *Teach and Learn*. Retrieved January 5, 2007, from http://www.slideshare.net/teachandlearn/classrooms-as-third-places

Glogowski, K. (2007). *Creating learning experiences.* Retrieved January 9, 2008, from http://www.teachandlearn.ca/blog/2007/08/16/creating-learning-experiences

Goldman-Carnegie Quest Program. (2006). *Inside teaching gallery.* Retrieved November 3, 2006, from http://gallery.carnegiefoundation.org/insideteaching

Grady, H. M., & Davis, M. T. (2005). Teaching well online in a collaborative, interactive mode. In K. C. Cook & K. Grant-Davie (Eds.), *Online education: Global questions, local answers* (pp. 101–122). Amityville, NY: Baywood.

Graham, S., Harris, K. R., Fink, B., & MacArthur, C. A. (2003). Primary grade teachers' instructional adaptations for struggling writers: A national survey. *Journal of Educational Psychology, 95,* 279–292.

Green, T. D., Brown, A., & Robinson, L. (2008). *Making the most of the Web in your classroom: A teacher's guide to blogs, podcasts, wikis, pages, and sites.* Thousand Oaks, CA: Corwin Press.

Grisham, D. L., & Wolsey, T. D. (2006). Recentering the middle school classroom as a vibrant learning community: Students, literacy, and technology intersect. *Journal of Adolescent & Adult Literacy, 49* (8), 648–660.

Guhlin, M. (2006, July 1). *Blogs: Webs of connected learning.* Retrieved July 9, 2006, from http://www.techlearning.com/story/showArticle.jhtml?articleID=189500884

Guzzetti, B. J., & Gamboa, M. (2004). Zines for social justice: Adolescent girls writing on their own. *Reading Research Quarterly, 39* (4), 408–436.

Haas, C., & Takayoshi, P. (2008, February 24). What is writing now? Paper presented at the 3rd International Santa Barbara Conference on Writing Research, University of California, Santa Barbara.

Hafner, K. (2006). *Growing Wikipedia revises its "anyone can edit" policy.* Retrieved June 20, 2006, from http://www.nytimes.com/2006/06/17/technology/17wiki.html?ei=5094&en=7f2dcfa9db8cc0ef&hp=&ex=1150603200&partner=homepage&pagewanted=print

Harrington, R., & Rekdal, S. (2007). *How to wow with PowerPoint.* Berkeley, CA: PeachPit Press.

Harris, J. (2006). *Rewriting; How to do things with texts.* Logan, UT: Utah State University Press.

Hayes, S. (2006). Technology toolkit: Improving writing; Online bulletin boards. *Voices From the Middle, 14* (2), 71–73.

Hecker, L., & Engstrom, E. U. (2005). *Multisensory teaching of basic language skills* (2nd ed.). New York: Brookes.

Hendron, J. G. (2008). *RSS for educators: Blogs, newsfeeds, podcasts, and wikis in the classroom*. Washington, DC: International Society for Technology in Education.

Hethering, M. (2006). *How to set up a student centered blog*. Retrieved May 30, 2006, from http://mhetherington.net/blogs/

Hewett, B. L. (2000). Characteristics of interactive oral and computer-mediated peer group talk and its influence on revision. *Computers and Composition, 17* (3), 265–288.

Hewett, S. M. (2006). Electronic portfolios and education: A different way to assess academic success. In L.T.W. Hin & R. Subramaniam (Eds.), *Handbook of research on literacy in technology at the K–12 level* (pp. 437–450). Hershey, PA: Idea Group.

Hicks, T., Russo, A., Autrey, T., Gardner, R., Kabodian, A., & Edington, C. (2007). Rethinking the purposes and processes for designing digital portfolios. *Journal of Adolescent and Adult Literacy, 50* (6), 450–458.

Hillocks, G. (2002). *The testing trap: How state writing assessments control learning*. New York: Teachers College Press.

Hocks, M. R. (2003). Understanding visual rhetoric. *College Composition and Communication, 54* (4), 629–654.

Hoechsmann, M., & Low, B. E. (2008). *Reading youth writing: New literacies, cultural studies & education*. New York: Lang.

Hosseini, K. (2004). *The kite runner*. New York: Riverhead Trade.

Hull, G., & Katz, M. (2007). Crafting an agentive self: Case studies of digital storytelling. *Research in the Teaching of English, 41* (1), 43–81.

Hunt, B. (2006). *Sample blog acceptable use policy. Bud the teacher's wiki*. Retrieved March 22, 2007, from, http://budtheteacher.com/wiki/index.php?title=Sample_Blog_Acceptable_Use_Policy

Hutchinson, Y. D. (2006). *A friend of their minds: Capitalizing on the oral tradition of my African American students*. Retrieved November 4, 2006, from http://gallery.carnegiefoundation.org/collections/quest/collections/sites/divans-hutchinson_yvonne/

International Society for Technology in Education. (2008). *2008 national education technology standards for teachers*. Retrieved June 30, 2008, from, http://www.iste.org/Content/NavigationMenu/NETS/ForTeachers/2008Standards/NETS_for_Teachers_2008.htm

Jacobi, T. (2007). The Zine Project: Innovation or oxymoron? *English Journal, 96* (4), 43–49.

Jenkins, H. (2006a). Confronting the challenges of participatory culture: Media education for the 21st century. *The MacArthur Foundation.* Retrieved October 25, 2006, from, http://www.digitallearning.macfound.org/site/c.enJLKQNlFiG/b.2108773/apps/nl/content2.asp?content_id={CD911571-0240-4714-A93B-1D0C07C7B6C1}&notoc=1

Jenkins, H. (2006b). *Learning by remixing.* Retrieved August 20, 2006, from http://www.pbs.org/mediashift/2006/07/learning_by_remixing.html

Jenkins, H. (2007). *What Wikipedia can teach us about the new media literacies: Confessions of an Aca fan.* Retrieved August 4, 2007, from http://www.henryjenkins.org/2007/06/what_wikipedia_can_teach_us_ab.html

Jocson, K. M. (2005). Teacher as learner in DV poetry: Toward a praxis of engaging literacies in alternative spaces for learning. *Current Issues in Education, 8* (5). Retrieved April 20, 2008, from http://cie.ed.asu.edu/volume8/number5/

Johnson-Eilola, J. (2004). The database and the essay: Understanding composition as articulation. In A. Wysocki, J. Johnson-Eilola, C. Selfe, & G. Sirc (Eds.), *Writing new media: Theory and applications for expanding the teaching of composition* (pp. 199–236). Logan, UT: Utah State University Press.

Kajder, S., Bull, G., & Albaugh, S. (2005). Constructing digital stories. *Learning and Leading With Technology, 32* (5), 40–42.

Kent, R. (2006). Room 109's portfolios and our high school writing center. *The Clearing House, 80* (2), 56–58.

Kies, D. (2006). *Evaluating grammar checkers.* Retrieved May 11, 2007, from http://papyr.com/hypertextbooks/grammar/gramchek.htm

Kilbane, C. R., & Milman, N. B. (2003). *The digital teaching portfolio handbook: A how-to-guide for educators.* Boston: Allyn & Bacon.

King, K. P., & Gura, M. (2007). *Podcasting for teachers: Using a new technology to revolutionize teaching and learning.* Charlotte, NC: Information Age.

Kolb, L. (2008). *Toys to tools: Connecting student cell phones to education in and out of the classroom.* Washington, DC: International Society for Technology in Education.

Krakauer, J. (2007). *Into the wild.* New York: Anchor.

Krause, S. D. (2006). Broadcast composition: Using audio files and podcasts in an online writing course. *Computers and Composition Online.* Retrieved May 6, 2007, from http://www.bgsu.edu/cconline/krause1/results.html

Kress, G. (2003). *Literacy in the new media age.* New York: Routledge.

Kress, G. (2007). Thinking about meaning and learning in a world of instability and multiplicity. *Pedagogies: An International Journal, 2* (1), 19–34.

Lamb, B. (2006). *BlogShop Lite.* Retrieved May 2, 2007, from http://careo.elearning.ubc.ca/cgi-bin/wiki.pl?BlogshopLite

Landow, G. P. (2006). *Hypertext 3.0: Critical theory and new media in an era of globalization.* Baltimore: Johns Hopkins University Press.

Lankshear, C., & Knobel, M. (2003). *New literacies: Changing knowledge and classroom learning.* Buckingham, England: Open University Press.

Lenhart, A., Arafeh, S., Smith, A., & MacGill, A. R. (2008). *Writing, technology and teens.* Washington, DC: Pew Internet & American Life Project. Retrieved April 24, 2008, from http://www.pewinternet.org/PPF/r/247/report_display.asp

Lenhart, A., & Madden, M. (2007). *Social networking websites and teens: An overview.* Washington, DC: Pew Internet & American Life Project. Retrieved January 28, 2007, from http://www.pewinternet.org.

Lessig, L. (2002). *The future of ideas: The fate of the commons in a connected world.* New York: Vintage.

Leuf, B., & Cunningham, W. (2001). *The wiki way: Quick collaboration on the Web.* Boston: Addison-Wesley.

Lewis, C., & Fabos, B. (2005). Instant messaging, literacies, and social identities. *Reading Research Quarterly, 40* (4), 470–501.

MacArthur, C. A. (2006). The effects of new technologies on writing and writing processes. In C. A. MacArthur, S. Graham, & J. Fitzgerald (Eds.), *Handbook of writing research* (pp. 248–262). New York: Guilford Press.

MacArthur, C. A., Graham, S., Haynes, J. A., & De La Paz, S. (1996). Spelling checkers and students with learning disabilities: Performance comparisons and impact on spelling. *Journal of Special Education, 21,* 22–42.

Mackey, R. (2007). Wikipedia to check I.D.'s. *The New York Times.* Retrieved March 8, 2007, from http://thelede.blogs.nytimes.com/2007/03/09/wikipedia-to-check-ids

Madden, M., et al. (2007). *Digital footprints: Online identity management and search in the age of transparency.* Pew Internet & American Life Project. Retrieved January 5, 2008, from http://www.pewinternet.org/PPF/r/229/report_display.asp

Mahiri, J. (2006). Digital DJ-ing: Rhythms of learning in an urban school. *Language Arts, 84* (1), 55–62.

Marttunen, M., & Laurinen, L. (2007). Collaborative learning through chat discussions and argument diagrams in secondary school. *Journal of Research on Technology in Education, 40* (1), 109–126.

McCloud, S. (2006). *Making comics: Storytelling secrets of comics, manga and graphic novels*. New York: Harper.

McNabb, M. L., Thurber, B. B., Dibuz, B., McDermott, P., & Lee, C. A. (2006). *Literacy learning in networked classrooms: Using the Internet with middle-level students*. Newark, DE: International Reading Association.

Merchant, G. (2007). Writing the future in the digital age. *Literacy, 41* (3), 118–128.

Monroe, B. (1998). The look and feel of the OWL conference. In E. Hobsen (Ed.), *Wiring the writing center* (pp. 3–24). Logan, UT: Utah State University Press.

Montgomery, D. J., Karlan, G. R., & Coutinho, M. (2001). The effectiveness of word processor spell check programs to produce target words for misspellings generated by students with learning disabilities. *Journal of Special Education Technology, 16,* 27–41.

Montgomery, D. J., & Marks, L. J. (2006). Using technology to build independence in writing for students with disabilities. *Preventing School Failure, 50* (3), 33–38.

Montgomery, K. Z., & Wiley, D. A. (2004). *Creating e-portfolios using PowerPoint: A guide for educators*. Thousand Oaks, CA: Sage.

Moore, M. (Director). (2007). *Sicko* [Film]. Dog Eat Dog Films.

Morgan, M. C. (2005). *Singing the praises of using a wiki to teach writing*. Retrieved March 6, 2007, from http://biro.bemidjistate.edu/~morgan/wiki/wiki.php/NoteBook/VirtuesOfWiki

Morgan, M. C. (2006a). *Wiki as presentation tool*. Retrieved May 2, 2007, from http://biro.bemidjistate.edu/~morgan/wiki/wiki.php/NoteBook/WikiPoint

Morgan, M. C. (2006b). *Wiki, blog, eFolio: How wikis and Weblogs trump eportfolios*. Retrieved April 26, 2007, from http://biro.bemidjistate.edu/~morgan/wiki/wiki.php/NoteBook/WikisBlogsAndEFol

Morris, A., & Swiss, T. (Eds.). (2006). *New media poetics: Contexts, technotexts, and theories*. Cambridge, MA: MIT Press.

Morris, T., Tomasi, C., & Terra, E. (2008). *Podcasting for dummies* (2nd ed.). Hoboken, NJ: Wiley.

Moulthrop, S. (1995). *Victory garden*. Cambridge, MA: Eastgate Systems. Retrieved August 18, 2008, from http://www.eastgate.com/VG/VGStart.html

Murrey, C. (2007). Translation tool tackles language barrier in schools. *eSchool News*. Retrieved May 8, 2007, from http://www.eschoolnews.com/news/showStory.cfm?ArticleID=7057

National Council of Teachers of English (NCTE). (2008). *Toward a definition of 21st-century literacies.* Retrieved April 16, 2008, from http://www.ncte.org/announce/129117.htm

National School Boards Association. (2007). *Creating & connecting: Research and guidelines on online social and educational networking.* Retrieved January 7, 2008, from http://www.nsba.org/site/pdf.asp?TP=/site/docs/41400/41340.pdf

Nerius, M. G. (2007). *Digital scrapbooking: Using your computer to create exciting scrapbook pages.* New York: Lark Books.

Nixon, A. S. (2008). *Digital storytelling and identity play in an after-school club.* Paper presented at the annual meeting of the American Education Research Association, New York.

November, A. (2008). *Web literacy for educators.* Thousand Oaks, CA: Corwin Press.

Ohler, J. B. (2007). *Digital storytelling in the classroom: New media pathways to literacy, learning, and creativity.* Thousand Oaks, CA: Sage.

Oldenburg, R. (2000). *Celebrating the third place: Inspiring stories about the "great good places" at the heart of our communities.* New York: Marlowe.

Olsen, S. (2008). Are wired kids well served by schools? *CNet News.* Retrieved April 25, 2008, from, http://www.news.com/8301-10784_3-9928174-7.html?tag=blogFeed

O'Reilly, T. (2005). What is Web 2.0? *O'Reilly News.* Retrieved January 20, 2007, from http://www.oreillynet.com/pub/a/oreilly/tim/news/2005/09/30/what-is-web-20.html

Parry, D. (2006). The technology of reading and writing in a digital space: Why RSS is crucial for a blogging classroom. *Blogs for Learning.* Retrieved August 13, 2008, from, http://blogsforlearning.msu.edu/articles/)

Pearson, M. (2007, March). *Screwing things up for your favorite team? Writing about collegiate sports online.* Paper presented at the annual meeting of College Composition and Communication, New York.

Peer Review of Teaching Project. (2007). Retrieved May 2, 2007, from http://www.courseportfolio.org/peer/pages/index.jsp?what=rootMenuD&rootMenuId=6

Pincus, M. (2006). *Infusing "main stage" with "second stage" drama performances.* Retrieved November 3, 2006, from http://gallery.carnegiefoundation.org/collections/quest/collections/sites/pincus_marshal

Pleasants, H. (2007). *Negotiating identity projects: Exploring the digital storytelling experiences of three African American girls.* Retrieved April 20, 2008, from, http://vectors.usc.edu/thoughtmesh/publish/106.php

Rainie, L., & Trancer, B. (2007). *Wikipedia: When in doubt, multitudes seek it out.* Washington, DC: Pew Internet and American Life Project. Retrieved May 1, 2007, from, http://pewresearch.org/pubs/460/wikipedia

Ray, B. B., & Hocutt, M. M. (2006). Reflection and the middle: School blogger; Do blogs support reflective practices? *Meridian: A Middle School Computer Technologies Journal, 9* (1). Retrieved January 10, 2008, from, http://www.ncsu.edu/meridian/win2006/MS_blogs/index.htm

Read, B. (2007). Middlebury College History Department limits students' use of Wikipedia. *Chronicle of Higher Education, 53* (24), A39.

Rice, J. (2004). *Writing about cool: Hypertext and cultural studies in the computer classroom.* New York: Longman.

Richardson, W. (2006). *Blogs, wikis, podcasts and other powerful Web tools for the classroom.* Thousand Oaks, CA: Corwin Press.

Romano, T. (2000). *Blending genre, Altering style.* Portsmouth, NH: Heinemann.

Satrapi, M. (2004). *Persepolis: The story of a childhood.* New York: Pantheon.

Scaletta, C. (2006). *"To whom are these texts valuable?": An inquiry into student blogging.* Unpublished report. University of Minnesota, Minneapolis.

Schoonmaker, M. (2007). *Cameras in the classroom: Educating the post-TV generation.* Lanham, MD: Rowman & Littlefield.

Shaffer, D. W. (2005). *How computer games help children learn.* New York: Palgrave Macmillan.

Shareski, D., & Winkler, C. A. (2005/2006). Are wikis worth the time? *Learning & Leading With Technology, 33* (3), 6–7.

Shipka, J. (2005). A multimodal task-based framework for composing. *College Composition & Communication, 57* (2), 277–306.

Siegle, D. (2006). Using hyperlinks to unleash the power of PowerPoint. *Gifted Child Today, 29* (3), 40–45.

Sirc, G. (2004). Box-logic. In A. Wysocki, J. Johnson-Eilola, C. Selfe, & G. Sirc (Eds.), *Writing new media: Theory and applications for expanding the teaching of composition* (pp. 111–146). Logan, UT: Utah State University Press.

Smith, C. (2006). Synchronous discussion in online courses: A pedagogical strategy for taming the chat beast. *Innovate: Journal of Online Education, 2* (5). Retrieved August 14, 2008, from, http://www.innovateonline.info/index.php?view=article&id=246&action=synopsis

Solomon, G., & Schrum, L. (2007). *Web 2.0: New tools, new schools.* Washington, DC: International Society for Technology in Education.

Spear, K. (Ed.). (1993). *Peer response groups in action: Writing together in secondary schools.* Portsmouth, NH: Heinemann.

Spiegelman, A. (1993). *Maus: A survivor's tale.* New York: Pantheon.

Spinuzzi, C. (2007). Collaboration for Keiretsu: A review of Google Docs. *Currents in Electronic Literacy.* Retrieved April 14, 2007, from, http://currents.cwrl.utexas.edu/node/16

Sprankle, B. (2006). Podcasting with purpose. *Principal, 85* (4), 62–63.

Stern, S. (2008). Producing sites, exploring identities: Youth online authorship. In D. Buckingham (Ed.)., *Youth, identity, and digital media* (pp. 95–118). Cambridge, MA: MIT Press.

Strickland, S. (1999). *The ballad of sand and Harry Soot.* Retrieved October 15, 2006, from http://wordcircuits.com/gallery/sandsoot/

Swiss, T. (Ed.). (2001). *Unspun: The Web, language, society.* New York: New York University Press.

Swiss, T., & Herman, A. (Eds.). (2000). *The World Wide Web and cultural theory: Magic, metaphor, power.* Oxford, UK: Routledge.

Swiss, T., & Nakamura, M. (2002). *Hey now.* Austin, TX: South By Southwest New Media Festival.

Thomas, A. (2004). Digital literacies of the cybergirl. *E-Learning, 1* (3), 358–382.

Thomas, A. (2006). Fictional blogs. In A. Bruns & J. Jacobs (Eds.), *Uses of blogs* (pp. 199–210). New York: Lang.

Torkelson, L., Petersen, C., & Torkelson, Z. (2002). *Programming the Web with Visual Basic.* Berkeley, CA: Apress.

Troia, G. A. (2006). Writing instruction for students with learning disabilities. In C. A. MacArthur, S. Graham, & J. Fitzgerald (Eds.)., *Handbook of writing research* (pp. 324–336). New York: Guilford Press.

Tufte, E. R. (2006). *The cognitive style of PowerPoint: Pitching out corrupts within* (2nd ed.). Cheshire, CT: Graphics Press.

Universal McCann. (2006). *The new digital divide: How the new generation of digital consumers are transforming mass communication.* New York: Author.

University of Chicago Press. (2003). *The Chicago manual of style* (15th ed.). Chicago: Author.

Utecht, J. (2007). *Online professional development.* Retrieved January 12, 2008, from, http://k12onlineconference.org/?p=205

Valenza, J. K. (2005/2006). Pathfinders, streaming video: Welcome to the 21st century school library. *Educational Leadership*.

Van Orden, J. (2006). *Promoting your podcast: The ultimate guide to building an audience of raving fans*. Larstan.

Verdi, R., & Hodson, S. (2006). *Secrets of video blogging*. Berkeley, CA: PeachPit Press.

Vrasidas, C., & Glass, G. V. (2007). Teacher professional development and ICT. In L. Smolin, K. Lawless, N. C.; Burbules (Eds.), *Information and communication technologies* (pp. 87–102). Malden, MA: Blackwell.

Warlick, D. (2007). *Classroom blogging* (2nd ed.). Morrisville, NC: LuLu.com.

Warschauer, M. (2006). *Laptops and literacy: Learning in the wireless classroom*. New York: Teachers College Press.

Watrall, E., & Ellison, N. (2006). *Blogs for learning: A case study*. Retrieved August 13, 2008, from http://www.higheredblogcon.com/teaching/watrall/blogs-for-learning2/player.html

Watson, L. (1993). *Montana 1948*. Minneapolis: Milkwood Press.

Weber, R. P. (1990). *Basic content analysis: Quantitative applications in the social sciences*. Thousand Oaks, CA: Sage.

Weinberger, D. (2007). *Everything is miscellaneous: The power of the new digital disorder*. New York: Times Books.

Wertsch, J. (1998). *Mind as action*. New York: Oxford University Press.

West, K. C. (2008). Weblogs and literary response: Socially situated identities and hybrid social languages in English class blogs. *Journal of Adolescent and Adult Literacy, 51* (7), 588–598.

Wilkinson, D. M., & Huberman, B. A. (2007). *Assessing the value of cooperation in Wikipedia*. Palo Alto, CA: HP Labs.

Willard, N. (2007). *Cyber-safe kids, cyber-savvy teens: Helping young people learn to use the Internet safely and responsibly*. San Francisco: Jossey-Bass.

Willinsky, J. (2006). Presentation. *OOOK Blog*. Retrieved October 25, 2006, from, http://oook.info/mt/archives/000319.html

Wissman, K. K. (2008). "This is what I see": (Re)envisioning photography as a social practice. In M. L. Hill & L. Vasudevan (Eds.). *Media, learning, and sites of possibility* (pp.13–46). New York: Lang.

Withrow, S., & Barber, J. (2005). *Webcomics: Tools and techniques for digital cartooning*. New York: Barons Books.

Woods, D., & Thoeny, P. (2007). *Wikis for dummies*. Hoboken, NJ: Wiley.

Wysocki, A. (2004a). The multiple media of texts: How onscreen and paper texts incorporate words, images, and other media. In C. Bazerman & P. Prior (Eds.), *What writing does and how it does it: An introduction to analyzing texts and textual practices* (pp. 123–163). Mahwah, NJ: Erlbaum.

Wysocki, A. (2004b). Open new media to writing. In A. Wysocki, J. Johnson-Eilola, C. Selfe, & G. Sirc (Eds.), *Writing new media: Theory and applications for expanding the teaching of composition* (pp. 1–41). Logan, UT: Utah State University Press.

Yancey, K. B. (2004). *Teaching literature as reflective practice.* Urbana, IL: National Council of Teachers of English.

Yang, G. L. (2007). *American born Chinese.* New York: First Second.

Index

A

Aby, M. S.
  classroom blog developed by, 224
    reflections on, 224–225
    research findings on, 225
    social studies teaching, concerns
      over, 223–224
Adams, J. *See also Conrad & Donaldson.*
  constructivist learning assump-
    tions, success of online learning
    through, 51
Allison, Paul
  Teachers Teaching Teachers podcast
    headed by, 139, 219–220
    student use of, example, 139–
      140
  Youth Wiki site developed by, 60, 79
American Society of Newspaper Editors
  online newspaper publishing spon-
    sored by, 171
Annan, Judy
  digital scrapbooks used by with
    students, 170–171

Anson, Chris
  formative feedback, new approaches
    to, 197–198
  plagiarism, student writing and,
    201–202
    technologies for subverting,
      202–203
  Web 2.0 technologies, discovery of
    many uses for in teaching, *xi*, 220
Anson, Chris M., & Beach, Richard. *See
  also Digital writing.*
  journals and writing, *viii, xi*

B

Barrett, H. C.
  e-portfolios, suggestions for student
    use, 217–218
Beach, Richard
  digital writing class of, 39–40
  inquiry-based learning, research
    on, 26
  media studies classes, use of blogs
    and wikis in, *xi*, 9, 22–23

245

About the Authors

Richard Beach is a professor of English education at the University of Minnesota, where he teaches and conducts research on media literacy methods, digital writing, and identity construction. He is the author and/or editor of 16 books, including *Teaching Literature to Adolescents, Teachingmedialiteracy.com: A Web-based Guide to Links and Activities, Journals in the Classroom: Writing to Learn*, and *A Teacher's Introduction to Reader Response Theories*. He is a former president of the National Conference on Research in Language and Literacy and a member of the National Council of Teachers of English Commission on Media.

Chris Anson is a university distinguished professor of English and director of the Campus Writing and Speaking Program at North Carolina State University, where he helps faculty in nine colleges to use writing and speaking in the service of students' learning and improved communication. He is the author and/or editor of 15 books, including *The WAC Casebook: Scenes for Faculty Reflection and Program Development; The Longman Handbook for Writers and Readers; Under Construction: Working at the Intersections of Composition Theory, Research, and Practice;* and *Journals in the Classroom: Writing to Learn*. He is past president of the Council of Writing Program Administrators.

257

Lee-Ann Kastman Breuch is an associate professor in the Department of Writing Studies at the University of Minnesota, where she teaches courses in first-year writing, technical communication, computer pedagogy, teacher training, and usability testing. Her research addresses writing theory and pedagogy in technical disciplines, composition, and online environments. As a fellow of the Digital Media Center at the University of Minnesota, she conducts online writing instruction. She is the author of *Virtual Peer Review: Teaching and Learning About Writing in Online Environments.*

Thom Swiss is professor of Culture and Teaching, University of Minnesota, where he teaches courses on new and/or digital media, media literacy, cultural studies, and popular music. His digital poems appear online and in art galleries. He is the author and/or editor of *New Media Poetics: Contexts, Technotexts, and Theories; Unspun: The Web, Language, Society;* and *The World Wide Web and Cultural Theory: Magic, Metaphor, Power.*